SOLARO

STUDY GUIDE

ence 6

SOLARO Study Guide is designed to help students achieve success in school. The content in each study guide is 100% curriculum aligned and serves as an excellent source of material for review and practice. To create this book, teachers, curriculum specialists, and assessment experts have worked closely to develop the instructional pieces that explain each of the key concepts for the course. The practice questions and sample tests have detailed solutions that show problem-solving methods, highlight concepts that are likely to be tested, and point out potential sources of errors. ***SOLARO Study Guide*** is a complete guide to be used by students throughout the school year for reviewing and understanding course content, and to prepare for assessments.

Rao,Gautam,1961 –
SOLARO STUDY GUIDE – Science 6 Ontario

1. Science – Juvenile Literature. I. Title

1 2 3 PP 15 14 13

Castle Rock Research Corp.
2410 Manulife Place
10180 – 101 Street
Edmonton, AB T5J 3S4

Publisher
Gautam Rao

Contributors
Mary-Ann Perras
Jennifer Walsh
Jill Hickson
Jared MacLeod
Pamela Brierley

CASTLE ROCK
RESEARCH CORP

Dedicated to the memory of Dr. V. S. Rao

SOLARO STUDY GUIDE

Each ***SOLARO STUDY GUIDE*** consists of the following sections:

Key Tips for Being Successful at School gives examples of study and review strategies. It includes information about learning styles, study schedules, and note taking for test preparation.

Class Focus includes a unit on each area of the curriculum. Units are divided into sections, each focusing on one of the specific expectations, or main ideas, that students must learn about in that unit. Examples, definitions, and visuals help to explain each main idea. Practice questions on the main ideas are also included. At the end of each unit is a test on the important ideas covered. The practice questions and unit tests help students identify areas they know and those they need to study more. They can also be used as preparation for tests and quizzes. Most questions are of average difficulty, though some are easy and some are hard—the harder questions are called *Challenger Questions*. Each unit is prefaced by a ***Table of Correlations,*** which correlates questions in the unit (and in the practice tests at the end of the book) to the specific curriculum expectations. Answers and solutions are found at the end of each unit.

Key Strategies for Success on Tests helps students get ready for tests. It shows students different types of questions they might see, word clues to look for when reading them, and hints for answering them.

Practice Tests includes one to three tests based on the entire course. They are very similar to the format and level of difficulty that students may encounter on final tests. In some regions, these tests may be reprinted versions of official tests, or reflect the same difficulty levels and formats as official versions. This gives students the chance to practice using real-world examples. Answers and complete solutions are provided at the end of the section.

For the complete curriculum document (including specific expectations along with examples and sample problems), visit http://www.edu.gov.on.ca/eng/curriculum/

SOLARO STUDY GUIDE *Study Guides* are available for many courses. Check www.castlerockresearch.com for a complete listing of books available for your area.

For information about any of our resources or services, please call Castle Rock Research at 1.800.840.6224 or visit our website at http://www.castlerockresearch.com.

At Castle Rock Research, we strive to produce an error-free resource. If you should find an error, please contact us so that future editions can be corrected.

CONTENTS

Key Tips for being Successful at School

KEY TIPS FOR BEING SUCCESSFUL AT SCHOOL

KEY FACTORS CONTRIBUTING TO SCHOOL SUCCESS

In addition to learning the content of your courses, there are some other things that you can do to help you do your best at school. You can try some of the following strategies:

- **Keep a positive attitude:** Always reflect on what you can already do and what you already know.
- **Be prepared to learn:** Have the necessary pencils, pens, notebooks, and other required materials for participating in class ready.
- **Complete all of your assignments:** Do your best to finish all of your assignments. Even if you know the material well, practice will reinforce your knowledge. If an assignment or question is difficult for you, work through it as far as you can so that your teacher can see exactly where you are having difficulty.
- **Set small goals for yourself when you are learning new material:** For example, when learning the parts of speech, do not try to learn everything in one night. Work on only one part or section each study session. When you have memorized one particular part of speech and understand it, move on to another one. Continue this process until you have memorized and learned all the parts of speech.
- **Review your classroom work regularly at home:** Review to make sure you understand the material you learned in class.

- **Ask your teacher for help:** Your teacher will help you if you do not understand something or if you are having a difficult time completing your assignments.
- **Get plenty of rest and exercise:** Concentrating in class is hard work. It is important to be well-rested and have time to relax and socialize with your friends. This helps you keep a positive attitude about your schoolwork.
- **Eat healthy meals:** A balanced diet keeps you healthy and gives you the energy you need for studying at school and at home.

How to Find Your Learning Style

Every student learns differently. The manner in which you learn best is called your learning style. By knowing your learning style, you can increase your success at school. Most students use a combination of learning styles. Do you know what type of learner you are? Read the following descriptions. Which of these common learning styles do you use most often?

- **Linguistic Learner:** You may learn best by saying, hearing, and seeing words. You are probably really good at memorizing things such as dates, places, names, and facts. You may need to write down the steps in a process, a formula, or the actions that lead up to a significant event, and then say them out loud.
- **Spatial Learner:** You may learn best by looking at and working with pictures. You are probably really good at puzzles, imagining things, and reading maps and charts. You may need to use strategies like mind mapping and webbing to organize your information and study notes.
- **Kinesthetic Learner:** You may learn best by touching, moving, and figuring things out using manipulatives. You are probably really good at physical activities and learning through movement. You may need to draw your finger over a diagram to remember it, tap out the steps needed to solve a problem, or feel yourself writing or typing a formula.

Scheduling Study Time

You should review your class notes regularly to ensure that you have a clear understanding of all the new material you learned. Reviewing your lessons on a regular basis helps you to learn and remember ideas and concepts. It also reduces the quantity of material that you need to study prior to a test. Establishing a study schedule will help you to make the best use of your time.

Regardless of the type of study schedule you use, you may want to consider the following suggestions to maximize your study time and effort:

- Organize your work so that you begin with the most challenging material first.
- Divide the subject's content into small, manageable chunks.
- Alternate regularly between your different subjects and types of study activities in order to maintain your interest and motivation.
- Make a daily list with headings like "Must Do," "Should Do," and "Could Do."
- Begin each study session by quickly reviewing what you studied the day before.
- Maintain your usual routine of eating, sleeping, and exercising to help you concentrate better for extended periods of time.

Creating Study Notes

Mind-Mapping or Webbing

Use the key words, ideas, or concepts from your reading or class notes to create a mind map or web (a diagram or visual representation of the given information). A mind map or web is sometimes referred to as a knowledge map. Use the following steps to create a mind map or web:

1. Write the key word, concept, theory, or formula in the centre of your page.
2. Write down related facts, ideas, events, and information, and link them to the central concept with lines.
3. Use coloured markers, underlining, or symbols to emphasize things such as relationships, timelines, and important information.

The following examples of a Frayer Model illustrate how this technique can be used to study vocabulary.

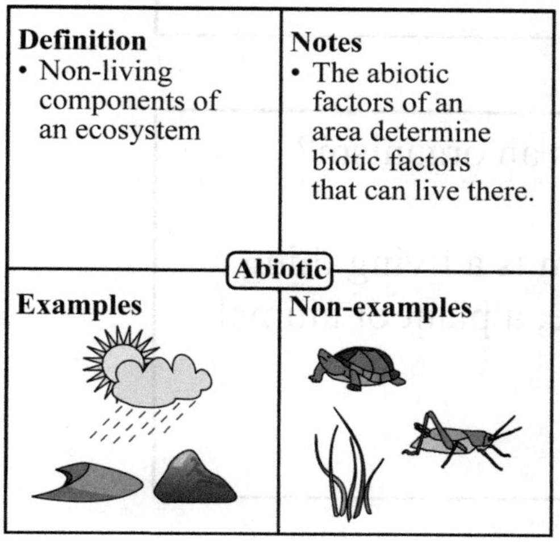

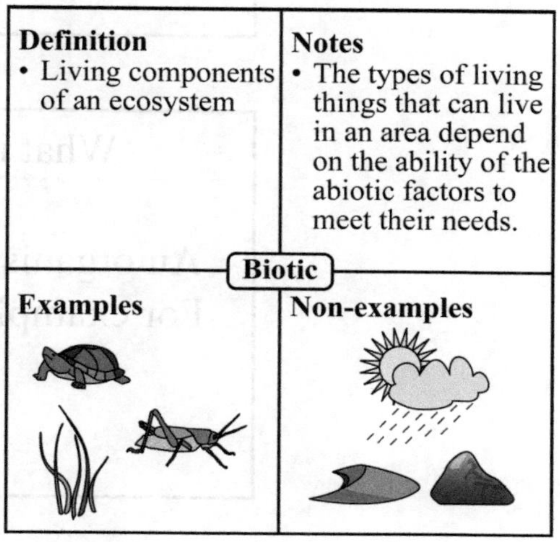

INDEX CARDS

To use index cards while studying, follow these steps:

1. Write a key word or question on one side of an index card.
2. On the reverse side, write the definition of the word, answer to the question, or any other important information that you want to remember.

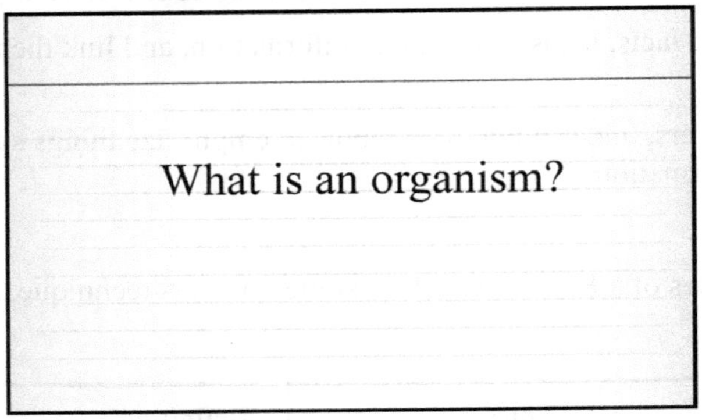

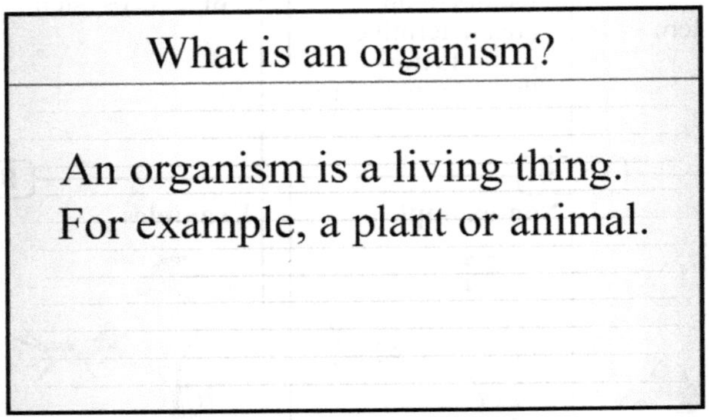

SYMBOLS AND STICKY NOTES—IDENTIFYING IMPORTANT INFORMATION

Use symbols to mark your class notes. The following are some examples:

- An exclamation mark (!) might be used to point out something that must be learned well because it is a very important idea.
- A question mark (?) may highlight something you are not certain about
- A diamond (◊) or asterisk (*) could highlight interesting information that you want to remember.

Sticky notes are useful in the following situations:

- Use sticky notes when you are not allowed to put marks in books.
- Use sticky notes to mark a page in a book that contains an important diagram, formula, explanation, or other information.
- Use sticky notes to mark important facts in research books.

Memorization Techniques

- **Association** relates new learning to something you already know. For example, to remember the spelling difference between dessert and desert, recall that the word *sand* has only one *s*. So, because there is sand in a desert, the word *desert* has only one *s*.
- **Mnemonic** devices are sentences that you create to remember a list or group of items. For example, the first letter of each word in the phrase "Every Good Boy Deserves Fudge" helps you to remember the names of the lines on the treble-clef staff (E, G, B, D, and F) in music.
- **Acronyms** are words that are formed from the first letters or parts of the words in a group. For example, RADAR is actually an acronym for Radio Detecting and Ranging, and MASH is an acronym for Mobile Army Surgical Hospital. HOMES helps you to remember the names of the five Great Lakes (Huron, Ontario, Michigan, Erie, and Superior).

- **Visualizing** requires you to use your mind's eye to "see" a chart, list, map, diagram, or sentence as it is in your textbook or notes, on the chalkboard or computer screen, or in a display.
- **Initialisms** are abbreviations that are formed from the first letters or parts of the words in a group. Unlike acronyms, an initialism cannot be pronounced as a word itself. For example, GCF is an initialism for **G**reatest **C**ommon **F**actor.

Key Strategies for Reviewing

Reviewing textbook material, class notes, and handouts should be an ongoing activity. Spending time reviewing becomes more critical when you are preparing for a test. You may find some of the following review strategies useful when studying during your scheduled study time:

- Before reading a selection, preview it by noting the headings, charts, graphs, and chapter questions.
- Before reviewing a unit, note the headings, charts, graphs, and chapter questions.
- Highlight key concepts, vocabulary, definitions, and formulas.
- Skim the paragraph, and note the key words, phrases, and information.
- Carefully read over each step in a procedure.
- Draw a picture or diagram to help make the concept clearer.

KEY STRATEGIES FOR SUCCESS: A CHECKLIST

Reviewing is a huge part of doing well at school and preparing for tests. Here is a checklist for you to keep track of how many suggested strategies for success you are using. Read each question, and put a check mark (✓) in the correct column. Look at the questions where you have checked the "No" column. Think about how you might try using some of these strategies to help you do your best at school.

Key Strategies for Success	Yes	No
Do you attend school regularly?		
Do you know your personal learning style—how you learn best?		
Do you spend 15 to 30 minutes a day reviewing your notes?		
Do you study in a quiet place at home?		
Do you clearly mark the most important ideas in your study notes?		
Do you use sticky notes to mark texts and research books?		
Do you practise answering multiple-choice and written-response questions?		
Do you ask your teacher for help when you need it?		
Are you maintaining a healthy diet and sleep routine?		
Are you participating in regular physical activity?		

Life Systems: Biodiversity

LIFE SYSTEMS: BIODIVERSITY

Table of Correlations

Specific Expectation		Practice Questions	Unit Test Questions	Practice Test
6LS1:STSE	Assess human impacts on biodiversity, and identify ways of preserving biodiversity;			
6LS1.1	*analyse a local issue related to biodiversity, taking different points of view into consideration, propose action that can be taken to preserve biodiversity, and act on the proposal*	1, 2	1, 2	24
6LS1.2	*assess the benefits that human societies derive from biodiversity and the problems that occur when biodiversity is diminished*	3, 4	3	25
6LS2:Skills	Investigate the characteristics of living things, and classify diverse organisms according to specific characteristics;			
6LS2.1	*follow established safety procedures for outdoor activities and field work*	19	4	26
6LS2.2	*investigate the organisms found in a specific habitat and classify them according to a classification system*	20, 21	5, 6	27
6LS2.3	*use scientific inquiry/research skills to compare the characteristics of organisms within the plant or animal kingdoms*	22, 23	7, 8	28
6LS2.4	*use appropriate science and technology vocabulary, including classification, biodiversity, natural community, interrelationships, vertebrate, invertebrate, stability, characteristics, and organism, in oral and written communication*	24, 25	9, 10	29
6LS3:Concepts	Demonstrate an understanding of biodiversity, its contributions to the stability of natural systems, and its benefits to humans.			
6LS3.1	*identify and describe the distinguishing characteristics of different groups of plants and animals, and use these characteristics to further classify various kinds of plants and animals*	5, 6, 7	11, 12, 13	30, 31
6LS3.2	*demonstrate an understanding of biodiversity as the variety of life on earth, including variety within each species of plant and animal, among species of plants and animals in communities, and among communities and the physical landscapes that support them*	8, 9	14	32
6LS3.3	*describe ways in which biodiversity within species is important for maintaining the resilience of those species*	10		33
6LS3.4	*describe ways in which biodiversity within and among communities is important for maintaining the resilience of these communities*	11	15	
6LS3.5	*describe interrelationships within species, between species, and between species and their environment, and explain how these interrelationships sustain biodiversity*	12, 13, 14	16, 17, 18	34
6LS3.6	*identify everyday products that come from a diversity of organisms*	15, 16	19	35
6LS3.7	*explain how invasive species reduce biodiversity in local environments*	17, 18	20	36

6LS1.1 *analyse a local issue related to biodiversity, taking different points of view into consideration, propose action that can be taken to preserve biodiversity, and act on the proposal*

THE EFFECTS OF HUMAN ACTIONS ON BIODIVERSITY

No other species changes the planet as much as humans do. Whenever people make changes to the environment, they risk changing the biodiversity of that space. **Biodiversity** refers to the variety of organisms found in the different ecosystems on Earth. An **organism** is any single living thing that can survive on its own. This includes all the plants and animals, but also smaller organisms, such as protists, bacteria, and fungi. All of these organisms are important for the ecosystem to continue working properly. People need to think about the biodiversity of the environment before they make changes to it. They need to think about what organisms live in that area.

Even a very small change could harm this wetland area and all the organisms that live there.

For example, suppose a company wants to clear a local forest to make room for a grocery store. The forest is home to many plants and animals. The plants will all be cut down. The animals that live there will need to find a new place to live. However, the people who live near the forest will finally have a grocery store nearby.

Constructing a new grocery store

Building a grocery store will affect the people and environment both negatively and positively.

Negative effects

- Fewer plants may lead to soil erosion in the area.
- Many animals will lose their homes and food sources.
- Extra traffic will bring more air pollution and noise to the area.
- Many plants will die during the construction of the grocery store.
- The current grocery store owner might lose customers when the new store opens.
- Hikers and bird watchers who use the woods may not want them to be destroyed.
- Smaller organisms that live in the dirt may die when the ground is cleared and dug for the building.

Positive effects

- The grocery store will create jobs for people who live nearby.
- People will not have to drive as far to get their groceries. This will mean less air pollution will be created by cars.

Before you make a decision about an issue, take some time to think the matter over. Do some research to find out what impact the planned change will have on the plants and animals that live in the area that will be affected. Think about how many people will benefit from the change. Discuss the issue with others. You can do this by

- talking to your parents and others to find out their points of view
- attending, or having a parent attend, the meetings about the issue
- writing a letter about your concerns and sending it to the newspaper, the mayor, or your member of Parliament

Use the following information to answer the next question.

Zebra mussels are accidentally introduced by boats into a northern Ontario lake. The zebra mussels begin to spread quickly, changing the original biodiversity of the lake.

Several people in a community by another nearby lake become concerned about the zebra mussels entering their lake because they depend on it for both food and jobs. The people decide to call a town meeting to discuss options for solving the mussel problem. Four main plans are voiced by people from the town:

1. Immediately pump chemicals that kill zebra mussels into the lake.
2. Find animals that eat zebra mussels and introduce them into the lake.
3. Begin a massive fishing operation to collect as many zebra mussels as possible from all the lakes.
4. Make new laws that require boaters to check their hulls and tanks for zebra mussels before entering the lake.

1. Which of the above plans would **best** protect the lake environment and help the people who live by the lake?

A. 1 **B.** 2

C. 3 **D.** 4

Use the following information to answer the next question.

An old logging mill in a northern Ontario town closes, leaving hundreds of people unemployed. A new company decides to invest in a new mill in the area; however, they will need to build the mill in a local forest ecosystem. This will require cutting the forest down to make room for the new facility. Citizens of the community were asked to provide any questions or concerns to the mayor of the town.
Citizens asked the following questions:

1. How will the plant affect the smell of the air?
2. What will happen to the animals in the forest?
3. How much of the forest will be cut down to build the new mill?
4. Will the construction of the plant increase jobs in the local economy?

2. Which question would **most likely** be the most important for this community?

A. 1 **B.** 2

C. 3 **D.** 4

6LS1.2 assess the benefits that human societies derive from biodiversity and the problems that occur when biodiversity is diminished

Benefits of Biodiversity

Humans have made use of the great diversity of species on Earth to meet many needs. Plants are grown for food as well as for fibre to make clothing, paper, and other products. Trees are used to make lumber and other building products. Animals are raised for food and other products such as clothing. Plants, fungi, and other organisms have been used to make medicines.

Food, lumber, and medicine are just a few of the materials made from Earth's many species.

The diversity of species in the world is complex and ever-changing. Every year, new species are found and classified while other species go **extinct**. This means that every member of that species in the world has died. Extinction is a normal part of Earth's cycles. However, the actions of humans have sped up the extinction rate on Earth. Many of these extinctions happen because habitats are destroyed.

With each extinction, people risk losing out on many important discoveries. For example, a species that has yet to be discovered could lead to cures for many diseases.

Other problems can occur when biodiversity dwindles. Many farms have experienced problems caused by a lack of diversity of species. For example, it is now common for farmers to plant only one type of crop. This is called a **monoculture**. A monoculture can be useful to a farmer. The farmer only needs to make the soil suitable for that particular crop. However, growing the same plant over and over in the same soil can take out all the useful nutrients. Over time, the plant may not grow as well because the soil is missing these nutrients.

Diseases and pests are also problems in monocultures. A few diseased plants in one field could kill the entire crop. A pest that likes to eat a certain crop will eat and multiply quickly if the plant is grown year after year. A farmer may use a pesticide to get rid of the pest. But pesticides have also created problems. They have polluted the air, water, and plants they are meant to protect. Pesticides sometimes kill helpful species. The pests can also grow resistant to pesticides, which means that they are not harmed by the pesticide and will continue to grow and reproduce.

Aerial view of different crops in Leamington, Ontario

Scientists are aware of the loss of biodiversity on the planet. They are working with different governments and groups to help stop or slow down the extinctions of organisms. The efforts of these people have helped to save many species from extinction.

3. One possible risk of planting a monoculture is that
A. it reduces the number of pests
B. a few diseased plants could kill the entire crop
C. only one type of soil is needed to grow the crop
D. several different types of soil are needed to grow the crop

Use the following information to answer the next question.

> Many scientists believe that human actions have increased the extinction rate of different species. Many of these extinctions happen because habitats are destroyed to make room for buildings or farms. The organisms that lose their habitat also lose their sources of food.

4. Which of the following statements explains a negative effect of the loss of biodiversity in an area?
A. It will cost less to produce food using fewer species.
B. Species will have to adapt to live with humans in their habitat.
C. Chemicals used to kill particular species will be more effective.
D. Possible cures for diseases found in undiscovered species may be lost.

6LS3.1 identify and describe the distinguishing characteristics of different groups of plants and animals, and use these characteristics to further classify various kinds of plants and animals

CLASSIFYING ORGANISMS BY THEIR CHARACTERISTICS

Scientists classify organisms into five kingdoms: Plantae, Animalia, Protista, Fungi, and Monera. The common names for the organisms in these five kingdoms are plants, animals, protists, fungi, and bacteria.

PLANTS

Most plants are multicellular organisms that cannot move on their own. They make their own food from sunlight through the process of photosynthesis. Plants can be put into two groups: vascular and non-vascular. **Vascular plants** have roots and tubes to move water and nutrients to all parts of the plant. They grow in many different environments and can be many different sizes. **Non-vascular plants** absorb water and nutrients through their roots, leaves, and stems. They grow best in shady places close to water, tend to be small, and reproduce by making spores.

Here is an example of plants put into a tree-classification system.

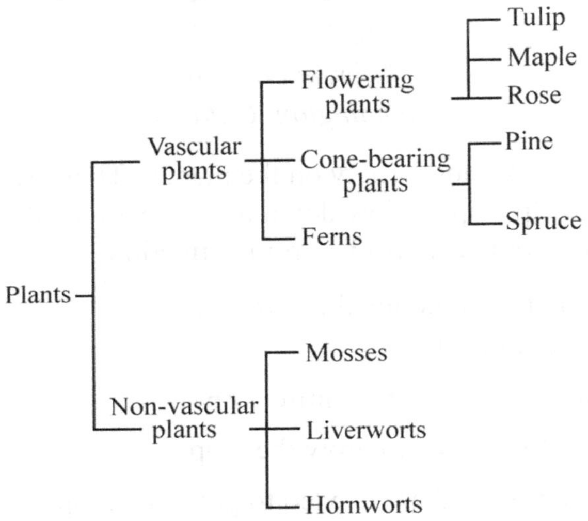

ANIMALS

Animals are multicellular organisms that cannot make their own food. They must eat plants or other animals for energy. Animals can move from place to place. They can be put into two groups: vertebrates and invertebrates.

- **Vertebrates** are animals that have a backbone and a skeleton inside their bodies. This skeleton may be made of bone, cartilage, or a combination of both.
- **Invertebrates** do not have backbones or internal skeletons. They might have a hard outer covering called an **exoskeleton**.

Vertebrates and invertebrates can also be classified into subgroups as shown in the tree chart below.

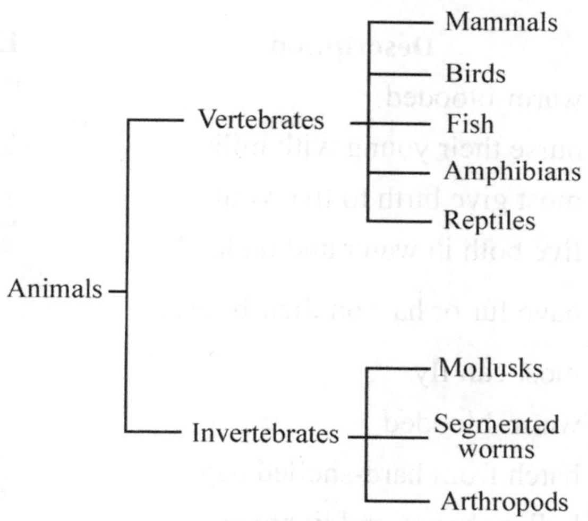

Each of these subgroups of vertebrates is also divided into subgroups. For example, mammals can be separated into many different groups, such as primates, carnivores, whales, and many others. Each group contains many different members. The whale group includes humpback whales, orcas, dolphins, and others. Below is an example of a tree classification showing three different groups of mammals and members of each group.

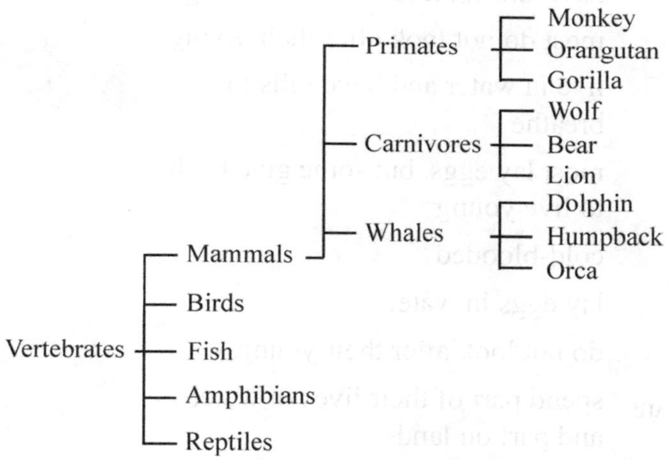

Different Vertebrates

Vertebrate Name	Description	Example
Mammals	warm-blooded	
	nurse their young with milk	
	most give birth to live young	
	live both in water and on land	
	have fur or hair on their bodies	
Birds	most can fly	
	warm-blooded	
	hatch from hard-shelled eggs	
	hollow bones and lightweight bodies	
	have wings, feathers, a beak, and two legs	
Fish	cold-blooded	
	have fins instead of arms and legs	
	most do not look after their young	
	live in water and have gills to breathe	
	most lay eggs, but some give birth to live young	
Amphibians	cold-blooded	
	lay eggs in water	
	do not look after their young	
	spend part of their lives in water and part on land	
	at different times in their life cycle, can breathe with gills, lungs, or even through their skin	
Reptiles	do not look after their young	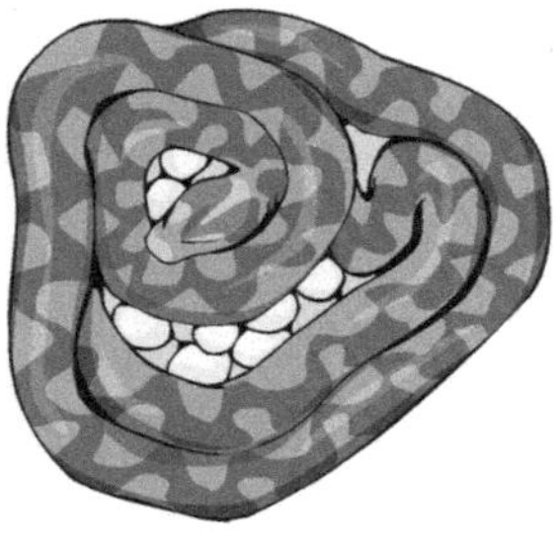
	covered in scales or hard plates	
	cold-blooded; warm themselves by sitting in the sun	
	most lay soft-shelled eggs; some snakes give birth to live young	

Different Invertebrates

Invertebrate Name	Description	Example
Mollusks	some have a shell for protection	
	some can live on land, as snails do	
	most live in water, like clams and squids	
	those that live in water have gills to breathe	
Segmented worms	soft bodied	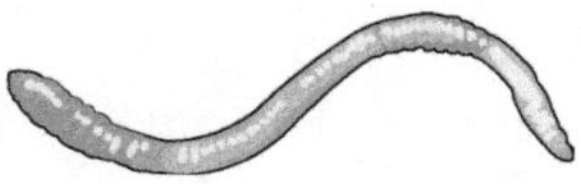
	found in damp places	
	bodies divided into segments	
Arthropods	legs have several joints	
	largest group of invertebrates	
	have an outer skeleton or shell	
	include insects, spiders, and lobsters	

PROTISTS

Most **protists** are single-celled organisms that have a nucleus and are so small they can only be seen with a microscope. Others can be multicellular and grow quite large. Kelp and seaweed are examples of protists that grow large. Protists usually live in water but may be found in damp areas on land. They can act like larger plants, fungi, or animals. Plant-like protists use sunlight to make their own food. Animal-like protists need to eat other single-celled organisms for energy. Fungi-like protists, such as slime molds, look like mold but act like animal-like protists. Slime molds can crawl around looking for bacteria to digest rather than breaking down matter as fungi would.

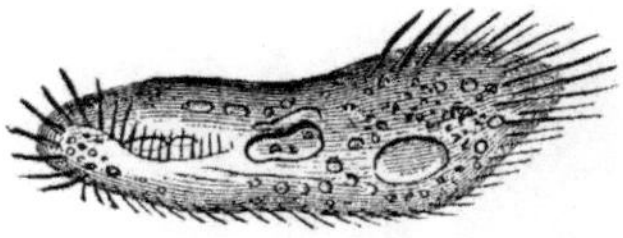

A paramecium is an example of an animal-like protist.

Scientists are still trying to decide how to classify many protists. For example, some scientists put green algae into both the plant and protists kingdoms. As scientists learn more about these organisms, they will be better able to classify them. Below is a tree chart that classifies different protists.

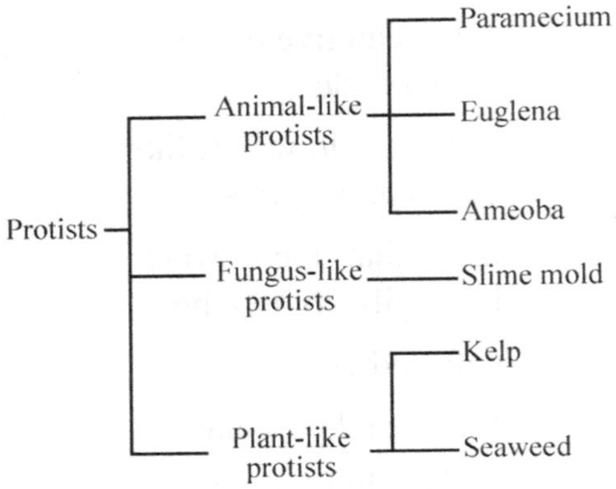

Fungi

Most **fungi** are multicellular organisms that cannot move from place to place. Fungi do not have chlorophyll and do not make their own food by photosynthesis as plants do. Instead, fungi feed on dead plant material. Mushrooms, molds, and yeasts are examples of fungi.

Monera

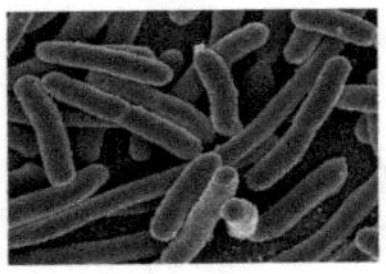

Monera are single-celled organisms that do not act like either plants or animals. Their cells do not have a nucleus. Bacteria belong to this kingdom. Bacteria are so small that you need a microscope to see them. One well known bacteria is *Escherichia coli*, better known as *E. coli*. This bacteria is found in the digestive tracts of mammals. Bacteria are found everywhere on Earth.

Use the following information to answer the next question.

5. Which of the following statements about fungi is true?

A. Fungi feed on dead plant material.

B. Fungi can only grow on the forest floor.

C. Fungi have chlorophyll to make their own food.

D. Fungi can transport themselves to other areas using the wind.

Use the following information to answer the next question.

Some plants are classified as non-vascular plants because they do not have tubes to transport water from the roots to the leaves. These plants absorb water and nutrients through their stems and leaves. They grow best in the shade and are usually small. Instead of producing seeds, these plants reproduce by making spores.

6. Which of the following plants is an example of a non-vascular plant?

A. 

B. 

C. 

D. 

Use the following information to answer the next question.

Earthworms and snakes both have tube-shaped bodies and both can be brown. However, they are not classified in the same subgroup of animals.

7. Which of the following statements explains why earthworms and snakes are **not** in the same subgroup of animals?
   A. Snakes are longer than earthworms, and they eat different food.
   B. Snakes' bodies have only one section, but earthworms have segmented bodies.
   C. They have similar physical features but different structural characteristics.
   D. They have similar physical features but need to live in very different habitats to survive.

6LS3.2 demonstrate an understanding of biodiversity as the variety of life on earth, including variety within each species of plant and animal, among species of plants and animals in communities, and among communities and the physical landscapes that support them

VARIETY WITHIN SPECIES AND COMMUNITIES

There are millions upon millions of different species on Earth. Each species is a group of similar individual organisms. An organism is any single living thing.

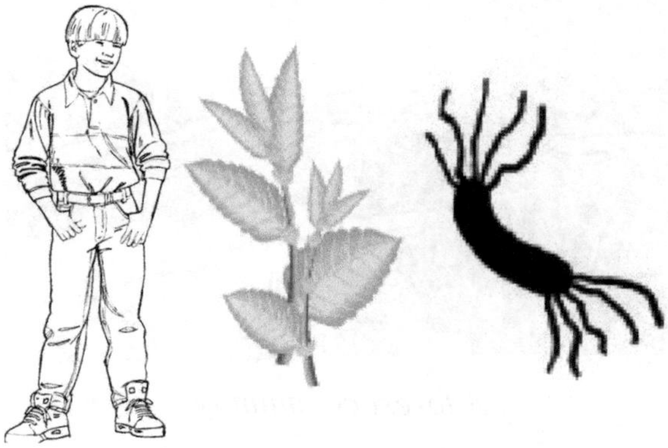

This boy, plant, and bacterium are organisms.

You can see variety in organisms of the same species. For example, zebras all have slight differences in the pattern of their stripes.

Zebras

Members of a species can show differences because of the differences in the environment and landscape. A pine tree at the bottom of a mountain will grow taller than the pines near the top of the mountain.

A tree of the same species may grow differently from another, depending on where it lives.

You can also see variety within communities. A **natural community** is made up of all the species that live together in the same area. It is made up of living things only. For example, a forest community is made up of all the different kinds of plants, animals, protists, fungi, and bacteria in the forest.

A forest community

Variety is important in communities. It helps to make sure that the community will survive under different conditions. For example, a fire can destroy a forest community in a matter of days. It can take many years before the forest grows back. However, there are populations that can help bring the community back quickly. Fireweed is a plant that grows quickly after a fire.

Fireweed is one of the first plants to appear after a forest fire.

Use the following information to answer the next question.

A pine tree grows in a low-lying forest as shown. There are many factors that contribute to the biodiversity of pine trees.

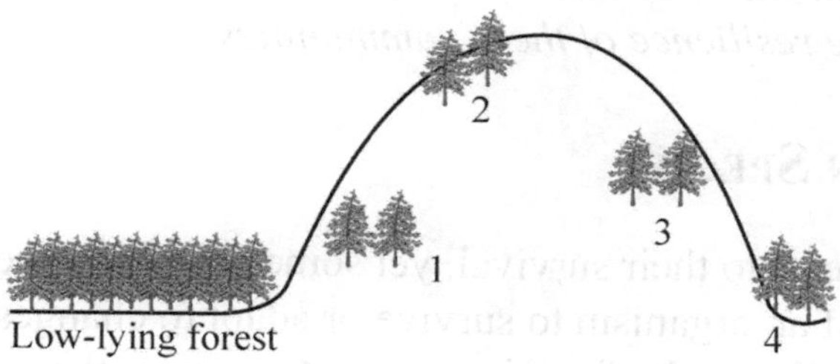

8. Which location on this map would **best** indicate a location where pine trees would grow much smaller than those in the low-lying forest?

A. 1 **B.** 2
C. 3 **D.** 4

Use the following information to answer the next question.

There is an enormous amount of biodiverse life on Earth. There are many different species of plants and animals. There are also differences within each group of plants and animals that make them very diverse.

9. Which of the following characteristics **best** shows a factor of biodiversity within humans?

A. Thumbs that help to grasp objects **B.** Different languages
C. Eye and hair colour **D.** Veins and arteries

6LS3.3 *describe ways in which biodiversity within species is important for maintaining the resilience of those species*

6LS3.4 *describe ways in which biodiversity within and among communities is important for maintaining the resilience of these communities*

Resilience Within Species

Organisms face many threats to their survival, yet some are resilient enough to survive. **Resilience** is the ability of an organism to survive or adapt to changes in its environment. An organism's resilience usually results from its genes. **Genes** are the genetic material found in an organism's cells. The genes from two parents combine in their offspring. This is why children usually look like their parents. An organism's genes also determine how its body will work. They help it survive in its environment.

The girl's genes gave her blond hair and light skin. The boy's genes gave him dark hair and dark skin.

The resilience of some animals can be seen when they get mange. Mange is a disease that can affect many animals. A mite causes mange when it burrows under the skin of an animal, causing itchiness and hair loss. Squirrels can be infected with mange. How badly they are infected depends upon their genes. The squirrels that show great resilience toward the disease are not bothered. Most likely, their young will not be affected by mange either. This is because the genes that protected them will be passed on to their offspring.

Some types of bacteria have become resistant to antibiotics over time. When antibiotics were first used, most of the bacteria died. However, a small number of them were not affected by the antibiotic, survived, and were able to reproduce and pass on this resilience to their offspring. Now that antibiotic is no longer effective at killing that type of bacteria.

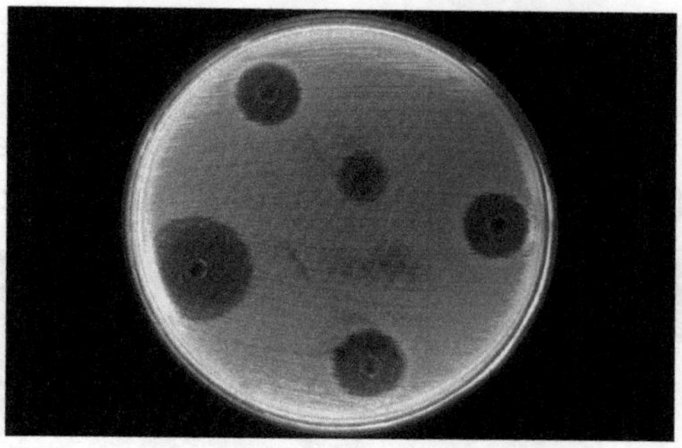

Testing bacteria for resistance to antibiotics

Resilience in Communities

Resilience is important in communities as well as in species. Suppose a farmer planted the same type of wheat in all his fields. That summer, disease killed all of his plants. However, other types of wheat were not affected by the disease. The farmer should have planted different types of wheat, rather than just one species. This way, he would have at least been able to bring in a small crop rather than none at all.

10. Which of the following examples **best** shows resilience?

A. Bacteria are killed by treatment with antibiotics.

B. A forest fire destroys all the organisms in an ecosystem.

C. Some dogs and their young are not greatly affected by fleas.

D. Several geese fly south for the winter in a V-shaped formation.

Use the following information to answer the next question.

There are many animals that live in communities all over the world. Some animals show more resilience toward diseases than others.

11. What is the major factor that explains why some animals are more resilient to certain diseases than other animals living in the same community?

A. Food

B. Genes

C. Weather

D. Location

6LS3.5 describe interrelationships within species, between species, and between species and their environment, and explain how these interrelationships sustain biodiversity

INTERRELATIONSHIPS

Organisms form connections with other organisms in nature. These connections are called **interrelationships**.

Interrelationships can occur within species. For example, wolves in a pack depend upon each other for survival. Together they defend their territory, hunt and bring down large prey, and raise the pups.

Wolves rely on each other to survive.

Interrelationships also occur between different species. A bee needs nectar from flowers to make honey. Some flowering plants need bees to pollinate their flowers. As a bee moves from flower to flower to look for nectar, it transfers the pollen from one plant to another. This allows the plants to reproduce.

Bee transferring pollen from one flower to another

Sometimes organisms compete with other organisms for things they need to survive. For example, water lilies and algae sometimes compete for sunlight. Algae grow very close to the surface of the water. Water lilies also grow on the surface of the water. Too many water lilies might block the sunlight from reaching the algae.

Water lilies floating on the water

12. Organisms form connections with other organisms in nature. A connection can be within a species or between different species. What is this type of connection called?

A. Food chain
B. Biodiversity
C. Interrelationship
D. Monoculture system

13. In which of the following situations does one organism benefit while the other is unaffected?

A. A bird lives in a hole in a tree.
B. A barnacle fastens itself to a whale.
C. A bee collects pollen from a flower.
D. A mosquito drinks blood from a cow.

14. Two species that live in the same area and share the same resources often compete with each other. Which of the following statements describes a situation where two species compete for the same resources?

A. A tree blocks sunlight needed by the undergrowth.
B. Lady bugs eat aphids from the leaves of a plant.
C. Ants build a colony near a rotting log in a forest.
D. Hummingbirds take nectar from a flower.

6LS3.6 identify everyday products that come from a diversity of organisms

Products That Come From Nature

People have always used materials from nature to meet their needs. Sometimes one type of organism is used to make many different products. For example, trees are used to make paper and lumber. Material from trees is also used in paint, chewing gum, nail polish, explosives, and cellophane. Sap from maple trees is used to make maple syrup.

Chewing gum, nail polish, paint, and cellophane all contain materials from trees.

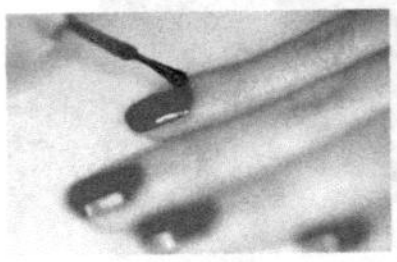

Many of the products you use every day come from plants. Flower pollen is used in vitamins, shampoos, toothpastes, and deodorants. White willow bark can be used as a pain reliever. Tofu is a food product that is made from soybeans. Wheat is used to make bread.

Seaweed is a form of algae. It is used as food or in medicines. Some forms of bacteria are also used in products. For example, bacteria are used to make yogurt.

Besides providing food for humans, animals also provide other useful products. Silk is made from the cocoons of silkworms. Sheep fleece is used to make wool, which is used to make clothing. Leather can also be used in furniture, belts, and sports equipment.

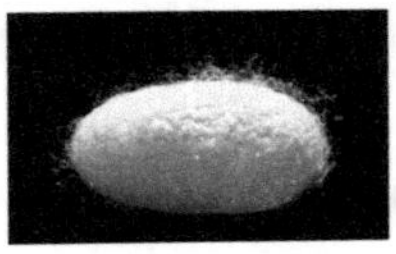

A silkworm cocoon

15. Tofu is a high protein food source enjoyed around the world. What is the primary source for making tofu?

A.

Soybean

B.

Cows

C.

Wheat

D.

Fish

16. Flower pollen collected by bees is used in all of the following products **except**

A. shampoo

B. deodorant

C. toothpaste

D. cellophane

6LS3.7 explain how invasive species reduce biodiversity in local environments

Invasive Species

An **invasive species** is a non-native species that has been introduced into a new environment and has taken over the habitat of native species. A **non-native species** is a plant or animal that has been brought in or placed into a new environment from somewhere else. Not all non-native species are invasive.

An environment that shows **stability** allows all species living within it to thrive. Invasive species can reduce the biodiversity of environments, making them unstable. An invasive species can kill off existing species in a habitat by using up all the available resources. They may also prey on native species. The native species may not have time to adapt to the change and may die out. There are several organisms in Canada that are considered invasive species.

Zebra mussels are fingernail-sized mussels that live in freshwater. They are originally from Asia and Eastern Europe. They have spread to the Great Lakes and other lakes in Ontario and Quebec. Zebra mussels are responsible for destroying many native mussels in North American lakes. They can attach to and kill native mussel and clam species. Zebra mussels also eat a great deal of phytoplankton and other microscopic organisms. Many native species often starve as they compete with the mussels for food. Scientists also believe that the zebra mussels are responsible for killing thousands of aquatic birds and fish. Zebra mussels are very good at cleaning water. However, toxins gather in their bodies. These toxins are passed down the food chain as they are eaten by fish, and the fish are eaten by the birds. The fish and birds die because of the concentration of these toxins.

Zebra mussel

Another very destructive invasive species is the Asian long-horned beetle, which originally came from China or Korea. It feeds on deciduous trees, such as poplar, elm, and maple. It lays its eggs in holes it makes in trees. The larvae burrow deeper into the tree and later come out of the tree as adults. Many beetles can kill a single tree in one or two years.The beetle is a great threat to forest habitats. The beetle only attacks certain trees. This could lead to forests that only grow trees that are resistant to the beetle, reducing the biodiversity of that habitat. The beetles are also a concern in cities. Large old trees that have stood for many decades are at risk of being infected. Infected trees are often replaced with species that are resistant to the beetle. This will reduce the diversity of trees found in a city's green areas.

Asian long-horned beetle

Another example of an invasive species is purple loosestrife, which is a plant that was brought to North America from Europe in the 1800s. It grows well in wetlands and places where soil has been disturbed. For example, it grows well in ditches by roads.Purple loosestrife is a great concern in wetland areas. It can quickly take over the habitat, choking out many native species of plants. Purple loosestrife is also a concern for farmers. It can clog canals and irrigation ditches. It can also grow as a weed in fields.

Purple loosestrife

Use the following information to answer the next question.

The zebra mussel was accidentally introduced into the Great Lakes and has reduced the biodiversity of the lakes.

17. How have zebra mussels reduced the biodiversity of the Great Lakes?

A. They use up all of the oxygen in the water.

B. They eat the eggs of fish native to the area.

C. They travel in large groups sweeping the lake bed of food.

D. They eat phytoplankton usually eaten by native species of the area.

18. Which of the following statements describes how the Asian long-horned beetle kills trees?

A. They eat all the tree's bark.

B. They eat all of the tree's leaves.

C. Their larva hatch and burrow farther into the tree.

D. The pupa use the leaves of the tree as their cocoons.

6LS2.1 follow established safety procedures for outdoor activities and field work

Safety Procedures for Outdoor Activities and Field Work

Before you go out into nature to do activities or study organisms, review the safety procedures your class has in place. These safety procedures might include the following guidelines:

- Research the organisms and habitats you will be exploring before you go outside.
- Always dress for the weather and the environment.
- Always stay together as a group or with a partner when exploring a habitat.
- Always stay on marked trails.
- Leave everything as you found it. Take only notes and photographs, or draw sketches. Never collect anything to bring back.
- Avoid going near bodies of water unless your teacher gives you permission first.
- Never approach animals in the wild.
- Only handle materials and organisms if your teacher gives you permission. This is for your safety and the safety of the animals and plants.
- Treat all living things with respect.
- Never eat anything you find in the environment. This includes berries and mushrooms.
- When you return to school or home, wash your hands.

Treat all living things with respect.

Some of your activities might take place in the classroom. Consider the following safety procedures:

- When studying organisms, always use equipment appropriately.
- Do not handle any organisms unless you have permission to do so.
- Follow any procedures that your teacher has for handling organisms.
- Always wash your hands before and after handling organisms. This is for your health and the health of the organism.

Use the following information to answer the next question.

Richard's class plans on exploring a forest habitat for their science class. They pick a partner to travel with and get ready to go.

19. Which of the following pairs of students is best prepared to explore a forest habitat in the summer?

A. 

B. 

C. 

D. 

6LS2.2 investigate the organisms found in a specific habitat and classify them according to a classification system

CLASSIFYING ORGANISMS IN HABITATS

There are many different ways you can **classify** living things. For example, you could classify them into the five different kingdoms: Animalia (animals), Plantae (plants), Fungi (fungi), Protista (protists), and Monera (bacteria).

Ava's class went on a field trip into a forest. While they were there, they saw all of the organisms shown in the following diagram.

Ava's teacher asked her to classify the organisms into the five kingdoms. She used a chart to do this.

Types of Organisms Found in a Forest Area

Monera	Protists	Fungi	Plants	Animals
Soil bacteria	Slime mold	Fungus Soil mold Toadstool Bracket fungi	Fern Moss Grass Oak tree Pine tree Berry bush	Fly Snail Toad Deer Crow Worm Beetle Rabbit Eastern cougar

After making the chart, Ava noticed there were many different kinds of animals. She decided to classify the animals further. She made the following tree chart to classify them.

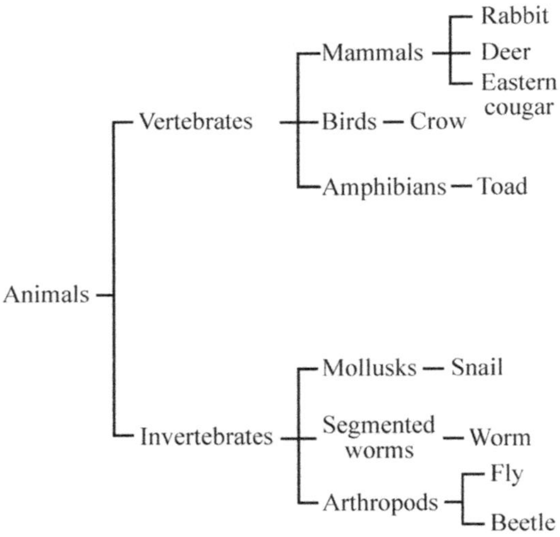

Ava also classified the plants further. She classified them according to whether they were vascular or non-vascular. Vascular plants have tubes within them to move liquid and nutrients to all parts of the plant. Non-vascular plants absorb liquid and nutrients through the different parts of the plant, like the leaves and stems.

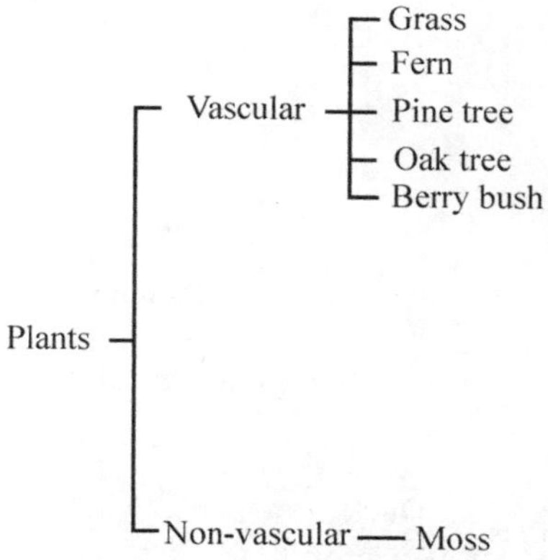

Use the following information to answer the next question.

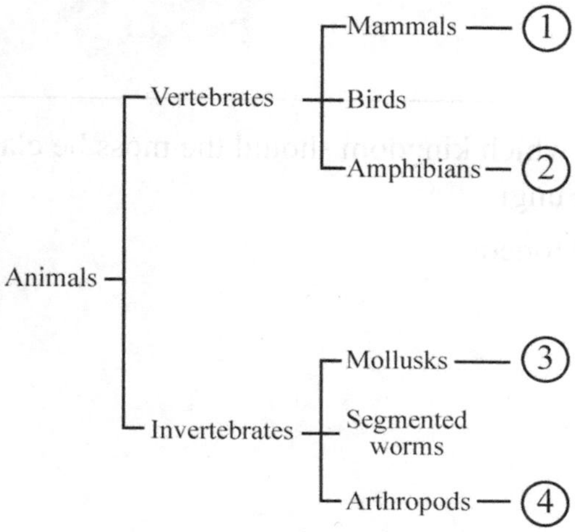

20. Which number in the chart correctly identifies the classification of the animal shown?

A. 1 **B.** 2

C. 3 **D.** 4

Use the following information to answer the next question.

Marcie visited a pond to study the plants and animals that lived there. She drew a picture of some of the things she saw so that she could classify the plants and animals.

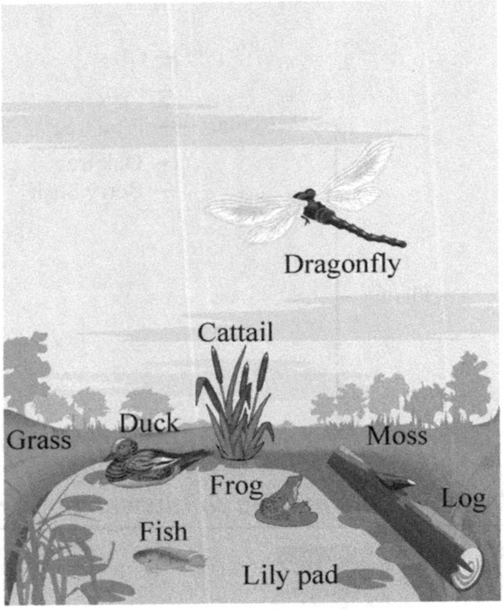

21. Into which kingdom should the moss be classified?

A. Fungi

B. Plants

C. Monera

D. Protista

6LS2.3 use scientific inquiry/research skills to compare the characteristics of organisms within the plant or animal kingdoms

Comparing Characteristics of Organisms

Characteristics of Plants

Plants can be classified into one of two groups based on their **characteristics:** vascular or non-vascular.

A flower is a vascular plant.

Moss is a non-vascular plant.

How are vascular and non-vascular plants the same and how are they different?

Vascular Plants	Non-vascular Plants
Have stems that hold the plant upright	Have stems that hold the plant upright
Have roots that keep the plant anchored to the ground	Have root-like parts that anchor the plant to a surface
Have tubes to take in water and nutrients from the ground	Absorb water and nutrients directly through the leaves and stems
Can be many different sizes; the largest members are trees	Are all very small
Have leaves filled with chlorophyll to capture the sun's energy to make food	Have leaf-like parts filled with chlorophyll to capture the sun's energy to make food
Can grow in many different environments, from moist forests to dry deserts	Grow in shady places, close to water
Three different groups, all of which reproduce differently: • Flowering plants—produce seeds in fruit, like sunflowers or apple trees • Cone-bearing plants—produce seeds in cones, like pine or spruce trees • Ferns—produce spores under leaves	Three different groups, all of which reproduce by making spores: • Mosses • Liverworts • Hornworts

This chart compares the characteristics of two vascular plants: a coniferous and a deciduous tree.

A coniferous tree

A deciduous tree

Characteristics of a Coniferous Tree and a Deciduous Tree

Coniferous Trees	Deciduous Trees
Vary in height, size, and age	Vary in height, size, and age
Needles are shed year-round	Leaves are shed in the fall; new leaves sprout in the spring
Have small, needle-like leaves	Have large, flat, broad leaves
Reproduce from seeds in cones	Reproduce from seeds inside fruit
Needles remain green year-round	Leaves change colour in the fall before being shed
Can grow in cold and dry climates, like on mountains or on the edge of deserts	Grow best in areas where the weather is warm and moist for at least part of the year

Characteristics of Animals

Animals are grouped by their characteristics. Animals can be classified into one of two categories: vertebrates or invertebrates.

Vertebrates	Invertebrates
Animals that have a backbone	Animals that do not have a backbone
Reproduce by live birth or laying eggs	Reproduce by laying eggs
Gain energy by eating other organisms	Gain energy by eating other organisms
Can be cold-blooded or warm-blooded	Are cold-blooded
Breathe oxygen from the air or in the water	Breathe oxygen from the air or in the water
Can move from place to place on land or in water	Can move from place to place on land or in water

This chart looks at the characteristics of two vertebrates: a mammal and a fish.

A mammal

A fish

Characteristics of a Mammal and a Fish

Mammal	Fish
Are warm-blooded	Are cold-blooded
Live in the water or on land	Live only in water
Most give birth to live young	Most lay eggs to reproduce
Nurse young with milk and care for young	Most fish do not look after their young
Have fur or hair at some stage of their life cycle	Most have scales covering their bodies

22. Which of the following lists contains three organisms considered vertebrates?

A. Elk, rabbit, hermit crab

B. Coyote, tree frog, salmon

C. Black bear, halibut, mayfly

D. Squid, beaver, salamander

23. Which of the following statements about deciduous and coniferous trees is **false**?

A. They both have seeds.
B. They both have leaves.
C. They both have flowers.
D. They both have woody stems.

6LS2.4 use appropriate science and technology vocabulary, including classification, biodiversity, natural community, interrelationships, vertebrate, invertebrate, stability, characteristics, and organism, in oral and written communication

BIODIVERSITY: VOCABULARY

Please refer to the glossary to find the definitions of the following vocabulary words: **biodiversity**, **characteristics**, **classification**, **interrelationship**, **invertebrate**, **natural community**, **organism**, **stability**, and **vertebrate**.

24. The word *organism* is best defined as

A. an organization that helps the environment
B. an organ found in the human body
C. a part in a keyboard instrument
D. a living thing

Use the following information to answer the next question.

A population of mice maintains a steady rate of growth and does not undergo any large decreases or increases in population.

25. The mouse population is **best** described as showing

A. stability
B. biodiversity
C. characteristic
D. interrelationship

ANSWERS AND SOLUTIONS
LIFE SYSTEMS: BIODIVERSITY

1. D	6. C	11. B	16. D	21. B
2. D	7. C	12. C	17. D	22. B
3. B	8. B	13. B	18. C	23. C
4. D	9. C	14. A	19. D	24. D
5. A	10. C	15. A	20. A	25. A

1. D

Making laws for boaters to check their ships for the mussels would best protect the lake environment.

Most of the points of view discussed require a change in the lake by adding chemicals or new species of animals or by requiring large scale fishing. All of these solutions are likely to harm the lake environment. So, none of these would be the best solution for a future zebra mussel problem in their lake.

2. D

The most important question for this community would be whether or not the mill will create jobs for the local economny. All of these questions are important and relevent. However, for the town to continue, hundreds of people need their jobs back.

The town already had a paper mill, so the people have already considered the environmental issues. Environmental damage may be considered less important by this community.

3. B

A few diseased plants could kill an entire crop. In a monoculture, all of the plants are the same. If some are infected, then all the rest are very likely to get the disease. This would ruin an entire crop for the farmers.

4. D

With fewer species, humans risk missing out on important discoveries.

There are species of plants and animals that have not been discovered yet that could cure diseases or provide humans with a cleaner source of fuel. If the habitat of these species is destroyed, the species and their medical and industrial properties could go undiscovered by people.

5. A

Fungi feed on decaying plants such as dead logs. They cannot make their own food, so they must feed on other organisms. Fungi are found in many different habitats.

6. C

Moss is an example of a non-vascular plant. Mosses absorb nutrients and water through their stems and leaves, and they usually grow in the shade, at the base of trees.

7. C

These animals have similar physical features, but different structural characteristics. They may have a similar body shape, but they are structurally different. Snakes have backbones, but worms do not have backbones.

8. B

The trees at location 2 will grow shorter, since they are growing on the top of a mountain. The environment and landscape can affect the size and population of the same species of trees.

9. C

Humans can have different coloured eyes and hair. There are many other differences in humans as well, such as skin colour or body size.

The use of different languages does not show biodiversity because language is learned, not inherited.

10. C

Some dogs are not bothered by fleas. These dogs' ability to adapt, survive, and reproduce despite the fleas shows the dogs' resilience, which is due to their genes. Their young will most likely have the same resistance.

11. B

An animal's genes carry genetic information from the parents to the offspring. They help animals to adapt and survive in their surroundings. Animals can pass these genes on to their offspring in the community, and they will most likely be resilient toward the same things.

12. C

The connection between two organisms in nature is called an interrelationship. Interrelationships are very important to maintaining biodiversity in species.

13. B

A barnacle fastens itself to a whale. The barnacle gets the chance to move around, giving it access to more food. The whale is not affected by the barnacle.

14. A

Both the trees and the undergrowth live in forests. Both compete for sunlight to live. This demonstrates a competitive interrelationship between species.

15. A

Tofu is made by processing soybeans. It is produced from curdled soybean milk.

16. D

Shampoo, deodorant, and toothpaste all contain flower pollen collected by bees. Cellophane is not made from flower pollen.

17. D

Zebra mussels eat phytoplankton that is usually eaten by native species of the Great Lakes. With less food to eat, these native species could starve. This reduces the biodiversity of the Great Lakes.

18. C

The larva of the Asian long-horned beetle hatch and burrow farther into the tree. This kills a tree over time.

19. D

The students wearing pants, long sleeve shirts, shoes, and hats are best prepared to explore the forest habitat, even in the summer. Try to avoid clothing that can catch on branches and twigs, and always wear a hat and sunscreen, even if it is cloudy.

20. A

The moose is classified into the mammal category. Moose are warm-blooded, have hair, give birth to live young, and feed their young with milk. These are all characteristics of mammals.

21. B

Moss is classified into the plant kingdom. Moss does not move and makes its own food by undergoing photosynthesis.

22. B

Coyotes, tree frogs, and salmon are classified as vertebrates. Vertebrates are organisms that have backbones. Fish, amphibians, reptiles, birds, and mammals are classified as vertebrates.

23. C

Only the deciduous trees have flowers. Both deciduous trees and coniferous trees have woody stems. They both have leaves, although the coniferous leaves are modified into needles. Both types of trees start from seeds.

24. D

An organism is any living thing. It can be a plant, animal, protist, fungus, or bacterium.

25. A

This population is showing stability. There are no sudden increases or decreases in population. The species maintains a steady growth in its environment.

UNIT TEST — LIFE SYSTEMS: BIODIVERSITY

Use the following information to answer the next question.

A mining company wishes to build a mine in southern Ontario. The area in which they wish to build contains many plants and animals that contribute to its biodiversity.

1. What action could the company take to **best** protect the biodiversity of the region?
   A. Get written permission from the government to build the mine
   B. Consult environmental experts on a course of action
   C. Bring in a team of lawyers to assess risk to the company
   D. Move all the plants and animals to a different area

Use the following information to answer the next question.

An environmental expert recommends that a logging company selectively-cut trees in a forest ecosystem instead of clear-cutting it. This picture shows an example of each cutting technique.

Selective-cutting

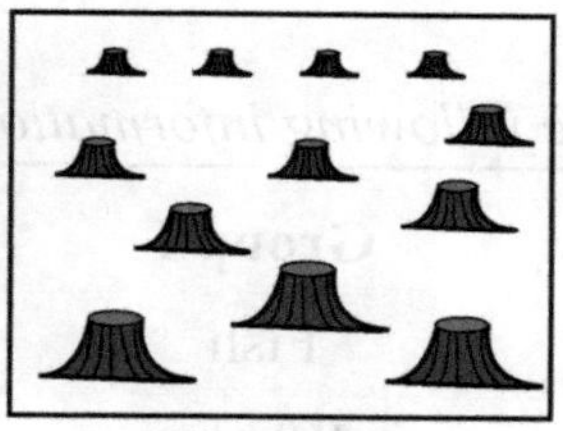
Clear-cutting

2. Which of the following statements describes a negative consequence to the company if it decides to selectively-cut the trees?
   A. Animals would still have shelter.
   B. There would be less soil erosion in the area.
   C. It could remove infested trees from a forest ecosystem.
   D. It would take more time and money to selectively cut the trees.

3. Which of the following statements **correctly** describes how the use of monocultures affects the environment?
   A. They add nutrients to the soil.
   B. They allow several species of crops to grow in one place.
   C. They use different types of soil that benefit only a few plants.
   D. They require pesticides because they allow the same pests to grow and multiply each year.

Use the following information to answer the next question.

Phil wants to explore and study the habitat shown.

4. To best protect this habitat while exploring, Phil should

A. collect living samples to study

B. only take notes and photographs and make sketches

C. walk off the trail to study as many areas as possible

D. leave behind the garbage so that it can be recycled into the soil

Use the following information to answer the next question.

Group I	**Group II**
Fish	Snail
Whale	Worm
Bear	Spider

5. What should be the titles of Group **I** and Group **II**?

A. Mammals and insects

B. Mammals and vertebrates

C. Vertebrates and invertebrates

D. Animals with fur and invertebrates

Use the following information to answer the next question.

Sherri was asked to classify the fish in the given diagram. She used the following chart to classify the fish.

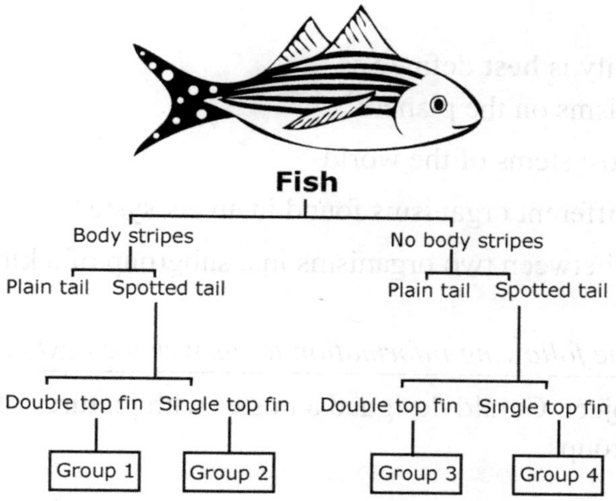

6. To which group does the fish belong?

A. 1 **B.** 2

C. 3 **D.** 4

Use the following information to answer the next question.

Trees like oak and maple have a tendency to shed their leaves and remain leafless for a part of the year.

7. Oak and maple belong to which of the following groups of trees?

A. Deciduous **B.** Evergreen

C. Rainforest **D.** Coniferous

8. Which of the following animals is a vertebrate?

A. 

Slug

B. 

Salamander

C. 

Crab

D. 

Starfish

9. Two organisms that depend on each other for survival can be described as having

A. a parasite
B. an adaptation
C. a modification
D. an interrelationship

10. The term biodiversity is **best** defined as

A. all of the organisms on the planet
B. the different ecosystems of the world
C. the variety of different organisms found in an ecosystem
D. the differences between two organisms in a subgroup of a kingdom

Use the following information to answer the next question.

For his science project, Gerald designed a poster with pictures of different organisms divided into two groups.

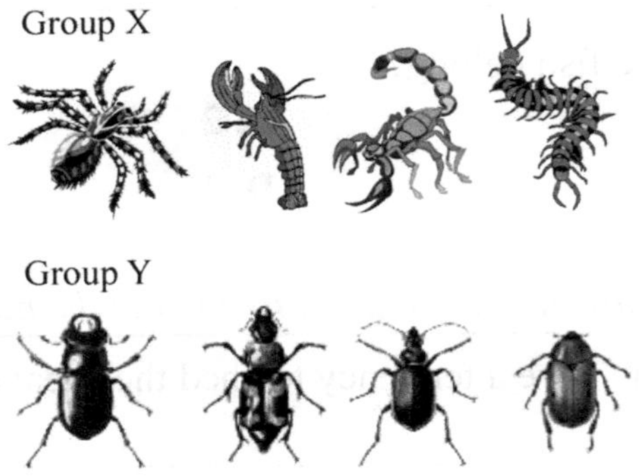

11. Which of the following organisms belongs to group Y?

A.

B.

C.

D.

12. Which of the following statements describes a difference between reptiles and amphibians?

A. Reptiles have scales on their bodies.

B. Reptiles are cold-blooded.

C. Reptiles have lungs.

D. Reptiles lay eggs.

Use the following information to answer the next question.

Lindee was looking at some pictures of plants that grow near her home. She wanted to classify the plants according to whether they produced flowers or not.

13. Which of the following pictures shows a flowering plant?

A. 

B. 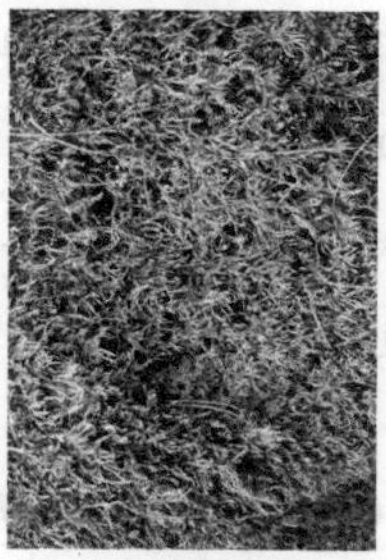

C. 

D. 

Use the following information to answer the next question.

This picture shows a group of zebras. Each zebra has many of the same characteristics; however, the pattern of stripes differs from zebra to zebra.

14. The different stripe patterns on each zebra **best** show an example of

A. physical mimicry

B. learned behaviours

C. its rank within the group

D. biodiversity within a species

Use the following information to answer the next question.

A farmer plants a monoculture of wheat in his entire field. That summer, a disease wipes out his entire crop. Other types of wheat on other farms remained unharmed.

15. What should the farmer have done to **best** protect against losing his entire crop?

A. Used large amounts of pesticides

B. Grown his wheat on the other farms

C. Planted several types of wheat instead of one

D. Harvested the wheat earlier to prevent the disease from spreading

16. Which of the following statements **best** describes the interrelationship wolves have within their species?

A. Wolves defend their territory together

B. Wolves kill and eat other animals

C. Wolves raise only their own pups

D. Wolves hunt individually

Use the following information to answer the next question.

A clownfish and a sea anemone are two different species that have an interrelationship.

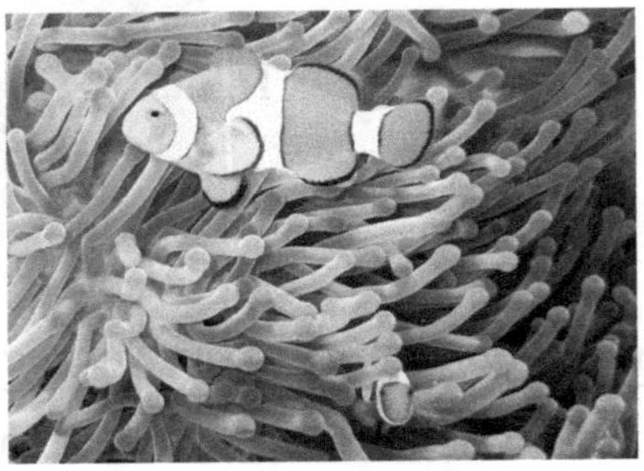

17. Which of the following statements **best** describes how their interrelationship works?

A. The clownfish eats the sea anemone.

B. The clownfish hunts other fish to help the sea anemone.

C. The sea anemone needs the clownfish to scare away predators.

D. The sea anemone needs the clownfish to attract prey that it eats.

Use the following information to answer the next question.

Sparrows pick up sticks and twigs from the ground and build nests in the branches of a tree. This is an interrelationship between species.

18. How does this interrelationship affect both the tree and the sparrows?

A. Both the tree and the sparrows benefit.

B. The tree benefits but the sparrows do not.

C. The sparrows benefit and the tree is harmed.

D. The sparrows benefit but the tree is unaffected.

19. From which part of the white willow tree are pain relievers derived?

A. Bark

B. Roots

C. Leaves

D. Flowers

Use the following information to answer the next question.

Some invasive species were deliberately introduced into Canada.

20. Which of the following plants was brought from Europe in the 1800s and can quickly take over a wetland habitat, choking out many of the plant species native to that area?

A. Cattails

B. Water lilies

C. Dandelions

D. Purple loosestrife

ANSWERS AND SOLUTIONS — UNIT TEST

1. B	5. C	9. D	13. C	17. D
2. D	6. A	10. C	14. D	18. D
3. D	7. A	11. D	15. C	19. A
4. B	8. B	12. A	16. A	20. D

1. B

Questions about changing the environment are often difficult to answer. Companies and governments often bring in environmental experts to help make decisions that impact the environment.

2. D

Selective-cutting takes more time and money than clear-cutting. It requires that certain trees are marked and cut, while others are left. This takes longer for the workers to do, and so it costs more money.

3. D

Monoculture means only one type of crop is grown. Monocultures often require the use of pesticides. A pest that eats a certain crop will grow and multiply when the same crop is grown in the same area over and over. This means pesticides will need to be used to kill them. Many pests can grow resistant to these chemicals and survive.

4. B

When exploring a habitat, you should take only notes, photographs and sketches. Never bring anything back. You should always leave the habitat the way you found it.

5. C

Group **I** should be named vertebrates and Group **II** should be named invertebrates. All of the animals in Group **I** are vertebrates because they have a backbone inside their bodies. All the animals in Group **II** do not have a backbone inside their bodies, so they would be called invertebrates.

6. A

This fish belongs in Group 1. It has a striped body, spotted tail, and two top fins, which puts it in this group.

7. A

Deciduous trees shed their leaves every fall. They remain leafless until spring, when new leaves sprout.

8. B

The correct answer is salamander.

A salamander has a backbone inside its body, so it is called a vertebrate. All of the other animals are called invertebrates because they do not have a backbone inside their bodies.

9. D

Interrelationships are formed when organisms come to depend on each other for survival. Interrelationships can occur within groups of the same organism or between two or more different organisms.

10. C

Biodiversity refers to the variety of different organisms found in the different ecosystems on earth. This includes all the plants and animals, but also smaller organisms, like protists, bacteria, and fungi. Even a small change to an area can make a difference to its biodiversity.

11. D

The insect should be classified in Group Y. Insects are invertebrates that have three body segments and six legs.

12. A

Reptiles have scales on their bodies while amphibians do not. Both amphibians and reptiles are cold-blooded, breathe through lungs, and lay eggs.

13. C

A water lily is an example of a flowering plant. A cedar tree is a plant that does not produce flowers, so it is considered a non-flowering plant. Neither lichen nor forest mushrooms are plants.

14. D

The different stripes on each zebra best shows biodiversity within a species. All zebras have stripes, but they do not all share the exact same pattern of stripes.

15. C

By planting several types of wheat instead of one, the farmer would have been able to harvest some wheat that showed resilience to the disease.

16. A

It is easier for wolves to defend their territory together. Wolves that live together in a pack need each other for survival.

17. D

The sea anemone needs the clownfish to attract its prey. It then stings the prey and uses it as food.

18. D

The sparrows benefits but the tree is not benefitted or harmed. The sparrows collect twigs that have already fallen from the trees. They use the trees to build a nest but do not harm the tree or do anything to help the tree live.

19. A

Traditional pain relievers are derived from the bark of the white willow tree.

20. D

Purple loosestrife was brought over from Europe in the 1800s as a medicinal herb. The plant was grown in gardens because of the beautiful purple flowers. Purple loosestrife can quickly take over a habitat, choking out many native species of plants. This affects the animals that live there, as they have come to rely on a great variety of plants to survive.

NOTES

Structures and Mechanisms: Flight

Chewing gum, nail polish, paint, and cellophane all contain materials from trees.

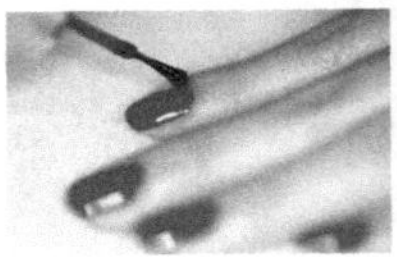

Many of the products you use every day come from plants. Flower pollen is used in vitamins, shampoos, toothpastes, and deodorants. White willow bark can be used as a pain reliever. Tofu is a food product that is made from soybeans. Wheat is used to make bread.

Seaweed is a form of algae. It is used as food or in medicines. Some forms of bacteria are also used in products. For example, bacteria are used to make yogurt.

Besides providing food for humans, animals also provide other useful products. Silk is made from the cocoons of silkworms. Sheep fleece is used to make wool, which is used to make clothing. Leather can also be used in furniture, belts, and sports equipment.

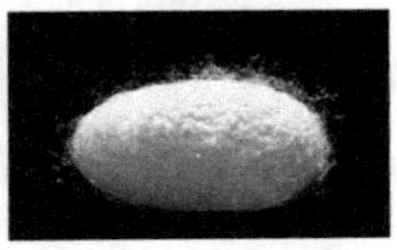

A silkworm cocoon

6SM1.1 assess the benefits and costs of aviation technology for society and the environment, taking different social and economic perspectives into account

The Benefits of Aviation

There are many people who benefit from the use of aircraft. Hospitals use airplanes to transport organs and other tissues from one place to another quickly. Helicopters and planes are also used as air ambulances. Police departments in larger cities have helicopters to help them spot criminals and to find missing persons.

An air ambulance

Travel is also easier and safer because of aircraft. People can travel all over the world in very little time. These people might be sightseeing, visiting friends or family, or travelling for work. Travellers bring in money to people who own hotels, businesses, and tourist attractions. Airplanes also move cargo like mail and parcels from one place to another.

This letter was delivered with the help of an airplane.

The Costs of Aviation

Aircraft create many different forms of pollution. Airplanes use fossil fuels, which release carbon dioxide, soot, and other pollutants into the atmosphere. Today's planes produce less pollution than planes did in the past. However, there are so many more planes flying now that pollution from airplanes has increased in the last few decades. Spilled airplane fuel can pollute soil and water. Airplanes also create noise pollution. This can be disturbing to people and to other organisms, especially if they live near an airport.

Because air travel is so much faster than earlier forms of travel, diseases are being spread by the people travelling. A sick person might not know they are sick and might accidentally introduce the disease to a place that has yet to experience it.

Use the following information to answer the next question.

Since the Wright brothers' first flight in 1903, the aviation industry has grown considerably. More and more people are able to travel to distant places in a short amount of time.

1. Which of the following results of increased air travel **most** benefits the economy?
A. More scientists have been hired to develop new technology for safer air travel.
B. Fewer people are driving, so fewer people are working in the auto industry.
C. The cost of travelling by airplane has gone down.
D. People spend money when they travel.

Use the following information to answer the next question.

Due to an increased demand for more flights, an airport is considering expanding and adding two new runways. Several environmental groups have asked the airport to wait on construction until further investigations can be done.

2. What would an environmental group consider to be the **most important** factor in building the new runways?
A. How long it will take to construct the runways
B. Where the contractor will get the materials from
C. The disruption it will cause the other flights at the airport
D. The amount of pollution the increased air traffic will create

6SM3.1 identify the properties of air that make flight possible

6SM2.2 use scientific inquiry/experimentation skills to investigate the properties of air

Properties of Air

Airplanes and helicopters can fly because they are designed to use some of the properties of air to lift these vehicles into the air. The following properties of air allow these vehicles to fly:

- Air has mass.
- Air takes up space.
- Air can be compressed or can expand.
- Air exerts pressure, or pushes, on objects.

Air Has Mass

You can perform tests and take measurements to prove that air does have mass. For example, use a scale to measure the mass of an uninflated basketball. Record the mass of the ball. Now fill the ball full of air and measure its mass. The ball is heavier when it is filled with air.

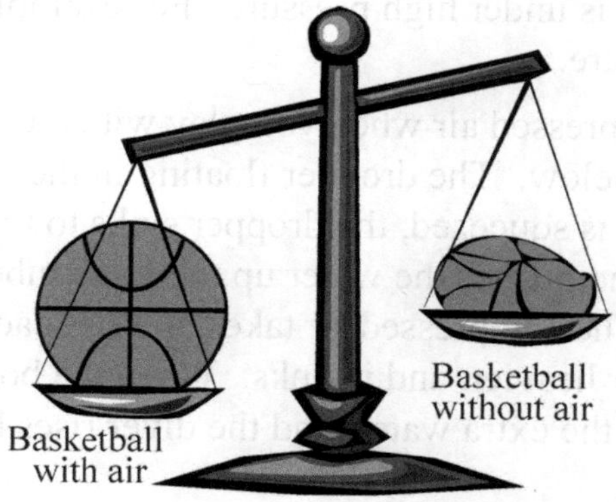

The basketball filled with air is heavier than the empty basket ball.

Air Takes Up Space

There is evidence that air takes up space. When you blow into a balloon, the air entering the balloon causes it to inflate. The air you put into the balloon requires space and causes the balloon to expand and change shape. This clearly demonstrates that air takes up space.

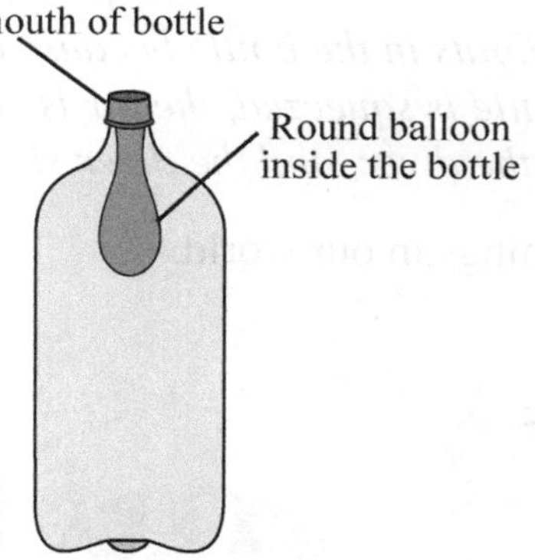

A student puts a balloon inside the mouth of a bottle. He then tries to blow up the balloon while it is inside the bottle. No matter how hard the student tries, he cannot blow much air into the balloon. This is because the bottle is already full of air. There is no room for the balloon to expand. The invisible air inside the bottle stops more air from entering the balloon.

Air Can Be Compressed

Air is made up of atoms of different gases. In a gas, these atoms are spread apart with lots of space in between. This makes it possible to squeeze air so that it takes up much less space. Air that has been squeezed to take up a smaller space has been **compressed**. When a lot of air has been compressed in a small space, it is under high pressure. For example, the air in an automobile or bicycle tire is under high pressure.

You can see the effects of compressed air when you play with a Cartesian diver, an example of which is shown in the picture below. The dropper floating in the closed bottle of water contains air and water. When the bottle is squeezed, the dropper sinks to the bottom. Squeezing the bottle applies pressure to the water and pushes the water up the glass tube. The air is trapped and compressed within the diver. The compressed air takes up less space, allowing more water to enter the diver. This makes the diver heavier, and it sinks. When the bottle is released, the compressed air expands again, pushing out the extra water, and the diver rises back to the surface.

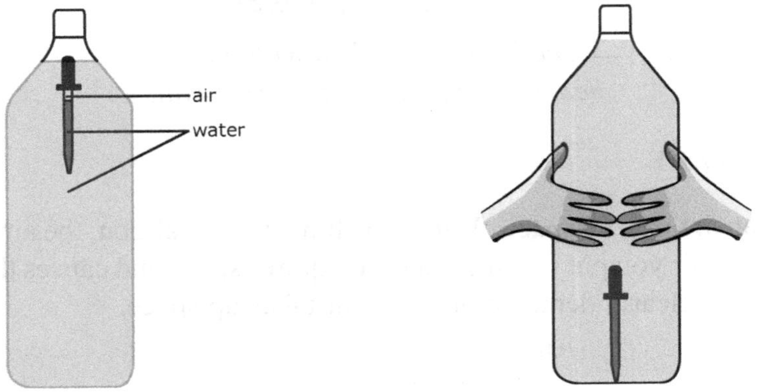

The Cartesian diver floats in the bottle because of the air trapped inside it (left). When the bottle is squeezed, the air is compressed. More water enters the diver, and the diver sinks (right).

Compressed air is used in many things in our world.

Aerosol cans, footballs, air tanks, and jack hammers all make use of compressed air.

Air Can Expand

Air can **expand**, or take up more space. This happens when air is heated. The molecules that make up air start to move faster and take up more space. When a constant amount of air takes up less space, it becomes less dense and floats. Warm air rises above cooler, denser air. This is what makes a hot air balloon float.

A hot air balloon

Air Exerts Pressure

Air exerts **pressure**, or pushes, on things. In the atmosphere, air presses with a force of about one kilogram per square centimetre. Air presses against things in all directions—downward, inward and even upward. Low and high pressure areas are constantly created in the atmosphere because air is a fluid. The higher the air pressure, the stronger the push.

Bernoulli's principle states that the faster air moves, the lower its pressure will be. Slow-moving air has high pressure, while fast-moving air has low pressure. So, slow-moving air has a stronger push than fast-moving air.

Bernoulli's principle is the main reason airplanes can fly. An airplane's wing is built to take advantage of these different air pressures. Air travels quickly over the top of the wing and slower under the bottom of the wing. This creates higher pressure air under the wing. It pushes on the bottom of the wing to help lift the plane off the ground. It also helps keep the plane in the air during flight.

Below is a picture of a cross-section of a wing. The air splits and moves above and below the wing. On top of the wing is fast-moving, low pressure air. Underneath the wing is slow-moving, high pressure air.

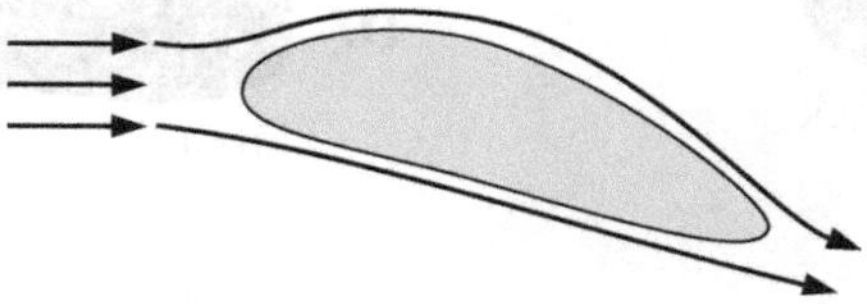

The air pressure above the wing is lower because the air on this surface travels faster than the air below the wing. The air pressure below the wing is higher because the air is moving slower there. High pressure air tends to move to areas of low pressure. This creates lift on the wings.

Use the following information to answer the next question.

Lonnie wanted to see what would happen if he attached two balloons to the opposite ends of a ruler. One balloon had air in it while the other balloon was empty. The ruler was hung so that the ends could move up and down.

3. What inference can be drawn from the picture of the balloons?

A. Air does not move most of the time.

B. Balloons do not hold air very well.

C. Air has mass.

D. Hot air rises.

4. Martin knows that wing design and air movement across the wings can affect the amount of lift on a plane. Which of the following wing designs will produce the **most** lift?

A.

B.

C.

D.

Use the following information to answer the next question.

Howard hooked two syringes together with some rubber tubing. He pressed down on one of the syringe plungers.

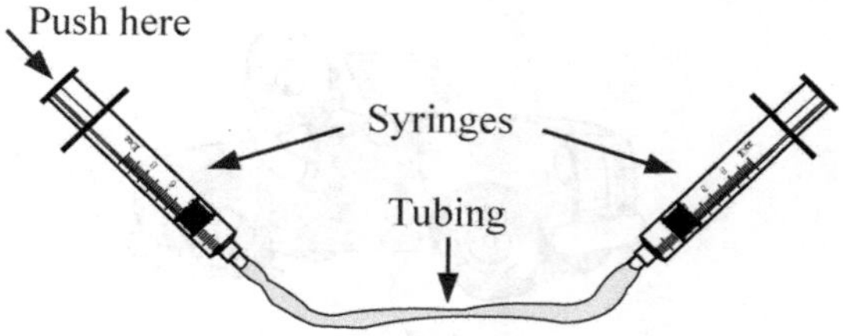

5. What **most likely** happened to the plunger on the other syringe?

A. It went up.
B. It went down.
C. It did nothing.
D. It went up and down.

Use the following information to answer the next question.

Debbie laid an empty bottle on its side and placed a feather inside the neck of the bottle. She then asked Glen to blow the feather into the bottle.

Glen blew directly into the mouth of the bottle. Instead of going into the bottle, the feather came flying out.

6. The reason that the feather came out of the bottle is that

A. Glen's breath was warm, which caused the feather to rise and come out of the bottle

B. the bottle and the feather were both positively charged, so the feather was repelled out of the bottle

C. the air in the bottle was under low pressure, which forced the feather out into the high pressure area outside the bottle

D. the bottle was full of air, so when Glen tried adding more air to the bottle, some of the air came back out with the feather

6SM3.2 identify common applications of the properties of air, such as its compressibility and insulating qualities

Applications of the Properties of Air

There are many objects and applications that use the properties of air. Two properties of air that are commonly used are its compressibility and its insulating quality.

When you squeeze air so that more can fit into a small space, you are compressing the air. Compressed air pushes on the object that it is trapped in. The air in car tires pushes on the tire, helping it to keep its shape. If there is not enough air in a car tire, or air leaks out of the tire, it does not hold the shape well, and it goes flat.

A flat tire

Heat naturally moves from a warmer place to a cooler place. Insulation is any material that helps slow down the transfer of heat from a warm area to a cooler area. Your home has insulation in its walls, floors, and ceiling. Insulation works because it has air trapped within it. The gases in the air do not transfer heat as well as solids because the particles of the gases are farther apart than in solids. The trapped air helps prevent heat from moving through it. Insulation prevents the warmth from your house from escaping outdoors in the winter. It also prevents the heat of the sun in the summer from moving into your house.

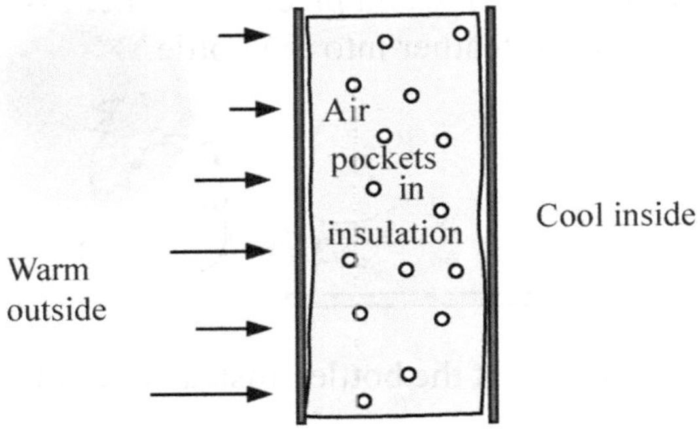

Cross-section at wall filled with insulation

In summer, air trapped in insulation helps prevent heat outside from entering a home.

A bird uses still air to stay warm on a cold day. It ruffles its feathers to trap air in between the feathers, preventing the loss of body heat.

A small bird keeps warm by trapping air in its feathers.

A sleeping bag is filled with material that traps air. This keeps the heat trapped inside the sleeping bag, keeping you warm. You can also stay warmer if you wear many layers of clothes in the winter. Air trapped between each layer of clothing acts as insulation.

A sleeping bag keeps you warm because air trapped inside it insulates you from heat loss.

Use the following information to answer the next question.

Many products that claim to improve energy efficiency in homes have some combination of foam or other air-trapping material covered with aluminum or some other shiny, metallic material. These products are intended to insulate things like walls, hot water pipes, dryer vents, or just about anything that can be wrapped or covered.

7. Which of the following statements **best** describes the function of the foam layer of insulation?

A. It reflects the heat back into the environment.

B. It slows the rate of heat transfer.

C. It stops the airflow.

D. It traps warm air.

Use the following information to answer the next question.

Cassandra conducted an investigation to learn about air compression. She dropped three basketballs onto a concrete floor to test their compressibility.

Basketball	Amount of Air
1	Barely filled with air
2	Half full of air
3	Completely full of air

8. The **best** prediction Cassandra could make about this investigation is that

A. basketball 1 will bounce the highest because it has the least air of the three balls

B. basketball 3 will bounce the highest because it has the most air of the three balls

C. basketball 2 will bounce higher than basketball 3 because it has less air than basketball 3

D. basketball 1 will bounce higher than basketball 2 because it has less air than basketball 2

6SM3.3 identify and describe the four forces of flight – lift, weight, drag, and thrust

6SM3.4 describe, in qualitative terms, the relationships between the forces of lift, weight, thrust, and drag that are required for flight

The Four Forces of Flight

There are four forces that affect flying objects such as aircraft, birds, and insects while they are in **flight**.

- **Lift**—the upward force that keeps a flying object in the air. Hot air balloons lift off the ground because the hot air in the balloon is less dense than the cool air that surrounds it. Airplanes get lift from their wings.
- **Thrust**—the force that gives the flying object a forward motion. The engines on an aircraft give it the thrust needed for flight.
- **Drag**—the force that acts to slow down an object as it moves through the air. Today, airplanes and other vehicles are often designed with smooth lines to cut through the air and overcome drag.
- **Gravity**—it is the force that pulls objects down to the ground. Gravity is related to weight; the heavier the object, the greater the gravitational pull on the object. For this reason, flying objects are often made of light-weight materials such as aluminum and plastic.

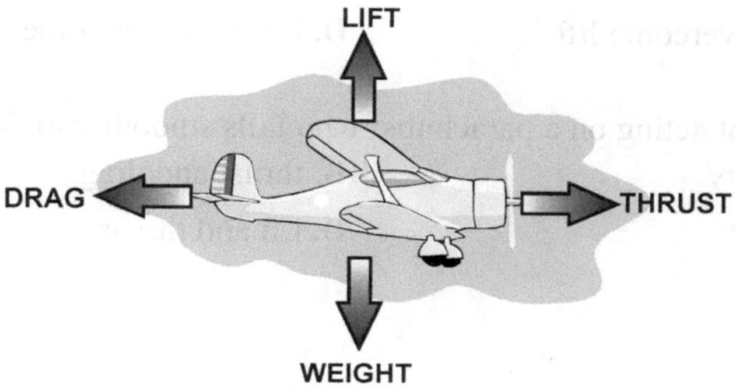

The four forces of flight

The forces of flight work in pairs. Weight, or gravity, opposes lift. Drag opposes thrust.

For example, think of an airplane in flight. If the plane's lift is greater than its weight, the plane goes up to a higher altitude. It will ascend, or climb in the air. If lift decreases, the plane goes down to a lower altitude. When lift and weight are equal, the aircraft will maintain a level flight.

Thrust and drag also oppose one another. If thrust is greater than drag, the plane moves forward. Increase the thrust and the plane moves forward faster. If drag is increased or thrust is decreased, the plane slows down. When thrust and drag are balanced, the plane moves forward at a steady rate.

For an airplane to take off, thrust and lift must be greater than drag and weight. To lower a plane to allow it to land, lift and thrust must be decreased until the drag and weight become greater. If all four forces are in balance, an aircraft such as a helicopter can hover in place.

Use the following information to answer the next question.

While learning about the principles of flight, some of the students in Mr. Jones' class came across an article about the gossamer albatross, a flying machine powered by the pedalling of the driver.

9. For this machine to increase its elevation,

A. drag must overcome thrust

B. thrust must overcome drag

C. gravity must overcome lift

D. lift must overcome gravity

10. The forces of flight acting on a parachutist who falls smoothly to the ground are

A. drag and gravity

B. thrust and drag

C. gravity and lift

D. lift and thrust

Use the following information to answer the next question.

This diagram shows a mosquito in flight. Each of the numbers represents a force acting on the body of the mosquito.

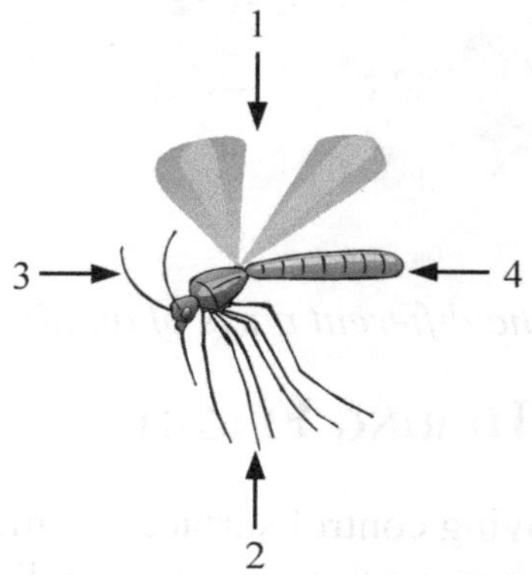

11. Which of the following rows **correctly** matches the force to its number in the diagram?

A.

1	2	3	4
Weight	Lift	Drag	Thrust

B.

1	2	3	4
Drag	Weight	Lift	Thrust

C.

1	2	3	4
Thrust	Weight	Drag	Lift

D.

1	2	3	4
Lift	Weight	Thrust	Drag

6SM3.5 describe ways in which flying devices or living things use unbalanced forces to control their flight

Airplane Parts and Control Surfaces

An aircraft is made up of several different parts that enable a pilot to have a successful flight. These are called the control surfaces of the plane.

- *Fuselage*—the main body of the aircraft.
- *Horizontal Stabilizer*—keeps the nose from moving up and down.
- *Vertical Stabilizer*—keeps the nose of the plane from swinging from side to side.
- *Wing*—extends out from the fuselage. The shape of the wing helps to create lift, allowing the plane to fly.
- *Rudder*—located on the tail of the plane. The rudder controls the left and right movement of the nose of the plane. This movement is called yaw.
- *Ailerons*—flaps located on the wings. They can be used to make the plane wings dip left or right. This movement is called roll. Ailerons work opposite each other.
- *Elevators*—located on the horizontal stabilizers of the plane. Elevators control the up and down motion of the nose of the plane. This movement is called pitch. The elevators work together.

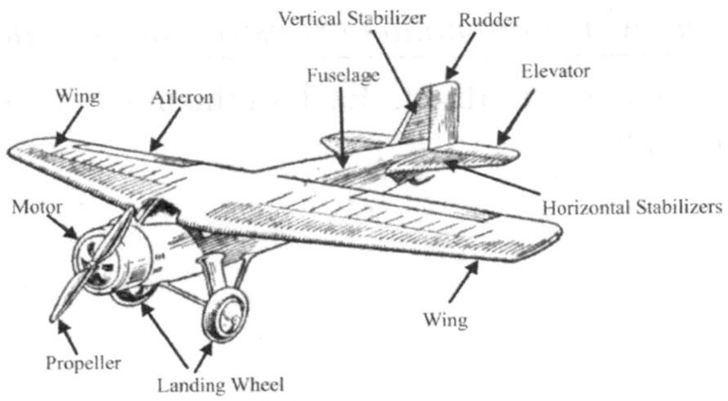

The different parts of an aircraft

MOVEMENT OF AIRCRAFT DURING FLIGHT

A pilot controls the aircraft by moving control surfaces, namely the ailerons, the rudder, and the elevators. There are three basic movements a pilot uses to direct an airplane: roll, pitch, and yaw.

Roll is used to bank a plane left or right. The pilot uses the ailerons to do this. For example, if the left aileron is raised and the right one lowered, the air moving over the upper surface of the left wing is slowed, thereby increasing the air pressure. As a result, the left wing dips and the plane banks to the left.

Roll of an aircraft

Pitch is the up and down movement of the nose of the plane using the elevators. When both elevators are down, the lift on the tail increases and the nose drops. When both elevators are up, the lift on the tail decreases. This makes the tail go down and the nose of the plane rises.

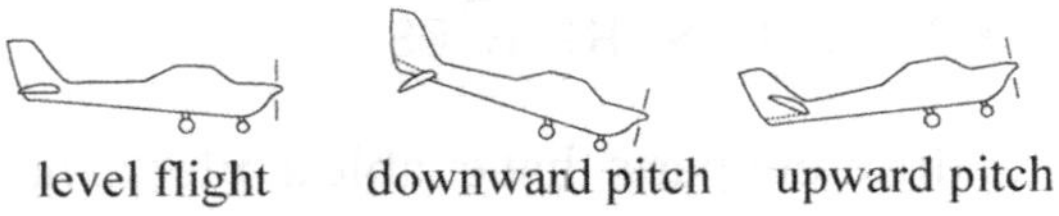

Pitch of an aircraft

Yaw is the left and right movement of the nose of the plane using the rudder. If the rudder is turned to the left, the nose of the plane turns left. If the rudder is turned to the right, the nose of the plane turns right. Pilots use both the ailerons and the rudder to turn the plane.

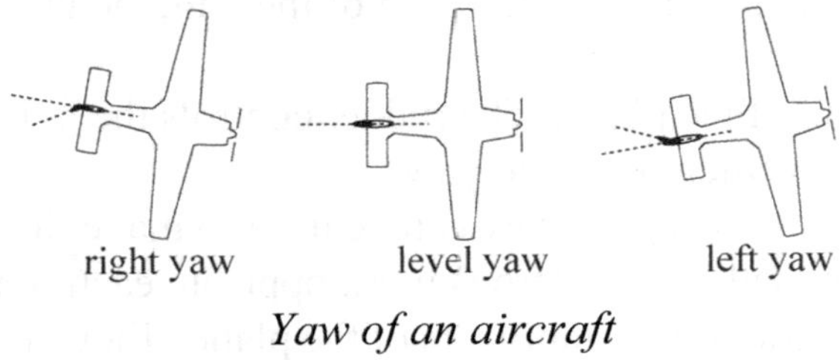

Yaw of an aircraft

Movement of Animals During Flight

A bird in flight

A bird uses body parts to move once it is in flight. For example, a bird uses its wings to provide lift and thrust.

A bird's feathers also help a bird with thrust and lift. Birds have two types of feathers: primary and secondary. The primary feathers are found at the tips of the wing and are used for thrust. The secondary feathers help give the wing the airfoil shape that a bird needs to get lift.

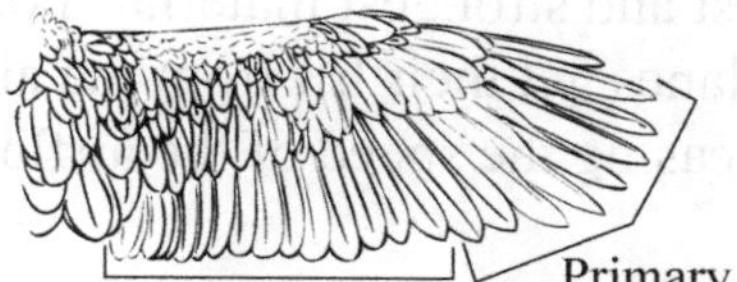

The primary and secondary feathers on a bird's wing

The tail of the bird is used to steer. The tail can be twisted and turned so that the feathers there act like the elevators and rudder on an airplane.

Use the following information to answer the next question.

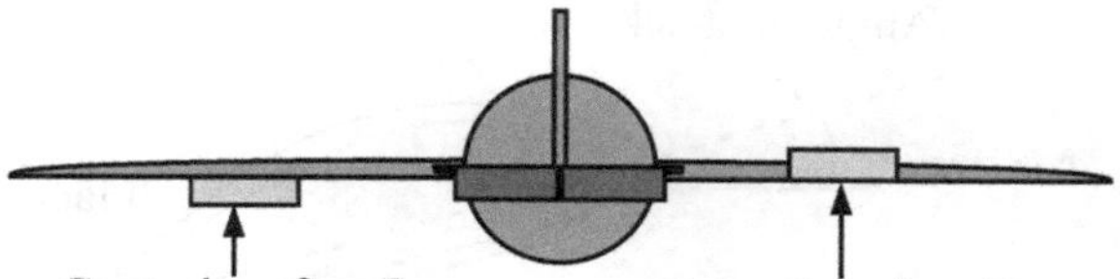

Rear view of an airplane in flight

12. If control surface **I** is in a downward position and control surface **II** is in an upward position, as shown in the diagram, the movement this airplane will make is a

A. yaw to the right
B. roll to the right
C. yaw to the left
D. roll to the left

Use the following information to answer the next question.

Jeremy noticed that the elevators on the horizontal stabilizer of an airplane had an airfoil shape.

13. Jeremy correctly concluded that when the elevators move to an upright position, the tail of the airplane will drop because the

A. movement of the elevators would disturb the overall balance of the airplane

B. air moving over the top surface of the elevators would be slowed down

C. extra weight of the elevators would make the tail end move downward

D. air over the vertical stabilizer would be split into two streams

6SM3.6 describe ways in which the four forces of flight can be altered

Aircraft Design and the Four Forces

Airplanes are designed with the four forces of flight and aerodynamics in mind. **Aerodynamics** is the study of how air moves over, under, and around an object.

Airplanes are built using the lightest and strongest materials possible so less lift force is needed to get the plane off the ground. Airplanes get their lift from the airfoil shape of their wings. Lift on the wings can be increased by increasing the speed of the airflow over the top surface of the wing or increasing the angle of attack.

Angle of attack refers to how the leading edge, or front, of the wing lines up with the flow of air. When the front of the wing points up into the airflow, the angle of attack increases. This increases lift. If the angle of attack is too great, lift cannot be achieved, and the plane is said to stall. When the wing is pointing down into the airflow, the angle of attack goes down. Here, the plane has less lift.

Image 1 shows an airplane wing that has a high angle of attack. Image 2 shows an airplane wing that has a low angle of attack.

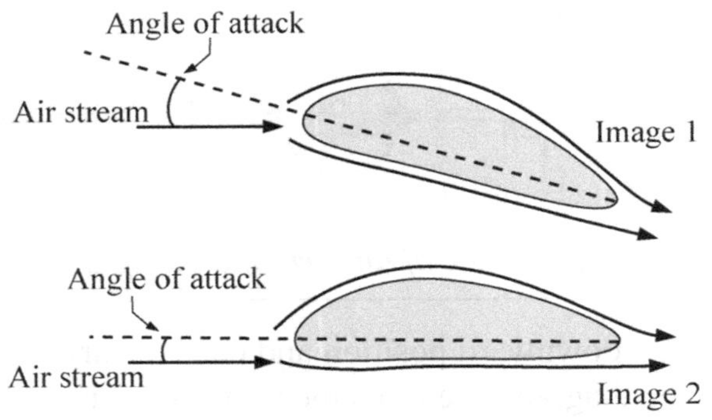

An airplane's jet or propeller engine provides different amounts of thrust. Thrust is caused by Newton's third law of motion. This law of motion states that, "For every action there is an equal and opposite reaction. A propellor or jet engine pushes air backward and the airplane moves forward. A lot of thrust is needed for takeoff and to keep the plane moving in the air. Less thrust is needed when the plane is landing.

An aircraft's shape is streamlined to reduce drag. For example, the nose of the plane is cone shaped so air can slip past it easily. Other parts of the airplane are designed to increase drag when needed. Movable control surfaces on an airplane's wings and tail help increase or reduce drag at certain times during the flight. This helps a plane to turn, to move up or down, or to slow down as the airplane lands. For example, on some airplanes an extra set of flaps may be found with the ailerons on the wings. These flaps help gain lift quickly on takeoff and act as brakes when landing.

Use the following information to answer the next question.

When the front of the wing lines up with the flow of air at different angles, the angle of attack is changing.

14. What happens when the angle of attack increases?

A. Lift increases **B.** Drag increases

C. Lift decreases **D.** Thrust decreases

Use the following information to answer the next question.

On some airplane's wings there are flaps used during takeoff and landing.

15. If the flaps on both wings are in an upright position, the plane will

A. go faster **B.** slow down

C. gain altitude **D.** turn to the right

6SM2.1 follow established safety procedures for working with electricity

SAFETY PROCEDURES: FLYING AND THROWING MODELS

Before you build or launch any model aircraft, review the safety procedures your class has in place. These safety procedures might include the following instructions:

- Always throw or launch your model away from other people. Injuries can happen if people are struck in the head.

Never launch or throw your model aircraft at people or other objects.

- Always follow instructions given to you on how to build and launch your models. Read all instructions carefully. If you are unsure about something, ask your teacher or another adult.
- Wear proper safety protection as provided by your teacher. For example, you may need to wear safety goggles if you are cutting wood. Do not take off any safety equipment until your teacher says it is safe to do so.
- Always cut away from yourself and others when using a knife or razor blade.
- Some glues and paints can give off strong smells. Use these materials in a room that has lots of airflow, or take them outside to use.
- Dispose of materials as directed by your teacher.
- Only fly kites in open areas. Do not launch kites near overhead power lines or trees. If your model gets stuck in a tree branch, ask an adult to help you get it down. Do not climb the tree to get it yourself.
- Always choose a safe place to launch parachutes and other models that are designed to fall. On top of your roof or the top of a ladder is not a safe place.
- Make sure that you have chosen an area where you are allowed to launch models. For most models, this is not a problem. However, some larger model airplanes that run on gas motors and are operated by remote control cannot be flown in the city. In some places it is illegal to launch model rockets. These models can also be very dangerous if you do not know how to use them. Always work with an adult when you use these types of models.

Take care when handling knives. Always make sure that your work space is free of clutter when you are building models.

Use the following information to answer the next question.

Andy finds an old model rocket kit in his garage. The instructions have been lost, but he decides to try to make the rocket anyway. Andy's father is concerned and tells him not to build the rocket.

16. What is the **most likely** reason Andy's father asked him not to use this rocket kit?

A. The glue in the kit might have hardened so he cannot use it.

B. The kit does not contain any materials to decorate the rocket.

C. If the rocket is not built properly it could hurt him when he launches it.

D. If the rocket falls apart before he can launch it, Andy will be disappointed.

6SM2.3 investigate characteristics and adaptations that enable living things to fly

Adaptations for Flight

In order for birds and insects to fly, they must create lift. They must also produce enough thrust to move through the air. Lift is an upward force that acts against the force of gravity. Thrust is the force needed by an object to propel itself forward. **Propel** means to move or push an object in a direction.

An **adaptation** is a change that a living thing undergoes so that it can better survive in its environment. Birds and insects have a number of adaptations that allow them to fly.

Birds have the following adaptations that allow them to fly:

- *Tail*—is used to steer the bird in flight.
- *Hollow bones*—help reduce a bird's weight, making it easier to fly.
- *Streamlined shape*—allows the bird to move through the air easily.
- *Powerful chest muscles*—needed to move the wings. These muscles do not tire easily.
- *Breathing system*—the lungs are attached to a group of air sacs that store and supply air to the bird's body. The air sacs ensure that the muscles receive a large amount of oxygen during flight. They also reduce the bird's body weight.
- *Feathers*—give birds thrust and lift. Primary feathers on the wings have a structure that gives the thrust for takeoff. The secondary feathers make the airfoil shape needed for lift once the bird is in the air. Some of the feathers also keep birds warm.
- *Wings*—are shaped by the feathers, and they allow a bird to achieve thrust and lift. The upper side of the wing bulges upward and the under side is flat like an airplane's wing. The wingspan is determined by the body size. Larger birds have large wingspans to create enough lift to carry the body upward.

Birds have many adaptations that allow them to fly.

Insects have the following adaptations that allow them to fly:

- *Double wings*—some insects have two sets of wings for added lift and thrust.
- *Light-weight bodies*—the bodies of insects are usually small and light-weight, making it easier to get lift.
- *Light-weight wings*—these wings are made up of a thin membrane supported by blood-filled veins. Insect wings are one of nature's lightest structures, lacking bone and muscle. They are made of chitin, an extremely tough material that is also part of an insect's hard outer skin. Like a bird's wing, an insect's wings are curved to help achieve lift.
- *Wing muscles*—these muscles, like a bird's, are very powerful. They allow the wings to flap up and down, but also to rotate. As the insect wing nears the end of a forward stroke, the wing rotates backward, twisting upside down, parallel to the ground. This rotation speeds up the flow of air over the wing. It also allows some insects to hover or fly backward.

An insect's wings and wing muscles help it to fly.

A bat is a mammal that is able to fly. It's wings are made of long, thin finger bones covered in a very thin membrane. The wing bones can bend easily without breaking. This lets the bat shape its wings so it can turn, bend, and shift easily while it flies.

A bat has adaptations that allow it to fly.

Plant Adaptations for Flight

Plants do not actually fly. However, some plants have made adaptations so that they can take advantage of moving air. The seeds from some plants can be caught by the wind and carried for great distances, so they can grow in different places. For example, a dandelion has seeds that act like parachutes. A maple tree seed has wings that can be carried on the wind.

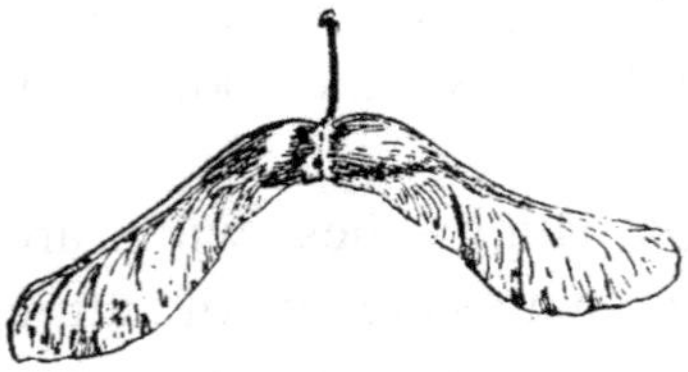

A dandelion seed (left) and a maple seed (right) are moved by the air.

Use the following information to answer the next question.

Birds have two kinds of feathers on their wings: primary feathers and secondary feathers.

17. The **main** function of the primary feathers is to

A. form an airfoil shape for flight

B. provide thrust through flapping

C. provide bigger wingspan to scare off predators

D. make the bird more attractive to potential mates

Use the following information to answer the next question.

All birds have wings. The function of wings is to help birds fly. However, some birds have smaller wings, which leaves them unable to fly.

18. Which of the following birds does **not** have functioning wings for flight?

A. Humming bird

B. Blue jay

C. Ostrich

D. Eagle

19. Which of the following adaptations of an insect's body **most** improves the thrust of a flying insect?

A. The leading edge of the flexible wing is much stronger than the rest of the wing.

B. Insects have developed powerful muscles to flap their wings.

C. Insects have exoskeletons instead of internal skeletons.

D. Sticky pads on the feet allow insects to walk upside-down.

6SM2.4 use technological problem-solving skills to design, build, and test a flying device

Designing and Testing a Paper Glider

Airplanes are designed to use the properties of air to fly. So are paper airplanes. A paper airplane does not really fly. Rather, it **glides**. An airplane uses an engine, while a glider uses some external force to get it into the air. Once it is in the air, the glider uses the lift from its wings to remain in the air. A glider will not glide well if it is not designed well. Here are some things to consider when designing and building a paper glider:

- Make the glider as light as possible.
- Make the fuselage as slim as possible. This will help decrease drag.
- Make your glider stable. Adding a vertical stabilizer onto your glider will help it fly straight and keep it stable in flight.
- The glider should have symmetry. This means that one side should be identical to the other in size and shape. Make your folds carefully. Make sure your wings and tail section are the same size and shape.
- Pay close attention to the design of the wings. A good wing design has a slight curve so that it takes on an airfoil shape. This allows high pressure air to build up under the wing and give the plane lift. The shape and size of the wings will also affect how the plane flies. Wings with a large surface area will give a glider a long, slow flight. Smaller more aerodynamic wings will give a glider a faster flight.

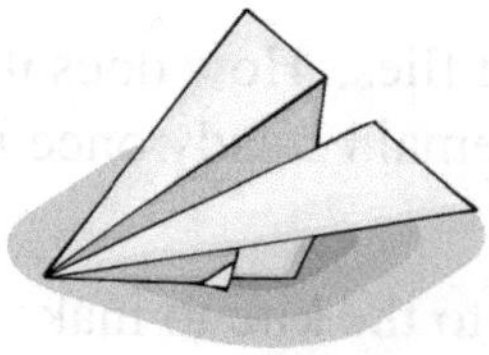

A paper glider needs to be designed and built well in order to fly well.

Observe your glider carefully once you launch it. What do you notice about its flight? Does it travel in a straight line, or does it swoop and turn?

Think of ways you can make changes to the glider so it will fly differently. For example, what would happen if you added a paper clip to the glider's nose? How about if you folded the edges of the wings up or down to make ailerons? After each change, watch how your glider flies. Did the change help its flight the way you hoped it would?

Look for different designs of paper airplanes on the Internet or in books. Each glider is designed to perform in a certain way. Some gliders are built to perform stunts, like loops or turns. Others are made to fly long distances.

Designing and Testing a Kite

Just like paper gliders, there are many different kite designs. A kite is designed to get lift or fly when the wind travels over its surfaces. Here are some other features to consider when designing and building a kite:

- Make your kite as light as possible. This will help it to achieve lift.
- The frame of your kite needs to be lightweight and sturdy. Wood or plastic dowels are often used for a kite frame.
- The sail that covers the frame helps a kite achieve lift. It also needs to be lightweight, but durable. Paper, fabric, and thin sheets of plastic have all been used on kites.
- A large wide kite provides lots of lift, but it is not very stable. A tail helps keep a kite stable as it flies. A kite that is shaped like a box is more stable. It often does not need a tail.

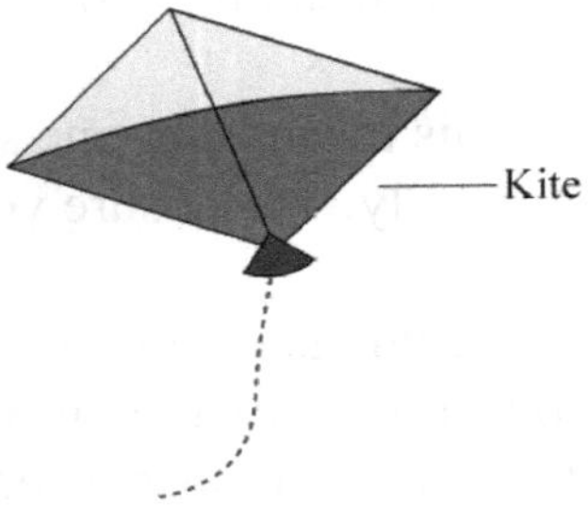

This kite has a tail to help keep it stable in flight.

Now try to fly your kite. Watch how it flies. How does it perform in weak winds? Strong winds? How high does the kite fly? Does it remain steady once it is in the air, or does it swoop from side to side? How sturdy is the kite?

Think about changes you could make to the kite to make it fly differently. What happens if you remove the tail from the kite or make it longer or shorter? How would the kite perform if you widened it or made it thinner? What materials could you use to make it sturdier? What changes could you make so it performs stunts in the air or flies in a steady pattern?

Take a look on the Internet or in books for more kite designs. Just like gliders, there are many different designs. You may also want to take a look at kites you can buy in a store. How are they designed? What materials do these kites use?

Designing and Testing a Hot Air Balloon

Here are some things to consider when designing and building a model hot air balloon:

- Use a thin, lightweight material for the balloon or bag. Tissue paper can be glued together to make a bag. A dry cleaner bag sealed at one end works very well.
- Attach several strings around the perimeter of the open end. Tie the other end of the strings to a light basket such as a strawberry basket. Remember to keep the weight light. The heavier the basket, the more hot air will be needed for the balloon to lift.
- Have someone gently hold the bag upside down so that the opening to the bag is at the bottom and the basket is hanging down.
- You will probably use a hair dryer to heat the air inside your balloon. Make the bottom opening larger than the nozzle of your hair dryer. A bit of the air needs to be able to escape the balloon as you heat it.
- Blow hot air into the bag until it fills up and puffs out. Release the hold on the balloon as it begins to lift.

Hot air balloons

Launch your hot air balloon outside in the morning or evening, when the air is cooler. Do not launch your balloon on a windy day. If your class has access to the gym, launch the balloons there.

Observe how your hot air balloon behaves once it is launched. Time how long it stays in the air. Estimate how high the balloon travelled. How could you make the balloon travel higher or stay in the air longer? What happens if you heat the air inside the balloon for 10 seconds? 40 seconds? 1 minute?

Once you have launched your hot air balloon a few times, think about ways you could make changes to your balloon. Can you make a similar balloon out of different materials? What would happen is you put a small hole somewhere in the balloon, perhaps at the top? Does the shape of the bag make a difference to how well the hot air balloon flies?

Use the following information to answer the next question.

Sonny was learning about hot air balloons. He set up the following apparatus to see what would happen if he heated the air below a plastic bag.

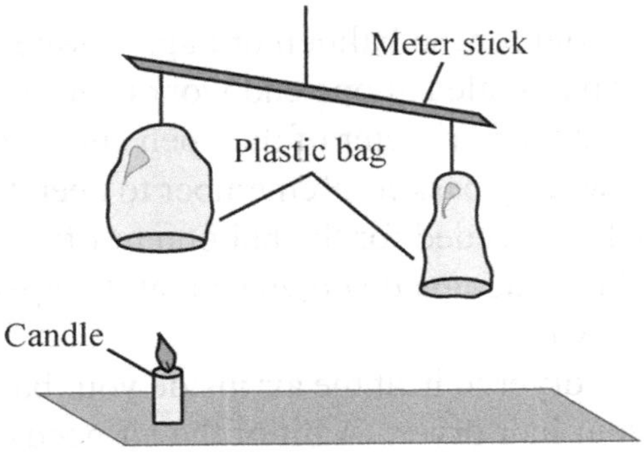

20. The bag over the candle puffed up and rose because the

A. plastic bag was very thin

B. hot air in the bag expanded

C. cool air rushed into the bag

D. hot air in the bag contracted

Use the following information to answer the next question.

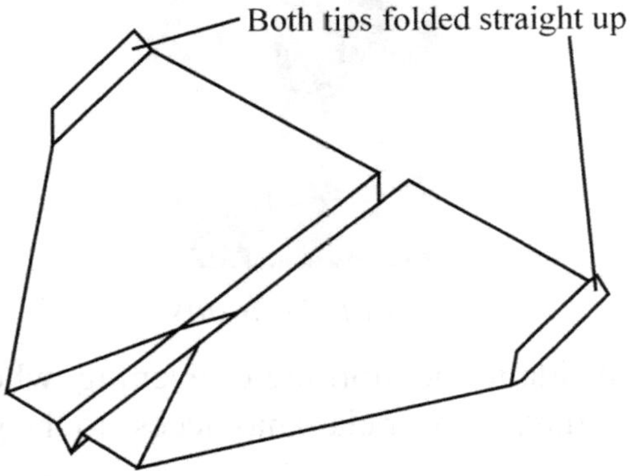

21. When this paper airplane is flown, it will probably

A. turn to the left

B. turn to the right

C. fall straight to the ground

D. glide forward through the air for a long distance

Use the following information to answer the next question.

Matt made two kites for his science fair project. He made each kite out of the following materials.

Kite 1	Kite 2
Cardboard	Nylon fabric
Plastic sticks	Wooden sticks
Clear tape	Masking tape
Nylon string	Cotton string

When Matt tested his two kites, he found that kite 1 did not fly as well as kite 2.

22. Kite 1 did not fly as well as kite 2 because

A. kite 1 was made with clear tape

B. the string used for kite 2 is cotton

C. the cardboard used for kite 1 is too heavy

D. kite 2 had wooden sticks instead of plastic

6SM2.5 use appropriate science and technology vocabulary, including aerodynamics, compress, flight, glide, propel, drag, thrust, and lift, in oral and written communication

Properties of Air and Principles of Flight: Vocabulary

Please refer to the glossary to find the definitions of the following vocabulary words: **aerodynamics, compress, drag, flight, glide, lift, propel,** and **thrust.**

23. In terms of flight, the word **aerodynamic** refers to the

A. thrust needed to get an airplane to fly

B. time a gliding object will remain in the air

C. shape of an object and how it moves through the air

D. noise generated by an object moving throught the air

ANSWERS AND SOLUTIONS
STRUCTURES AND MECHANISMS: FLIGHT

1. D	6. D	11. A	16. C	21. D
2. D	7. B	12. B	17. B	22. C
3. C	8. B	13. B	18. C	23. C
4. D	9. D	14. A	19. B	
5. A	10. A	15. B	20. B	

1. D

When people travel, they spend money on things such as hotels, meals and entertainment. This provides the most benefit to the economy.

2. D

An environmental group would consider the amount of pollution the increased air traffic will create to be the most important factor in building the new runways. Once the runways are built, there will be a greater number of airplanes using the airport. This will greatly increase the amount of pollution in the area.

3. C

This picture shows that air has mass.

The mass of the filled balloon is greater than the mass of the empty balloon because of the mass of the air inside the filled balloon. Because the filled balloon has a greater mass, the ruler is pulled down on that side.

4. D

The wing shape in alternative D will produce the most lift. This shape has the greatest surface area at the front, so the air travelling over top of the wing will move faster than the air moving underneath. The air moving fast over top of the wing creates an area of low pressure, and the slower-moving air under the wing creates high pressure. It is the high pressure air under the wing that creates lift.

5. A

The plunger in the first syringe compressed the air in the syringe. This compressed air pushed on the air in the tubing. The air in the tubing pushed the air in the other syringe. The plunger of the other syringe moved upward.

6. D

The feather came out of the bottle because the bottle was already full of air. When Glen tried to add more air to the bottle by blowing into it, some of the air came back out with the feather.

7. B

The foam or air-trapping layer of insulation slows the rate of heat transfer. By wrapping hot water pipes, hot water tanks, or dryer vents with this type of insulation, less heat is transferred or lost.

8. B

Basketball 3 will bounce the highest because it contains the most air. The greater the amount of compressed air, the higher the basketball will bounce. This will hold true for any ball that is filled with compressed air.

9. D

Lift is what makes a flying machine go up. Gravity is what makes a flying machine go down. To increase elevation, lift must overcome the effect of gravity.

10. A

The forces of flight acting on a parachutist are gravity and drag. Gravity is pulling the parachutist down. The canopy of the parachute catches the air and holds the parachute back, making the parachutist fall slower.

11. A

The forces in correct order from 1 to 4 are weight, lift, drag, and thrust. Weight refers to the pull of gravity. Lift is the force needed to overcome gravity. Thrust is the force needed to overcome drag, to increase speed.

12. B

With the ailerons in the positions shown in the diagram, the airplane would roll to the right. This is because control surface **II** slows the air moving over top of the wing on that side of the plane. When the air movement over the right wing slows, the pressure increases. The higher pressure on the top of the wing on this side of the plane makes this side dip, causing it to roll to the right.

The aileron on the left wing slows the air movement under the wing, increasing the pressure on the bottom of the wing. So, the left wing is pushed up at the same time as the right wing is pushed down.

13. B

The tail of the plane will drop when the elevators are in the upright position because air moving over the top surface of the elevators would be slowed down. When the air movement over the stabilizer slows, the pressure increases. The higher pressure on the top of the stabilizer makes the tail dip, causing the plane to pitch upward.

14. A

When the angle of attack increases, the lift increases. When the angle of attack is high, the air is moving much slower under the wing than over the wing. So, there is more pressure under the wing, and the lift is great.

15. B

When the flaps are moved up, the air resistance or drag increases. This increase in drag will cause the plane to slow down.

16. C

Andy should not build the rocket without a set of instructions. If the rocket is not built properly, it could hurt him when he launches it. For example, if the fins are not attached correctly, the rocket will not fly straight and it might hit someone or something when it is launched.

17. B

The main purpose of the primary feathers is to provide thrust when the wings are flapping.

18. C

The ostrich has wings that are too small to allow the bird to fly. Ostrichs have adapted their legs for running instead.

19. B

Insects have developed powerful muscles to flap their wings. By pushing the air backwards, the insect's body moves forward.

20. B

The candle flame heats the air in the bag. The warmer air expands, and the balloon puffs up and rises.

21. D

The design of this paper airplane will allow it to glide forward through the air for a long distance.

22. C

Cardboard is not a good material for making a kite because it is too heavy. Kite 1 would not have flown as well as Kite 2 because cardboard is much heavier than nylon fabric.

23. C

The word aerodynamic refers to the shape of an object and how it moves through the air. Streamlined shapes move through the air easier because there is less drag.

UNIT TEST — STRUCTURES AND MECHANISMS: FLIGHT

Use the following information to answer the next question.

Environmentalist are concerned about the aviation industry. Sometimes an airplane is over its landing weight or it develops mechanical problems and the pilot must make an emergency landing. When this happens, the pilot dumps some of the fuel through special vents in the wings.

1. Why would environmentalists be concerned when an airplane dumps fuel before landing?

A. The fuel could land on a house and cause a fire.

B. Fuel is expensive, and dumping it is a waste of money.

C. The fuel pollutes the water and land and harms organisms.

D. Fuel that is dumped could land on people and poison them.

Use the following information to answer the next question.

Justin wants to test the parachute he made for his science fair project.

2. The safest place for Justin to drop his parachute is from the

A. top of a ladder

B. roof of his house

C. highest branch of a tree

D. highest window of his house

Use the following information to answer the next question.

Mrs. Knot took her Grade 6 class to the science lab. She asked students to set up an experiment. Each group placed an empty plastic bottle underneath very hot running water. When the bottle was heated, the students quickly screwed the cap on tightly. As the bottle cooled, it collapsed inward. Students were asked to think about what they had seen and explain what was happening to the air in the bottle when the hot water was running over it.

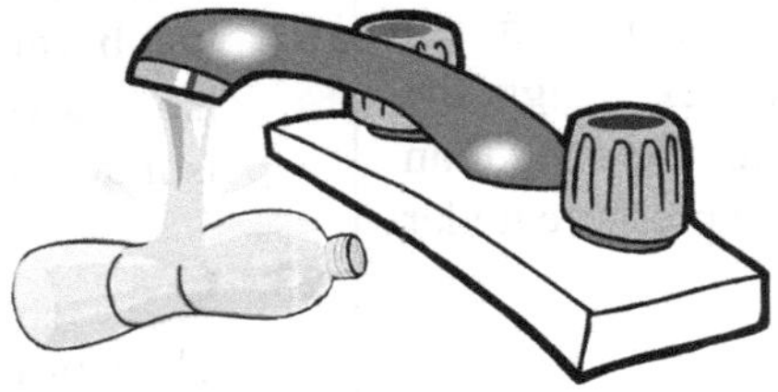

3. As the hot water was running over the bottle, the air inside the bottle

A. expanded and stayed inside the bottle

B. contracted and stayed inside the bottle

C. contracted and moved out of the bottle

D. expanded and moved out of the bottle

Use the following information to answer the next question.

To learn more about the properties of air, Tom performs the following experiment.

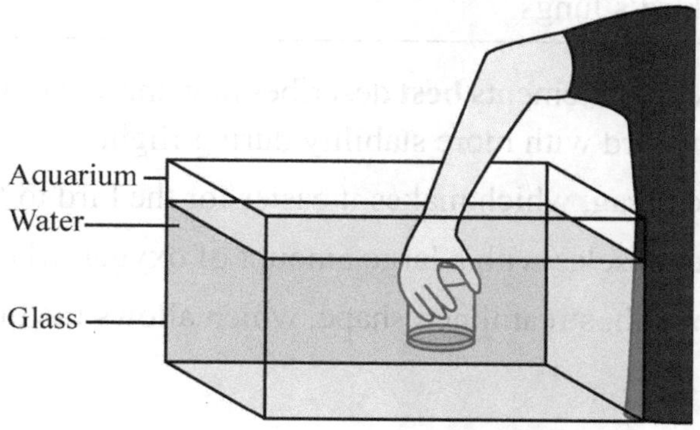

4. The glass will **not** fill with water because

A. air takes up space

B. air is lighter than water

C. water is heavier than air

D. gravity pulls down on the water

Use the following information to answer the next question.

Mrs. Perras set up the following apparatus for her science class.

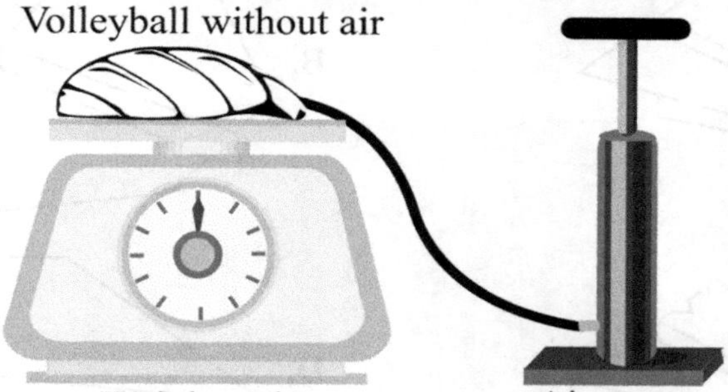

5. Mrs. Perras asked the class to predict what would happen to the weight of the volleyball as the volleyball is pumped up. Chrissy correctly predicted that the weight will

A. decrease as the air pressure inside the ball decreases

B. decrease as the air pressure inside the ball increases

C. increase as the air pressure inside the ball decreases

D. increase as the air pressure inside the ball increases

Use the following information to answer the next question.

Birds have many adaptations that allow them to fly. One adaptation is the air sacs that are attached to the bird's lungs.

6. Which of the following statements **best** describes how these sacs help a bird during flight?
   A. They provide the bird with more stability during flight.
   B. They help reduce drag, which makes it easier for the bird to fly.
   C. They supply the muscles with a large amount of oxygen when the bird is flying.
   D. They make a smooth, streamlined shape, which allows the bird to move through the air easily.

7. A bird uses its tail feathers to
   A. change the direction of flight
   B. increase the speed of flight
   C. fly in a fixed place
   D. resist air currents

8. Eric constructed four paper gliders. Which of the following designs shows the paper glider that should stay in the air for the longest time?

A. 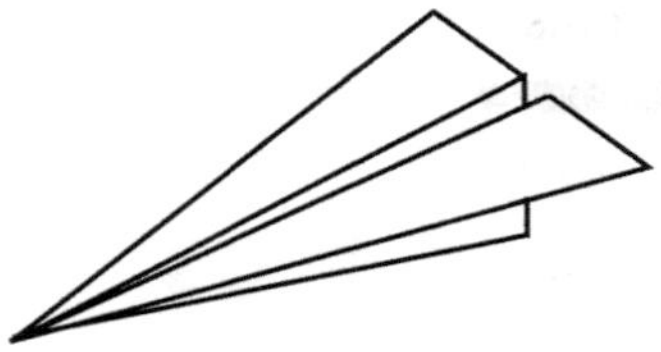

B. 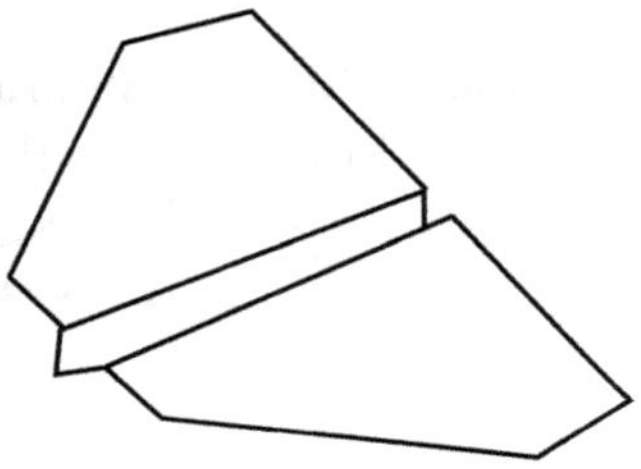

C. 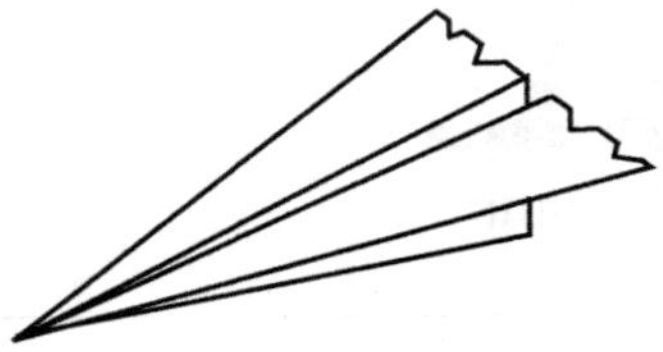

D. 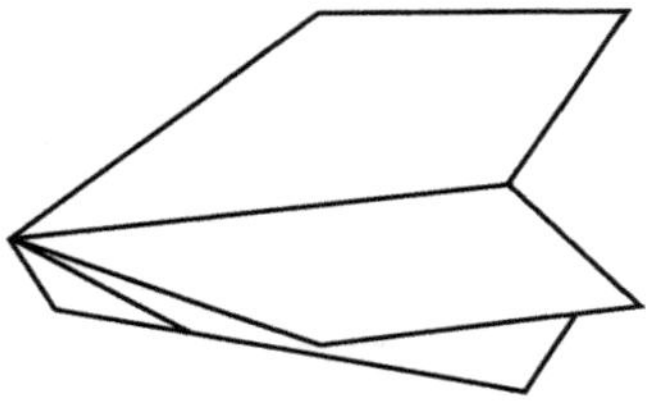

Use the following information to answer the next question.

Jane was at a kite festival with her father. She enjoyed watching all the different shaped kites soar high in the air. Jane decided that she was going to design and build her own kite when she got home. She wants to make a kite that has the most lift possible so that it goes high in the air.

9. What would be the most important factor that Jane should consider when she is designing her kite?

A. To make the kite out of thick and durable material such as cardboard.

B. To construct the kite from lightweight and durable materials.

C. To attach a very long string to the kite to hold when flying it.

D. To build the frame using pieces of steel or aluminum pipe.

10. In terms of flight, the word **glide** means to

A. fly without any air resistance

B. move higher and higher in the air

C. fly through the air without stopping

D. move through the air without propulsion

Use the following information to answer the next question.

11. A kite achieves lift because there is low pressure air located in the area on the illustration that is labelled

A. 1

B. 2

C. 3

D. 4

Use the following information to answer the next question.

12. The children at Jared's party saw a hot air balloon in the sky. When the children asked how the balloon was able to float in the air, Christina correctly replied that

A. air takes up space and pushes upward during summer weather

B. air pressure inside the balloon equals the air pressure outside

C. cold air is less dense than hot air and rises

D. hot air is less dense than cold air and rises

Use the following information to answer the next question.

When wheels were first invented, they were made out of stone or wood. Now, tires have an outer shell made of rubber and are filled with a compressed gas.

13. The **most likely** reason that tires are filled with a compressed gas and not made of solid rubber is that

A. using compressed gas in the tire makes the tire last longer

B. the compressed gas in the tire cushions the ride and makes it smoother

C. solid rubber tires would break apart easier than tires with compressed gas

D. there would be more litter on the roadways from rubber tires that break apart

Use the following information to answer the next question.

Alesha was going for a walk. She did not think her fleece sweater would be warm enough, so she put on a down vest as well.

14. How will the down-feathered vest help Alesha stay warm?

A. The material of the outside layer blocks any cold air from getting through.

B. The feathers rub together as she walks to create friction.

C. The vest will reflect the heat from the sun.

D. The feathers trap air between them.

Use the following information to answer the next question.

The arrows in the diagram below show the forces that act on an airplane.

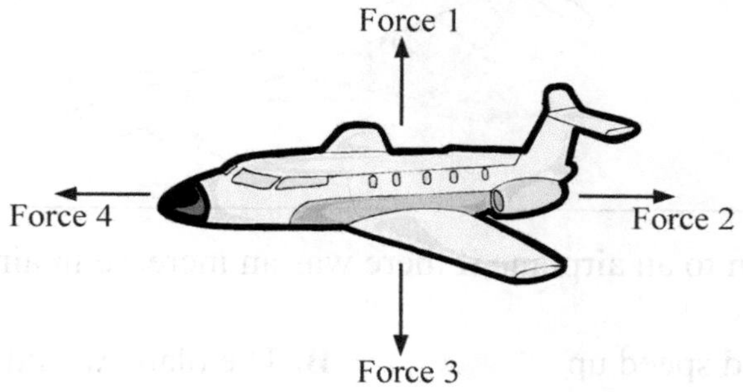

15. There are four forces at work on an aircraft as it flies. What force is labelled Force 4?

A. Lift

B. Drag

C. Thrust

D. Weight

Use the following information to answer the next question.

16. A hot air balloon moves toward the ground when the

A. air inside the balloon is being heated

B. weight of the balloon is greater than its lift

C. air outside the balloon is heated by the sun's rays

D. weight of the balloon is greater than its drag

Use the following information to answer the next question.

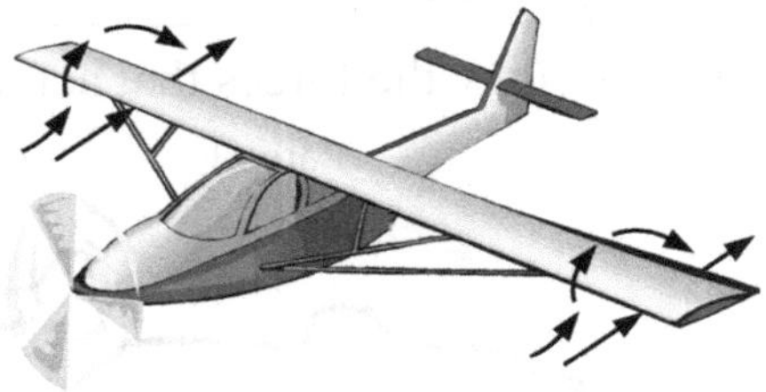

17. What would happen to an airplane if there was an increase in air resistance along both wings?

A. The plane would speed up

B. The plane would slow down

C. The plane would gain altitude

D. The plane would bank to one side

Use the following information to answer the next question.

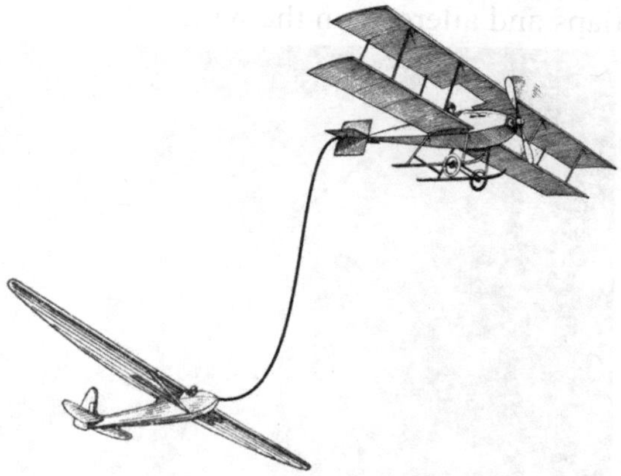

A glider is a lightweight aircraft that does not have an engine. A glider is tethered to an aircraft that takes the glider up into the air. When ready, the glider pilot releases the tether and the glider begins its flight. A glider has all the control surfaces that an airplane has.

18. The part that makes a glider curve upward when it flies is its

A. rudder
B. ailerons
C. fuselage
D. elevators

Use the following information to answer the next question.

This mechanic is constructing wings that will be attached to the fuselage of an airplane. He uses lightweight metal to form the wings.

19. If a heavy material is used for the wings, the plane will

A. not be as aerodynamic

B. become more unstable

C. use less lift force to get it into the air

D. need a greater lift force to get it into the air

Use the following information to answer the next question.

Some airplanes have flaps and ailerons on the wings.

20. When a plane is landing, the main purpose of the flaps is to

A. increase drag and slow the plane down

B. decrease drag so the plane will slow down

C. increase lift by changing the angle of attack

D. decrease the angle of attack so the plane will remain level

ANSWERS AND SOLUTIONS — UNIT TEST

1. C	**5. D**	**9. B**	**13. B**	**17. B**
2. D	**6. C**	**10. D**	**14. D**	**18. D**
3. D	**7. A**	**11. C**	**15. C**	**19. D**
4. A	**8. B**	**12. D**	**16. B**	**20. A**

1. C

Dumping fuel before landing pollutes the environment and harms organisms. While it is the safest procedure for the pilot to follow during an emergency landing, environmentalists are concerned about the impact the fuel has on the environment.

2. D

The safest place for Justin to drop his parachute would be the highest window of his house. It would not be safe for him to drop the parachute from his roof, the top of a ladder, or the highest branch of a tree.

3. D

When air is heated, it expands. As the hot water ran over the bottle, both the bottle and the air inside it were heated. As the air in the bottle expanded, it needed more room. This caused the air in the bottle to flow out of the bottle, where there was more room.

When the cap was placed on the bottle, the air flow was restricted. As the bottle cooled, the air inside of it cooled and needed less space. Since the air pressure outside of the bottle was greater than the air inside the bottle, the bottle collapsed inward.

4. A

The glass will not fill up with water because air takes up space. The air inside the jar pushes on the water, so the water does not fill the jar.

5. D

Air has mass. A mass of air has weight because of the force of gravity acting on it. The more air that is pumped into the ball, the heavier the ball will get. The more air that is pumped into the ball, the greater the air pressure inside the ball will be.

6. C

The air sacs attached to a bird's lungs help the bird by supplying the muscles with a large amount of oxygen during flight.

7. A

The tail of a bird is covered with feathers. These tail feathers help the bird to change direction during flight.

8. B

The airplane with the greatest surface area on its wings will stay in the air the longest. The airplane in alternative B has the greatest surface area.

9. B

Jane wants a kite that will have the maximum amount of lift. In order to do this, she should design a kite that is make from lightweight and durable materials

10. D

To glide means to move through the air without propulsion. Neither an airplane glider nor a hang glider have engines, so they cannot propel themselves through the air.

11. C

The kite achieves lift because there is low pressure above the top surface of the kite. The high pressure air below the bottom surface of the kite creates lift.

12. D

The hot air rises. The air inside the balloon is heated by the balloon's flame. The heated air expands and is less dense than the air surrounding the outside of the balloon. Since the air inside the balloon is less dense than the air outside the balloon, the hot air balloon rises.

13. B

The compressed gas in a tire cushions the ride because the tire can conform to the shape of the road.

14. D

The feathers in the down vest help by creating air pockets. The trapped air in these pockets will not transfer the heat of Alesha's body very well. The heat stays close to her body and helps to keep her warm.

15. C

The force labelled Force 4 is thrust. The four forces of flight are gravity, lift, thrust, and drag. Gravity opposes lift. Drag opposes thrust.

16. B

When the weight of the balloon becomes greater than its lift, the balloon will begin to decend.

17. B

The airplane would slow down if there was an increase in air resistance along both wings.

18. D

The elevators on the tail can be adjusted upward to cause the glider to turn or pitch upward.

19. D

The heavier the material used to build an airplane, the more lift force it will require to get it into the air.

20. A

When an airplane is landing, the flaps increase drag and slow the plane down. These flaps act as brakes when the plane is landing.

Matter and Energy: Electricity and Electrical Devices

MATTER AND ENERGY: ELECTRICITY AND ELECTRICAL DEVICES

Table of Correlations

Specific Expectation		Practice Questions	Unit Test Questions	Practice Test
6ME1:STSE	Evaluate the impact of the use of electricity on both the way we live and the environment;			
6ME1.1	*assess the short- and long-term environmental effects of the different ways in which electricity is generated in Canada, including the effect of each method on natural resources and living things in the environment*	1, 2	1, 2	37
6ME1.2	*assess opportunities for reducing electricity consumption at home or at school that could affect the use of non-renewable resources in a positive way or reduce the impact of electricity generation on the environment*	3, 4	3	38
6ME2:Skills	Investigate the characteristics of static and current electricity, and construct simple circuits;			
6ME2.1	*follow established safety procedures for working with electricity*	22, 23	4	39
6ME2.2	*design and build series and parallel circuits, draw labelled diagrams identifying the components used in each, and describe the role of each component in the circuit*	18, 19, 20	5, 6, 7	40
6ME2.3	*use scientific inquiry/experimentation skills to investigate the characteristics of static electricity*	7	8	
6ME2.4	*design, build, and test a device that produces electricity*	24, 25	9	41
6ME2.5	*use technological problem-solving skills to design, build, and test a device that transforms electrical energy into another form of energy in order to perform a function*	13	10	42
6ME2.6	*use appropriate science and technology vocabulary, including current, battery, circuit, transform, static, electrostatic, and energy, in oral and written communication*	26, 27	11	43
6ME3:Concepts	Demonstrate an understanding of the principles of electrical energy and its transformation into and from other forms of energy.			
6ME3.1	*identify the properties of air that make flight possible*	5	12	44
6ME3.2	*use the principles of static electricity to explain common electrostatic phenomena*	6	13	45
6ME3.3	*identify materials that are good conductors of electricity and good insulators*	8, 9, 10	14, 15	46
6ME3.4	*describe how various forms of energy can be transformed into electrical energy*	11, 12	16	47
6ME3.5	*identify ways in which electrical energy is transformed into other forms of energy*	14	17	
6ME3.6	*explain the functions of the components of a simple electrical circuit*	15	18	48
6ME3.7	*describe series circuits (components connected in a daisy chain) and parallel circuits (components connected side by side like the rungs of a ladder), and identify where each is used*	16, 17	19	49
6ME3.8	*describe ways in which the use of electricity by society, including the amount of electrical energy used, has changed over time*	21	20	50

6ME1.1 assess the short- and long-term environmental effects of the different ways in which electricity is generated in Canada, including the effect of each method on natural resources and living things in the environment

Environmental Effects of Electricity Generation in Canada

Energy is the ability to do work. The energy most used by people and industry is electrical energy. The demand for electricity is increasing all across Canada.

There are many ways that electricity is created in Canada. Many of these methods use **renewable resources**. These are resources from nature that can be used and replaced quickly. Electricity can also be created from **non-renewable resources**. These are resources from nature that cannot be replaced within a human lifetime.

In Canada, electricity is generated in coal and natural gas power plants, nuclear power plants, as well as in hydroelectric, geothermal, wind, and solar power facilities. In Ontario, most of the electricity is made in nuclear, hydroelectric, and thermal power plants. Each method of creating electricity can affect the environment. These effects can be short-term or long-term.

Thermal Power (Burning Fossil Fuels)

Thermal power is the burning of fossils fuels, such as coal and natural gas. These fuels are burned and the heat generated is used to create electricity. Fossil fuels are non-renewable resources because their supplies will eventually run out.

Short-Term Effects to the Environment

- Mining coal and extracting natural gas from the earth cause environmental problems. If the coal is strip-mined, large areas of earth are ripped up to expose the coal for mining. Natural gas is found near or with oil deposits. Getting to the oil sites, extracting the natural gas, and then shipping it to refineries can also cause a lot of environmental damage.

Long-Term Effects to the Environment

- Burning fossil fuels pollutes the environment by adding smoke and other chemicals to the air. This can pollute the air and add gases to the air that make Earth's atmosphere warmer. This is called global warming. Pollution from fossil fuels can also mix with water in the air to make acid rain.
- The machinery that remove these materials also pollute the environment. They need to burn fuel to operate, which causes air pollution.
- Coal and natural gas are fossil fuels that will eventually run out. As the amount of fossil fuels available decreases, it becomes more difficult to find them, causing costs to rise.
- Some people find it hard to breathe air that contains smoke and particles from coal or natural gas plants. This pollution can cause respiratory problems such as asthma. People who have asthma often have trouble breathing.

Nuclear Power

In a nuclear power plant, nothing is burned. Instead, uranium atoms are split apart. This creates a great deal of heat, which is used to produce electricity.Nuclear power is a non-renewable source of energy.

CANDU Reactor – Image created by Atomic Energy of Canada Limited

Short Term Effects to the Environment

- A great deal of electrical energy is made with a small amount of uranium. Nuclear power plants release steam into the air so there is no air pollution. The cost of running a nuclear power plant is much less than the cost of operating other types of power plants.

Long-Term Effects to the Environment

- Mining the uranium used in nuclear power plants causes long-term damage to the environment.
- The waste from nuclear power plants is poisonous and difficult to remove. It is stored in airtight lead containers underground. A leak can leave poisonous materials in the environment for hundreds of years.
- Uranium ore will eventually run out, so the cost will increase as it becomes more difficult to find it.

Hydroelectric Power

Hydroelectric power uses the energy from rivers to create electricity. A dam is built across a river. This creates a lake behind the dam, called a reservoir. The water in the lake is directed through tunnels in the dam to turn turbines, producing electricity. This electricity is then sent to homes and other buildings through power lines.

Hydroelectric power is renewable because the source water is continually recycled in the environment.

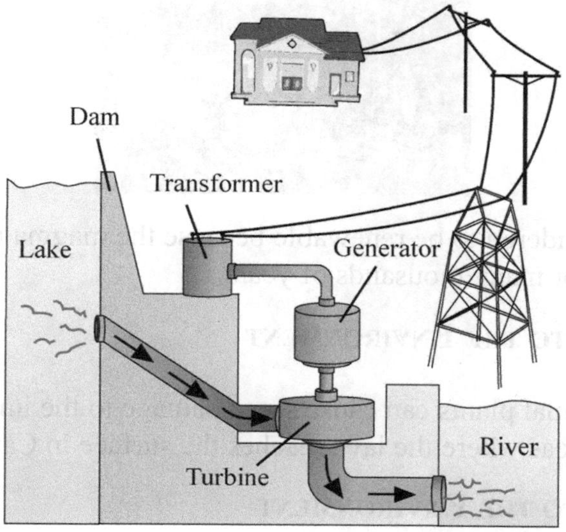

Short-Term Effects to the Environment

- Building the dam can cause some damage to the area. This is normal with any kind of construction. Once the dam is built, this pollution ends. Using the dam to make electricity creates no pollution.

Long-Term Effects to the Environment

- Many kilometres of land need to be flooded to create the reservoir for the dam. This means the destruction of many habitats in the area. This land is home to many different plants, animals, and even humans. All these organisms are either removed from the area or die when the flooding takes place.
- The habitats downstream from the dam are also affected. The water flow of the river is greatly reduced when a dam is put in place. Areas that have always been wet may suddenly dry up. Animals and plants that relied on the river as a source of water may have to find other water sources.
- Fish that travelled on the river to reach spawning grounds might be blocked by the dam. Many of the fish die before being able to lay their eggs. This can mean smaller numbers of fish in future generations.

Geothermal Energy

Geothermal energy is the thermal (heat) energy within the planet. Sometimes, steam comes out of the ground. Other times, hot water underground is heated even more in a power plant until it can make steam. This steam can be used to spin turbines. Geothermal energy can also be used directly to heat buildings. Hot water from the earth is pumped through pipes. These pipes give off heat, keeping the building warm.

Geothermal energy is considered to be renewable because the magma under Earth's surface will continue to provide heat for many thousands of years.

Short-Term Effects to the Environment

- Construction of geothermal plants can cause some damage to the immediate environment. There are not enough areas where the lava reaches the surface in Canada.

Long-Term Effects to the Environment

- Some power plants give off small amounts of carbon dioxide and other harmful gases. However, some new plants are trapping these gases and sending them back into the earth.
- Some power plants add water to hot dry rock to make steam. These areas of rock have never been exposed to water before. Some scientists are concerned about using natural water sources on hot dry rock to make steam. They are not sure how this could affect the environment.
- Some power plants have used up the heat energy in the section of Earth they are on. This forces the plants to shut down.

Wind Power

Wind energy is the energy of moving air. This energy can be captured by windmills. The blades of a windmill turn when the wind blows, creating electricity.

Wind power is a renewable source of energy.

Short-Term Effects to the Environment

- Damage to the environment is created when the windmills are constructed.
- Large numbers of windmills in one location can make a once scenic area look unattractive.

Long-Term Effects to the Environment

- Fields of windmills are called wind farms. They take up a lot of space in the environment. This space may have once been a natural area. Animals and plants that lived in this space would have had to find new homes and habitats to live in.
- Wind farms regularly kill bats and birds that happen to fly into the blades of the wind mills.
- Windmills also create a lot of noise while in use.

Solar Power

Solar power uses the energy of the sun to produce electricity. Special devices called solar cells change sunlight into electricity. You can see solar cells on calculators that use light for power.

Many large solar cells can be put together to make solar panels. These panels can be placed on a roof or other places that will get a lot of sunlight. Solar energy can also be used to heat buildings in northern climates. These buildings use insulation to prevent heat from leaving. They may also place large windows on the south side of the building, facing the sun's path through the sky. The building captures the heat energy from the sun. The insulation in the building helps keep the heat within. Unfortunately, the amount of useful sunlight varies from season to season in parts of Ontario. Weather conditions, such as rain, can also decrease the amount of light.

Solar energy is a renewable source of energy.

Short-Term Effects to the Environment

- Pollution is created when the solar panels are made.

Long-Term Effects to the Environment

- The sun produces large amounts of energy and will do so for a long time into the future. Solar power produces no pollution.
- They need a lot of space to generate a substantial amount of electricity.

Use the following information to answer the next question.

The Nipigon River drains Lake Nipigon into Nipigon Bay in Lake Superior. The river was once well known for the size of brook trout it contained. Between 1918 and 1950, four dams have been built on the Nipigon River.

1. What is the **most likely** long-term effect on the population of brook trout in the Nipigon River since the construction of the dams?

A. It has increased.
B. It has decreased.
C. It has remained the same.
D. It has increased significantly.

Use the following information to answer the next question.

Aluminium production requires vast amounts of electricity.

2. What are two energy sources available in Ontario to supply the electricity needed to produce aluminum?

A. Hydroelectric and nuclear
B. Solar and hydroelectric
C. Wind and geothermal
D. Nuclear and wind

6ME1.2 assess opportunities for reducing electricity consumption at home or at school that could affect the use of non-renewable resources in a positive way or reduce the impact of electricity generation on the environment

Reducing Electricity Use

The demand for electricity is higher now than it ever has been. To help meet this demand, scientists are looking for new sources of electricity. Some people are trying to encourage people to save energy. Some electrical companies ask that people try not to use a lot of electricity during peak hours, which is usually in the morning and late afternoon to early evening. Using less electricity also helps to conserve the natural resources that are used to create the electricity. You can also save electricity by reducing, reusing, and recycling the things you use. By doing this, fewer new products need to be made, and less electricity is used. Companies are also inventing devices that use less electricity than older products. For example, new fluorescent light bulbs use a lot less energy than the older incandescent light bulbs.

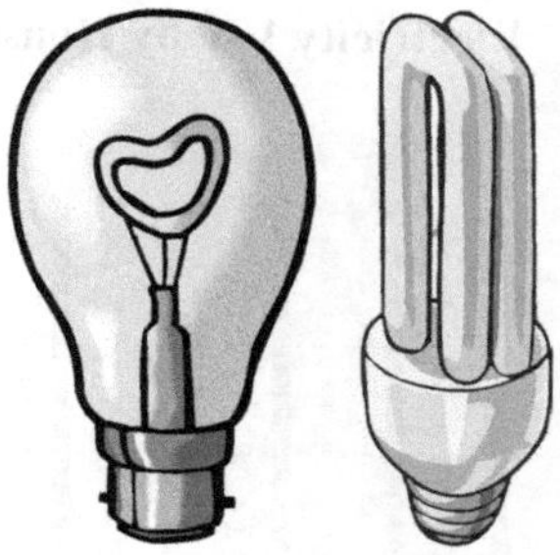

An incandescent bulb (left) uses more electricity than a fluorescent bulb (right).

There are some very simple things that you can do at home or at school to help reduce the electricity you use.

- When you leave a room, turn off the lights.
- Replace incandescent light bulbs with fluorescent bulbs.
- Wash the dishes by hand instead of using the dishwasher.
- Turn off computers and televisions when they are not being used.
- Hang wet clothes on a clothesline instead of using a clothes dryer.
- Turn down the heat in your home at night or when you will be out of the house during the day.
- Use air conditioners only when necessary because they use a lot of electricity. Use a fan instead.

3. Which of the following actions does **not** save energy?

A. Switching off televisions and stereos when they are not in use

B. Avoiding the use of vehicles for transportation whenever possible

C. Disabling the sleep mode feature on computers in order to save electricity

D. Using solar power instead of electricity to provide light and heat in homes

Use the following information to answer the next question.

William compared the electricity use of two identical-looking houses in his neighbourhood over one year.

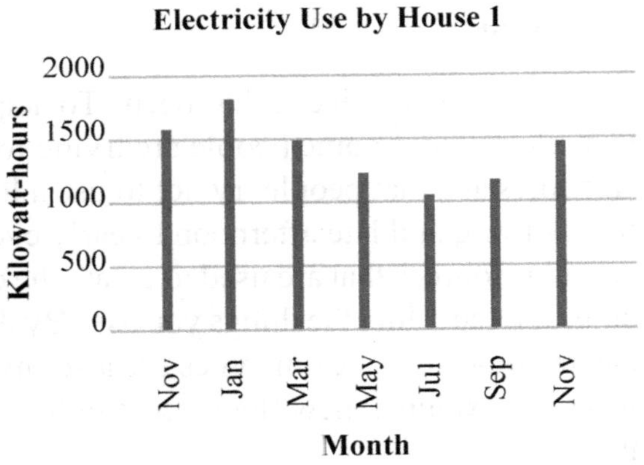

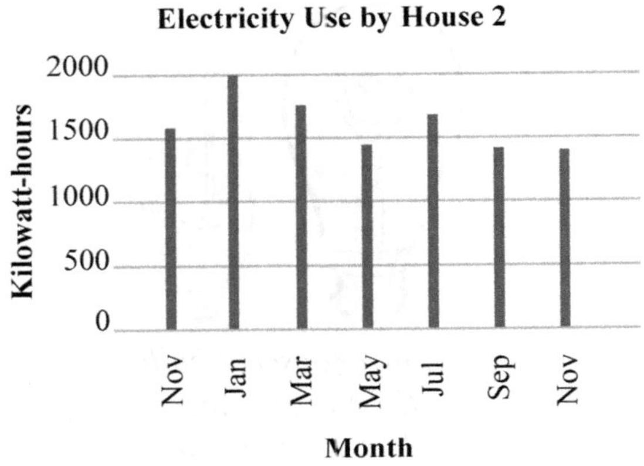

4. Which of the following inferences **best** explains why House 2 used more electricity in the summer months than House 1?

A. House 2 used an air conditioner, while House 1 did not.

B. Fewer people lived in House 1 than House 2, so House 1 did not need to use as much electricity.

C. The people in House 2 read more than the people in House 1 and needed the lights on more often.

D. House 2 was shaded with tall trees so the owners turned on more lights, whereas House 1 was not.

6ME3.1 identify the properties of air that make flight possible

Current Electricity Versus Static Electricity

Electricity is the flow of **electrons** from one area to another. **Current electricity** is the continuous flow of electrons through a conductor. A **conductor** is a material that easily allows electricity to travel through it. There are two types of current electricity: alternating current and direct current. Alternating current is the electricity made at power stations. Direct current is made when chemicals in a battery combine to make electricity. Current electricity can only flow when there are no breaks or gaps in a circuit. Current electricity is used to power the devices in your home and school.

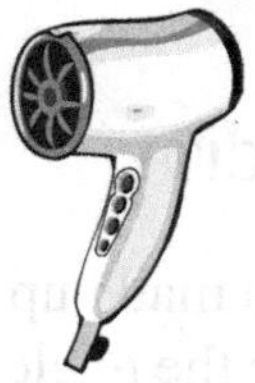

A hairdryer is a device that runs on current electricity.

Static electricity is a buildup of electrons on the surface of an object. The electrons or negative charges can potentially move to another charged object. Under the right circumstances, the negative charges will move in sudden bursts. Static electricity does not need a conductor to travel from one place to another. It can move across small gaps easily. However, it does not flow continuously as current electricity does. Static electricity cannot be used to power devices in your home or school.

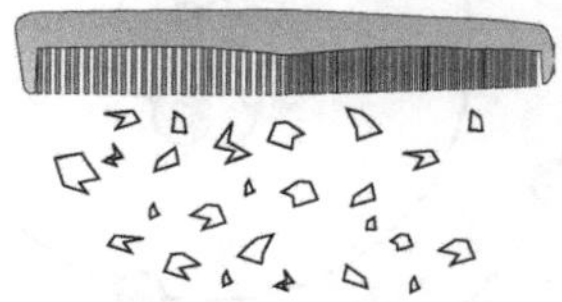

Small pieces of paper are attracted to the comb because of static charges.

5. Tony is learning about static and current electricity. He learned that rubbing a balloon on his hair generates static electricity and not current electricity because

A. the negative electrons are attracted to the negatively charged balloon

B. static electricity is a continuous flow of electrons

C. the electricity does not move across gaps easily

D. electrons build up and move in sudden bursts

6ME3.2 use the principles of static electricity to explain common electrostatic phenomena

6ME2.3 use scientific inquiry/experimentation skills to investigate the characteristics of static electricity

STATIC ELECTRICITY

Static electricity is a buildup of electrons on the surface of an object. The electrons or negative charges can potentially move to another charged object. The study of static electricity is a special branch of physics called electrostatics. **Electrostatics** looks at how static charges move from one object to another.

THE SOURCE OF STATIC ELECTRICITY

All matter is made up of atoms. An atom is made up of three parts: **electrons**, **neutrons**, and **protons**. The neutrons and protons make up the nucleus, which is the centre of the atom. Electrons move around the nucleus.

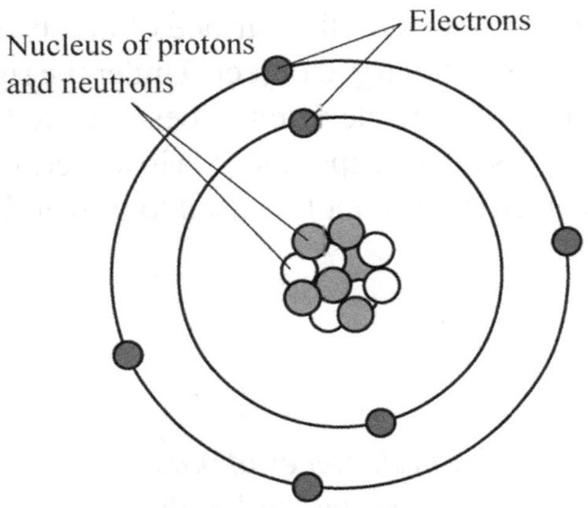

Diagram of an atom

Each atom usually has an equal number of neutrons, protons, and electrons. The protons are the positively charged particles of the atom and the electrons are the negatively charged particles. Neutrons do not have a charge. Because the protons and electrons are equal in number, atoms of objects are usually stable. Sometimes the negative charges (electrons) rub off or are added to another object. The negative charges (electrons) build up on the surface of an object.

Electricity is the movement of electrons from one place to another. Static electricity occurs when electrons move from one object to another. Electrons are too small to be seen from one place to another. The spark you see or the crackling noises you hear are the result of static electricity.

EXAMPLES OF STATIC ELECTRICITY

Static means the state of staying still or not moving. **Static electricity** is not really static because it can move from one place to another. Suppose two objects have opposite charges, one negative and one positive. Opposite charges are attracted to each other. If the differently charged objects move close enough together, some of the electrons on the negatively charged object will jump to the positively charged object. You may have noticed this happen when you walk on a carpet while wearing socks. Electrons build up in your body. When you touch a metal door knob, some of the electrons move from your body to the door knob.

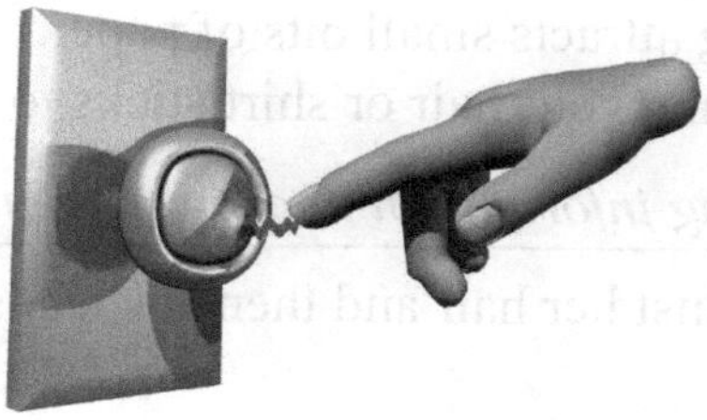

Sometimes you can feel static electricity when you touch metal objects.

Similar charges do not attract as opposite charges do; instead they repel one another. In the picture below, the boy is holding onto a Van de Graaff machine. The Van de Graaff machine is an electrostatic generator. Static electricity enters the boy's body. Each strand of hair on his head becomes negatively charged and is repelled by the other hairs.

Static electricity from the electrostatic generator causes the boy's hairs to repel each other.

Holding Static Charge

Some objects will hold static charges better than others. Their atoms easily accept electrons from other objects. These atoms hold a static charge well. Examples include metals like steel, copper, and brass as well as wood, many types of plastics, and hard forms of rubber. Other materials have atoms that give up electrons instead. These objects do not hold a static charge well. Examples include rabbit fur, human hair, paper, aluminum, and fabrics such as wool, silk, cotton, and nylon.

The following events are the result of static electricity:

- Clothes tumbled in a dryer cling together.
- Swirling storm clouds produce lightning bolts.
- A plastic ruler rubbed with a rag attracts small bits of paper.
- An inflated balloon rubbed against your hair or shirt sticks to the wall.

Use the following information to answer the next question.

Laura rubs two balloons against her hair and then suspends them with pieces of string to study static electricity.

6. Which of the following pictures shows the position of the balloons after they have been suspended?

A. 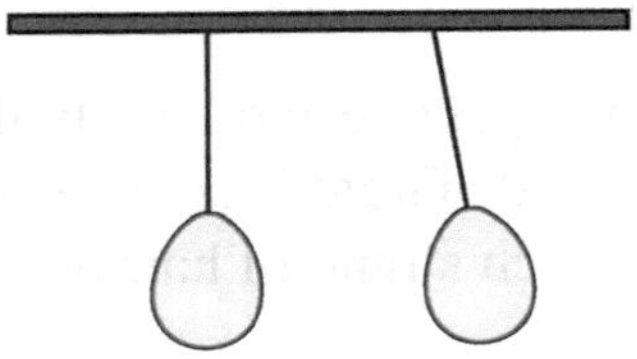

B. 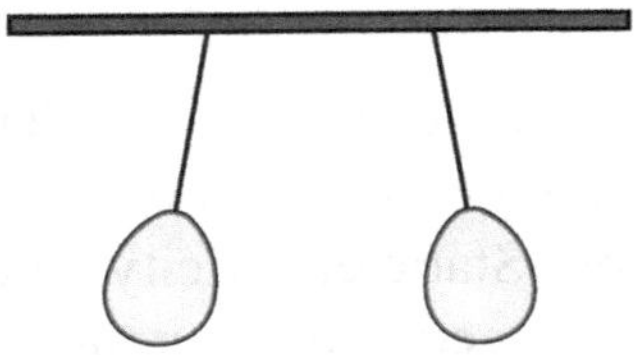

C. 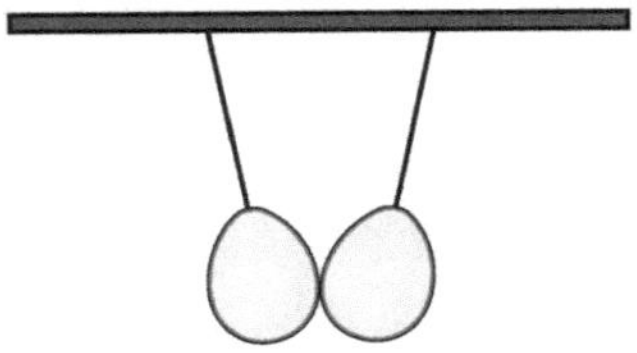

D. 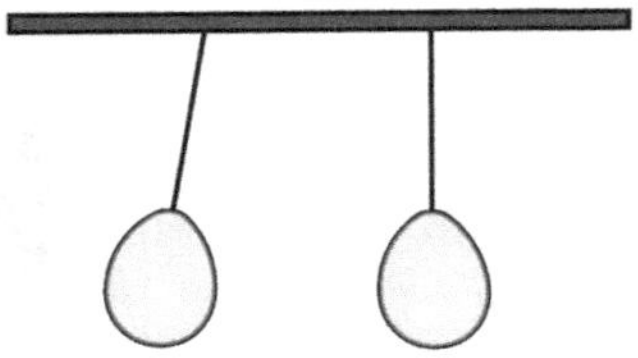

7. Which of the following situations is a result of static electricity?

A. A doorbell rings when the button is pressed.

B. Pieces of clothing tumbled in a dryer cling together.

C. The filament in a toaster gets hot when the knob is pushed down.

D. A thermostat switches on the furnace motor when the room temperature drops.

6ME3.3 identify materials that are good conductors of electricity and good insulators

Conductors and Insulators

A conductor is a material that electricity flows through easily. Metals are good conductors of electricity, so copper and aluminum wires are used in homes. Gold and silver are also used in electronics like stereos. Minerals in water help to conduct electricity through the water.

Here are some examples of objects that conduct electricity:

Paper-clip

Pencil lead

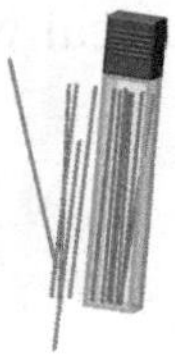

Metal Key

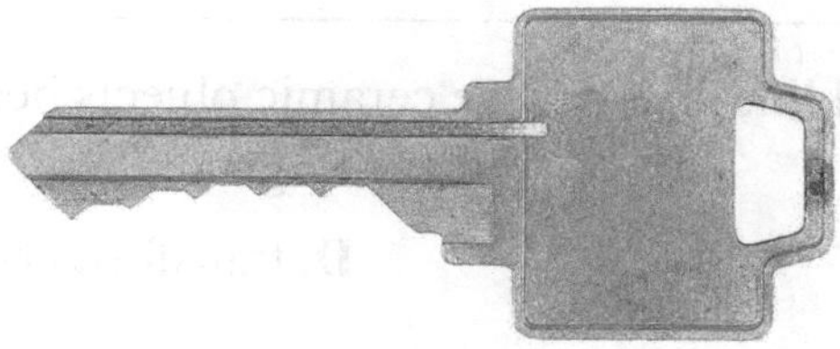

Insulators are materials that do not allow electricity to flow through them easily. The plastic and rubber used on the outside of wires are examples of insulators. The plastic stops the electricity from leaving the wire.

Here are some examples of materials that are insulators:

Rubber

Plastic

Glass

Wood

8. While working with electrical circuits, it is important to only touch rubber objects because rubber is a

A. poor conductor of heat
B. good conductor of heat
C. poor conductor of electricity
D. good conductor of electricity

Use the following information to answer the next question.

Margaret notices that ceramic objects are attached to the overhead electrical lines near her house. Electrical wires pass over the ceramic objects shown in the picture.

9. The overhead electrical lines have these ceramic objects because these objects are

A. insulators
B. generators
C. conductors
D. transformers

10. Which of the following rows **correctly** classifies a good conductor and a poor conductor of electricity?

A.

Good Conductor	Poor Conductor
Wood	Iron

B.

Good Conductor	Poor Conductor
Iron	Copper

C.

Good Conductor	Poor Conductor
Copper	Plastic

D.

Good Conductor	Poor Conductor
Plastic	Rubber

6ME3.4 describe how various forms of energy can be transformed into electrical energy

Transforming Energy into Electricity

Different forms of energy can be changed into electricity. A **battery** changes energy from chemical reactions into electricity. Batteries contain chemical liquids or pastes. These chemicals react with metals in the battery to release electrons. When the batteries are connected to complete circuits, the electrons flow through the circuit and back to the battery.

A battery transforms chemical energy into electrical energy.

A **generator** is a device that changes the energy of motion into electricity using magnets and coils of wire. If you spin a coil of wire through a magnetic field, you can generate electricity. In power plants, generators are attached to turbines. A **turbine** is a device that has blades like a windmill. When the blades turn, they make the turbine spin. The turbine then moves the coil or magnet in the generator to produce electricity.

Coal and natural gas plants use turbines to generate energy. The coal or gas is burned to heat water in a boiler. The water changes to steam, which rises against a turbine. The blades of the turbine spin, which causes a generator to spin. The generator produces electricity.

Turbines are used in hydroelectric dams. Water travels through tunnels in a dam to spin a turbine to turn a generator. Moving water from ocean tides turns turbines attached to generators. Other technologies use large buoys in the ocean to generate electricity. The buoy moves up and down with the ocean waves, which move a piston inside the buoy. This creates electricity in a generator inside the buoy.

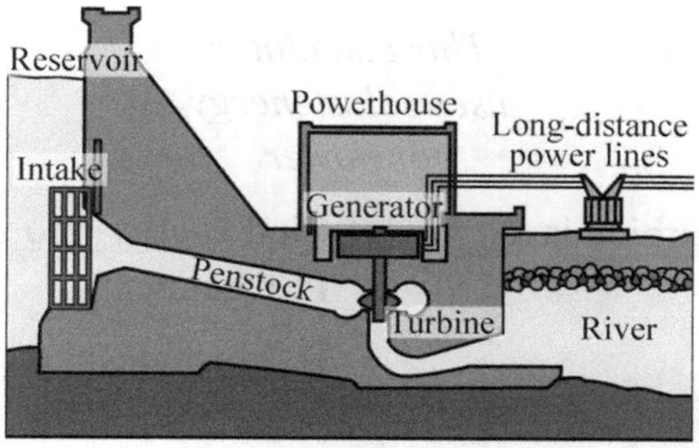

A hydroelectric dam

A windmill uses wind power to turn a turbine. The wind pushes against the blades of the windmill or wind turbine, causing them to turn. This movement spins the generator to create energy.

Wind turbines

In a nuclear power station, steam is used to spin a turbine. Uranium molecules are split, creating a great deal of energy. This energy is used to heat water and produce steam. The steam spins the blades of the turbine. The attached generator creates electricity.

The energy from the sun can also be used to generate electricity. To do this, a **solar cell** is used. It contains special layers that change the light from the sun to an electrical current. You can see solar cells on calculators that use light for power. Many large solar cells can be put together to make solar panels.

This calculator uses solar energy for power.

11. The purpose of a wind turbine is to convert wind energy into what other type of energy?

A. Solar
B. Chemical
C. Electrical
D. Mechanical

Use the following information to answer the next question.

Tom visits the Sir Adam Beck power stations in Niagara Falls, Ontario. He observes that a huge amount of water is stored at a height. When this water is released, it comes down with great force.

12. How does this moving water generate electricity?

A. The water rotates turbines, which generate electricity.

B. The movement of the water pushes air, which generates electricity.

C. Fast-flowing water moves through pipes that lead back to the reservoir.

D. A large buoy with a piston connected to a generator moves up and down with the water.

6ME3.5 identify ways in which electrical energy is transformed into other forms of energy

6ME2.5 use technological problem-solving skills to design, build, and test a device that transforms electrical energy into another form of energy in order to perform a function

ELECTRICITY IS ENERGY

Electricity is a form of energy. When electricity reaches your home, it is changed, or **transformed**, into other forms of energy. For example, a light bulb changes electricity into heat and light. Electricity passes through the filament of the bulb. This heats it up and makes it glow.

Glowing filament in a light bulb

Some devices change electricity into sound energy. A doorbell, a CD player, and a loud speaker change electricity into sound.

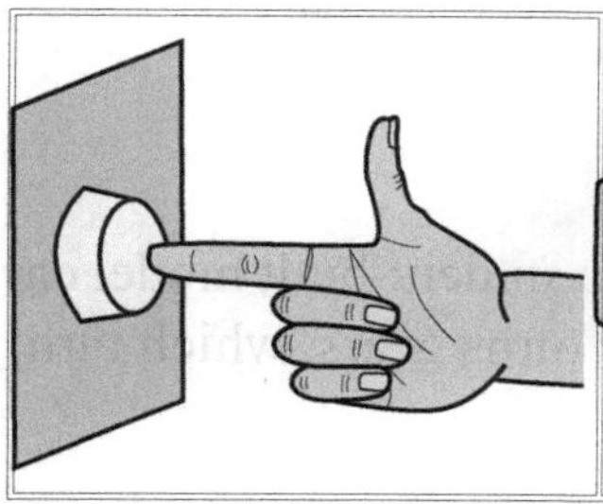
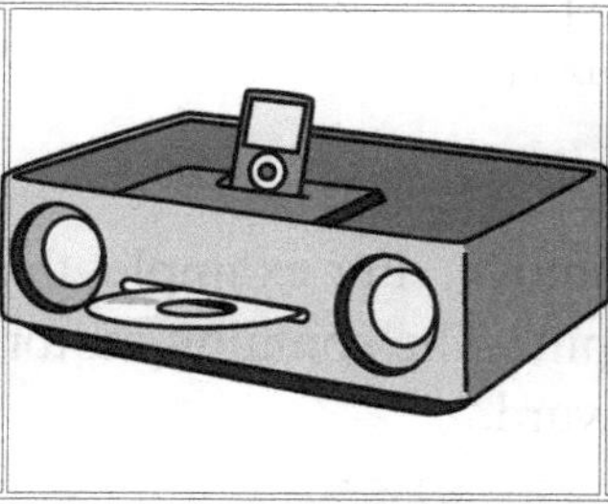
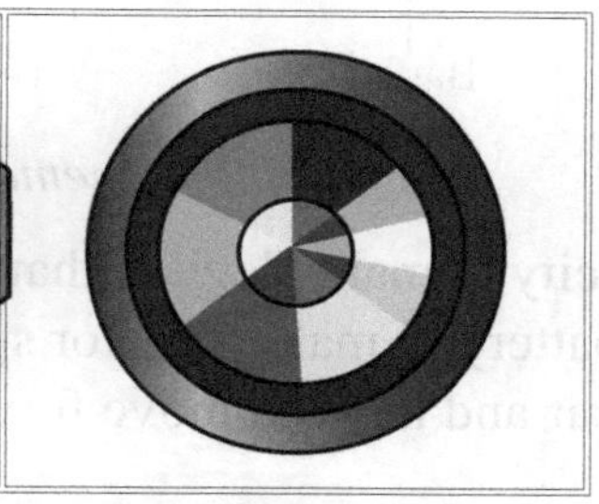

Some devices change electricity into thermal energy, or heat. A heater, curling iron, and waffle iron all change electricity into heat.

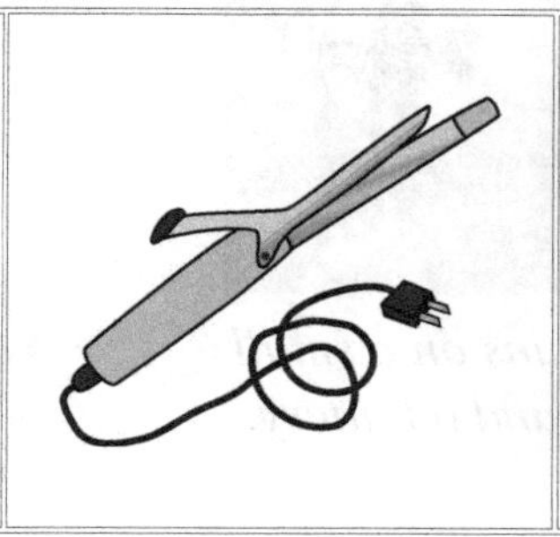

Building Devices that Change Electricity into a New Form of Energy

Usually when you design and build a circuit, you will change electrical energy into a new form of energy. One device that many students build is a burglar alarm. This is a device that gives a warning of some kind when someone is trying to break into a home or building. Usually this warning is in the form of an alarm from a buzzer or speaker. Below is an example of a student-built window alarm. When the pieces of foil meet, the circuit is complete, and the buzzer sounds.

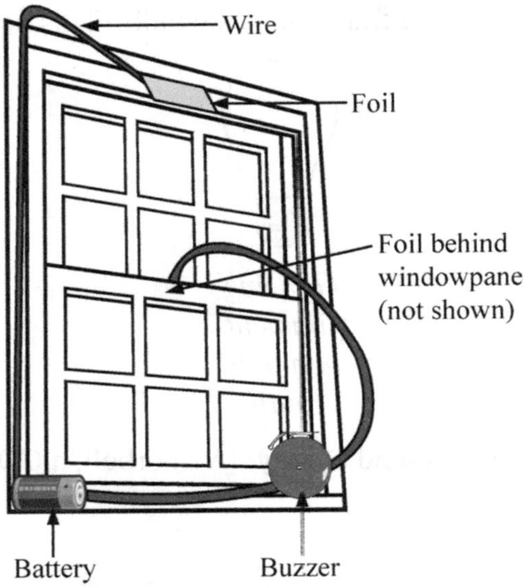

A sample homemade window alarm

You can also use electricity to make devices that move. For example, this student-built model car uses electricity from a battery to make a motor spin. The spinning motor turns gears, which turn the back wheels of the car and make it move forward.

A model car runs on a small hobby motor and a battery.

Use the following information to answer the next question.

Timothy built a burglar alarm and set it outside his bedroom door under the mat. When someone steps on the device, the electricity from the battery turns the light bulb on.

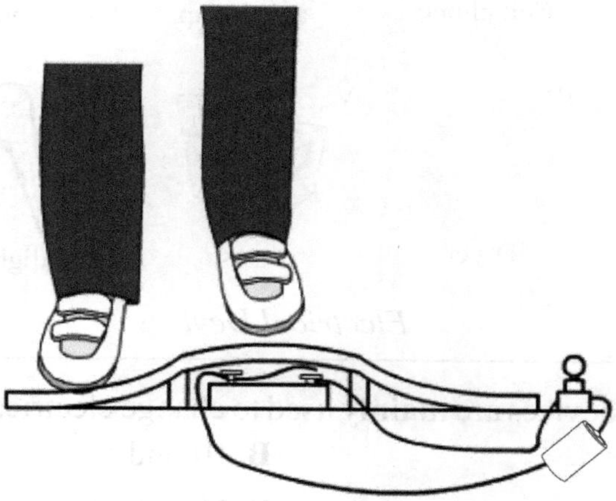

13. To make this an effective burglar alarm, the **best** place for Timothy to put the light and battery is

A. next to the mat on the floor outside his bedroom door

B. on the wall away from the door inside his bedroom

C. on the wall at eye level outside his bedroom door

D. next to the door on the floor inside his bedroom

Use the following information to answer the next question.

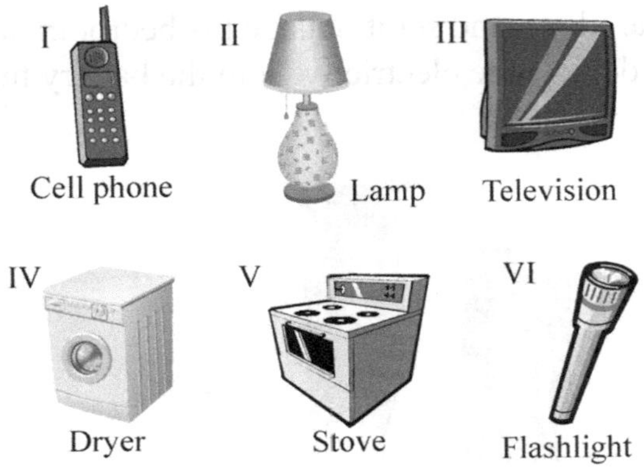

Electrical Devices

14. Which two electrical devices are **mainly** used to change electrical energy into heat energy?

A. I and IV

B. III and V

C. IV and V

D. V and VI

6ME3.6 explain the functions of the components of a simple electrical circuit

PARTS OF A SIMPLE CIRCUIT

The path an electric current follows is called an electric **circuit**. The simple circuit shown here is an example of an electric circuit. In order to work, the circuit must be closed, with no gaps or openings. In the picture the switch is open. When the switch is closed, the circuit will be complete.

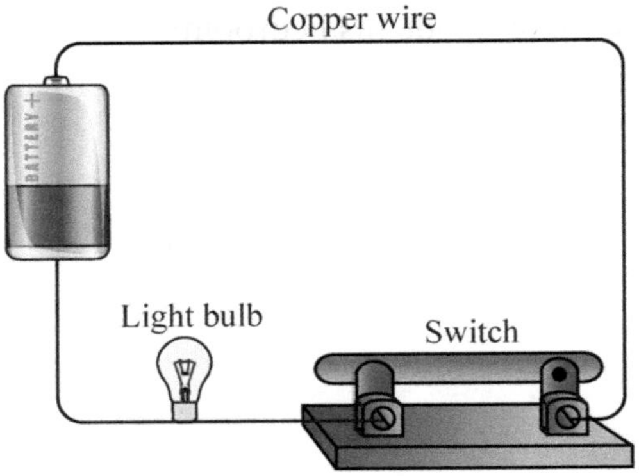

A simple circuit

This simple circuit is made up of four parts: a power source, wires, a switch, and a light bulb. A **power source** provides electricity to the circuit. In this case, the power source is a battery. The **load** is the device that will use the electricity to do something. In this case, the load is the light bulb. A **switch** is used to turn the flow of electricity on or off by opening or closing the circuit. Wires are used to connect the switch, load, and power source together. **Wires** conduct the electricity from one place to another.

You can draw a circuit using symbols. Here are some common symbols used in circuit diagrams.

Circuit symbols used in diagrams

Circuit Part	Symbol
Bulb	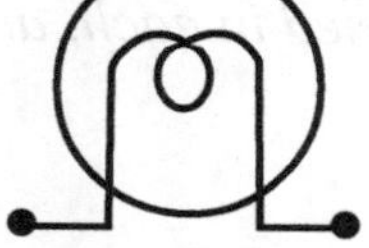
Battery	
Switch	
Wires	

A simple circuit can be drawn with these symbols, as seen below.

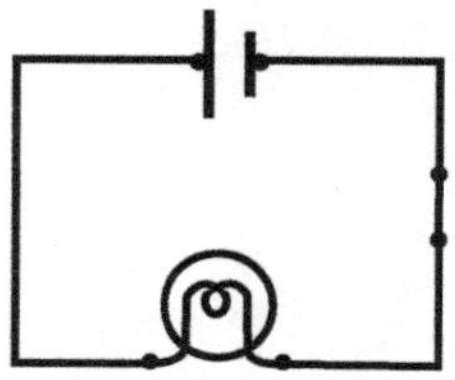

Use the following information to answer the next question.

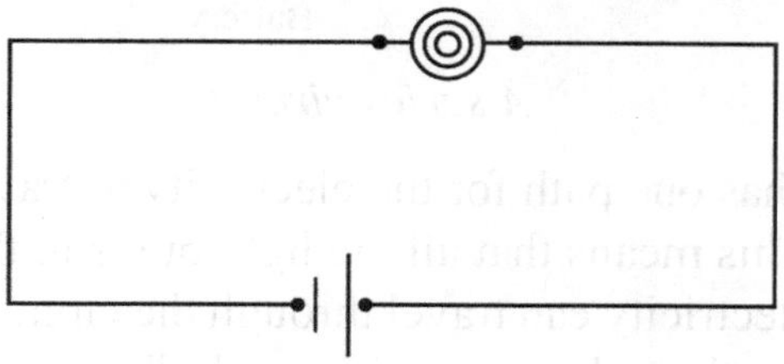

Brad designed this window alarm.

15. What important part is missing from Brad's design?

A. Switch

B. Buzzer

C. Battery

D. Light bulb

6ME3.7 *describe series circuits (components connected in a daisy chain) and parallel circuits (components connected side by side like the rungs of a ladder), and identify where each is used*

6ME2.2 *design and build series and parallel circuits, draw labelled diagrams identifying the components used in each, and describe the role of each component in the circuit*

Series Circuit

A **series circuit** is a circuit that has one path for the electricity to follow. Two or more bulbs or batteries in a row are wired to each other. Patio lights are sometimes wired in a series circuit. A series circuit looks like a necklace with all the beads strung onto one string. Like all circuits, the two ends of the wires have to touch one another for the electricity to flow. If there is any gap in the circuit, or if the switch is open, no electricity will flow through the circuit and the lights will not glow.

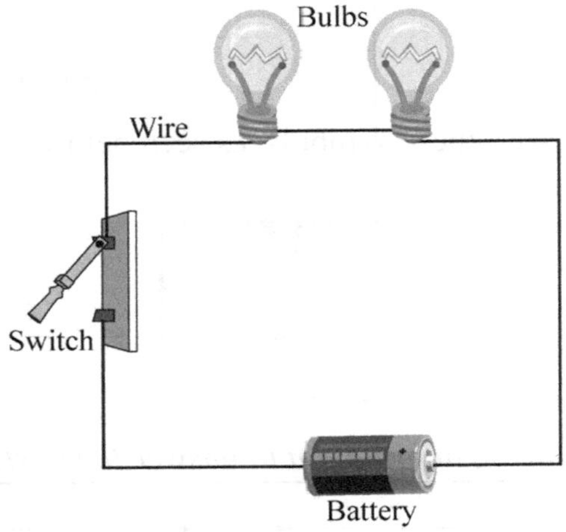

A series circuit

Because a series circuit only has one path for the electricity to travel, a broken or burnt out bulb creates a gap in the circuit. This means that all the light bulbs in the circuit will go out. Once the broken bulb is replaced, the electricity can travel through the circuit again. All the lights will come back on again. You will notice that when you wire two bulbs in a series circuit, the light given off from one bulb will be dimmer than the other. If you add another bulb to the circuit, the light from the third bulb will be even dimmer. This happens because the electricity has to push through one bulb after the other in a row.

You can draw the series circuit above using symbols.

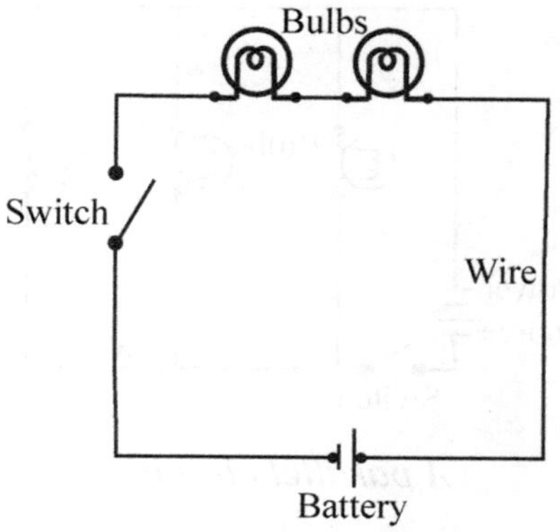

A series circuit drawn using symbols

Parallel Circuits

A **parallel circuit** provides at least one other path for the electricity to follow. Each bulb or battery is wired in seperately. A parallel circuits looks a little like a ladder. All the parts of the circuit are placed on the rungs. The legs of the ladder connect the rungs together.

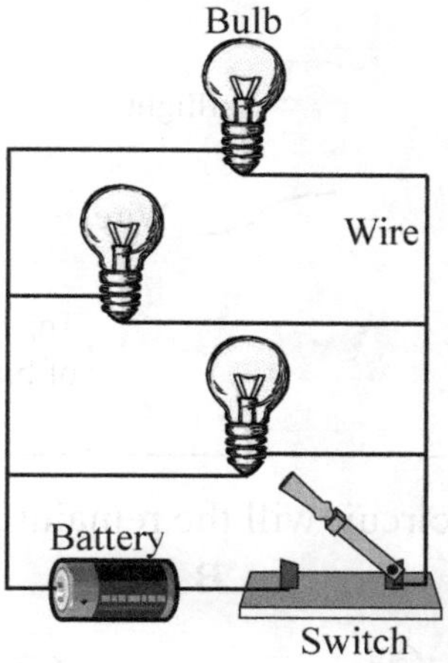

A parallel circuit

In a parallel circuit, if one bulb burns out, the others will remain lit. This is because the electricity has another path to follow. The electricity travels to each bulb seperately. This means that each bulb will give off the same amount of light and will not grow dim when another bulb is added.

A circuit similar to the one given above can also be drawn with symbols.

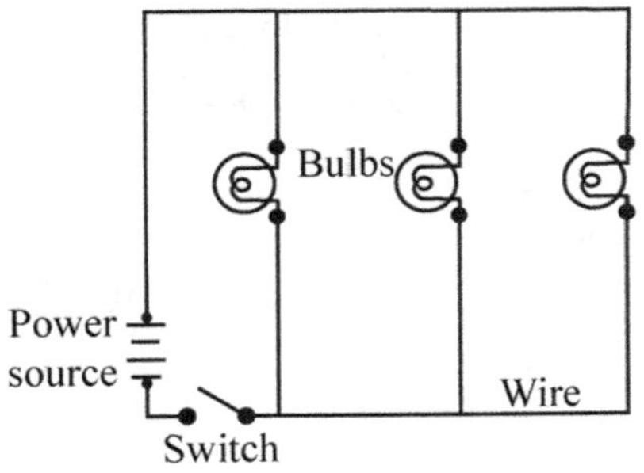

A parallel circuit

Use the following information to answer the next question.

Omid and Anne take long bike rides. To make their bicycles safer to ride at night, they want to attach lights. Omid is testing four circuits.

Legend

	Battery
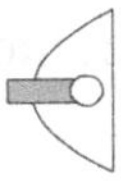	Headlight
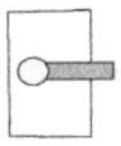	Taillight
	Wire
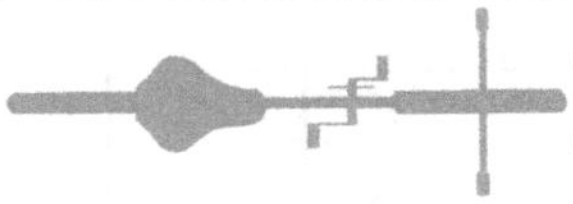	Top view of bicycle

16. If one bulb burns out, in which circuit will the remaining bulb stay on?

A.

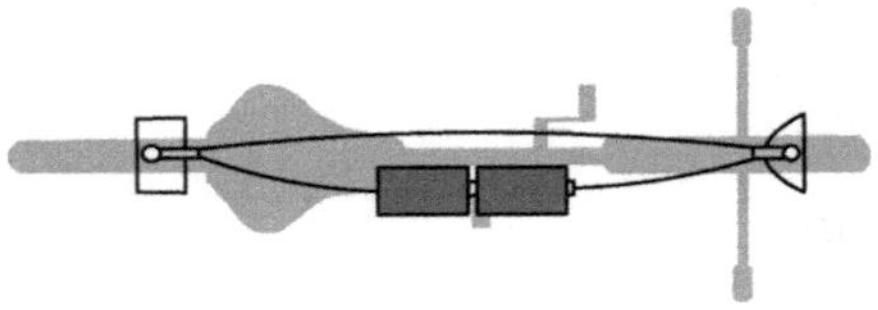

B.

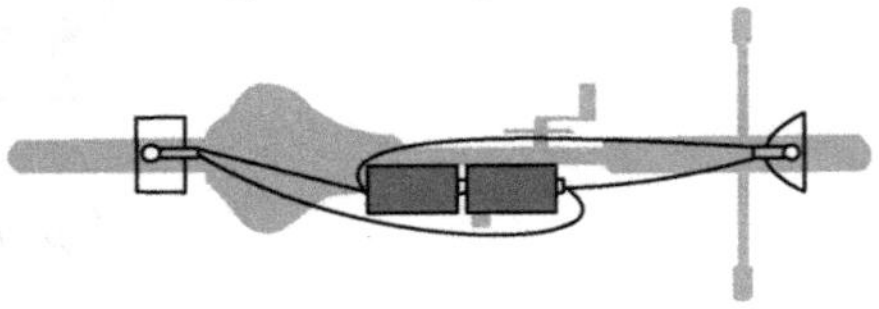

C.

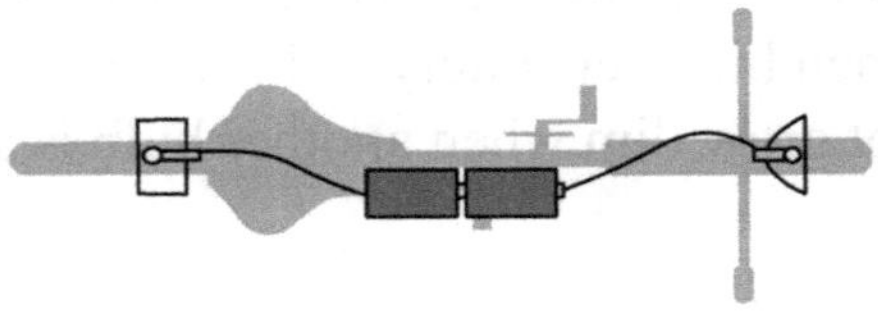

D.

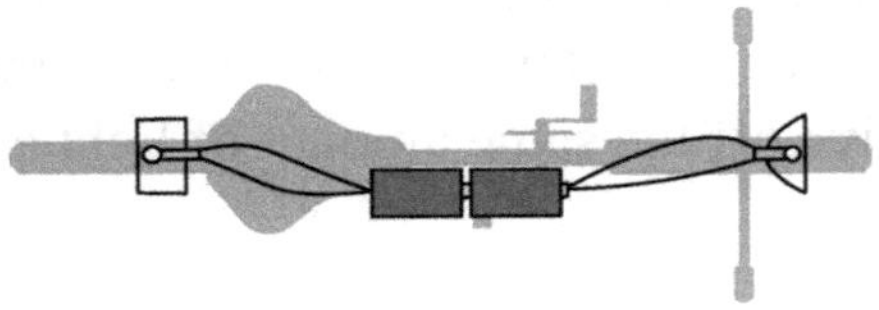

Use the following information to answer the next question.

This figure shows a circuit consisting of six bulbs and a battery.

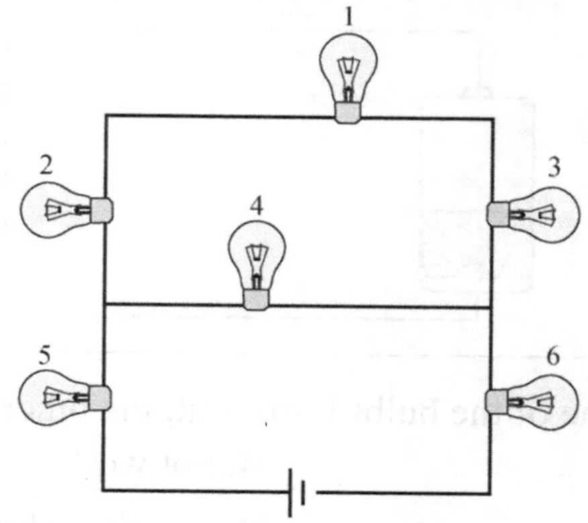

17. If bulb 4 burns out, which type of circuit remains?

A. Open circuit
B. Series circuit
C. Simple circuit
D. Parallel circuit

18. In which of the following circuits will **both** lights go on and off together?

A.
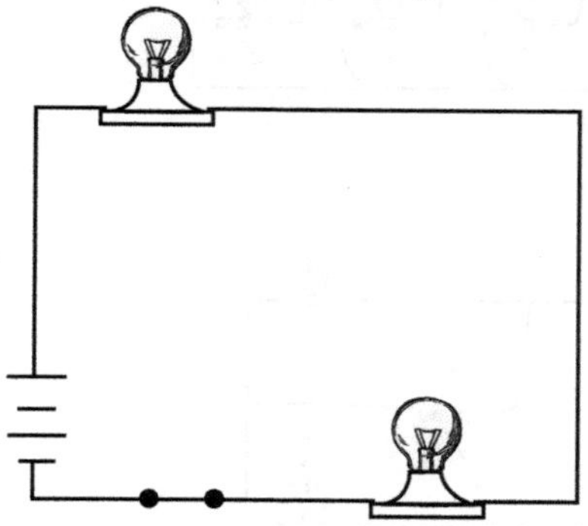

B.
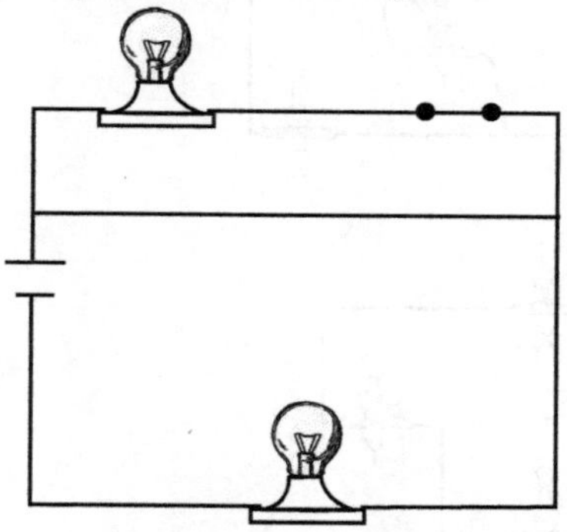

C.
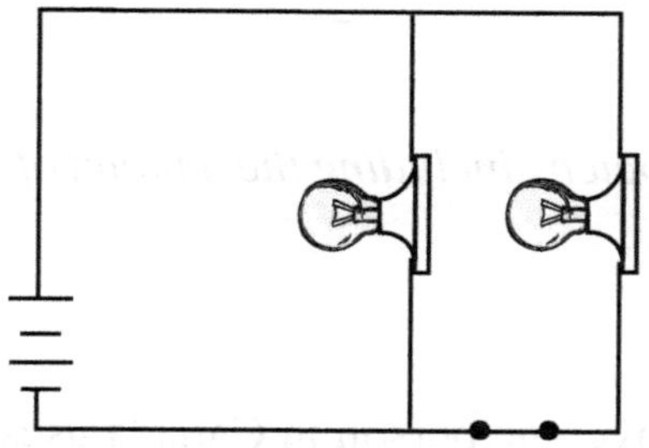

D.
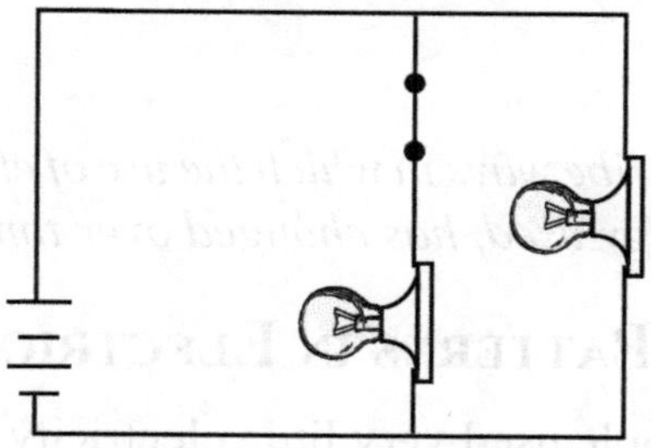

Use the following information to answer the next question.

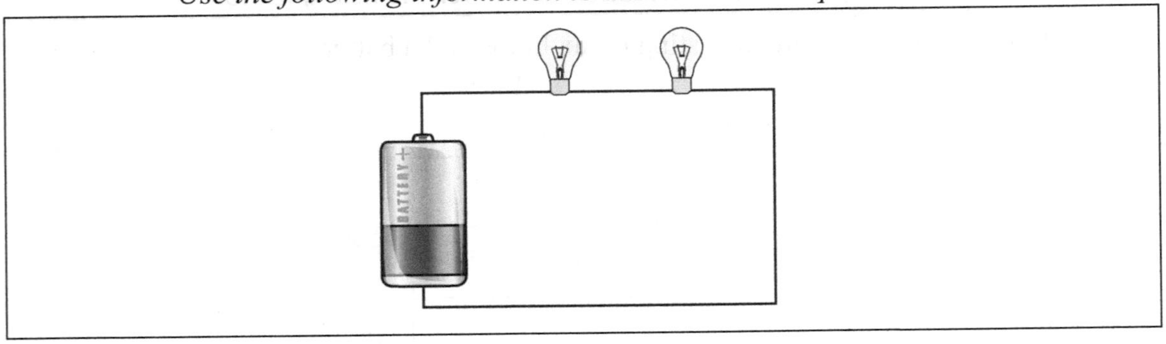

19. In the circuit shown, if one of the bulbs burns out, the other bulb will

A. burn out **B.** not work

C. become dimmer **D.** remain as bright

20. In which of the following circuits would bulb **Z** remain lit if **both** bulbs **X** and **Y** burned out?

A.
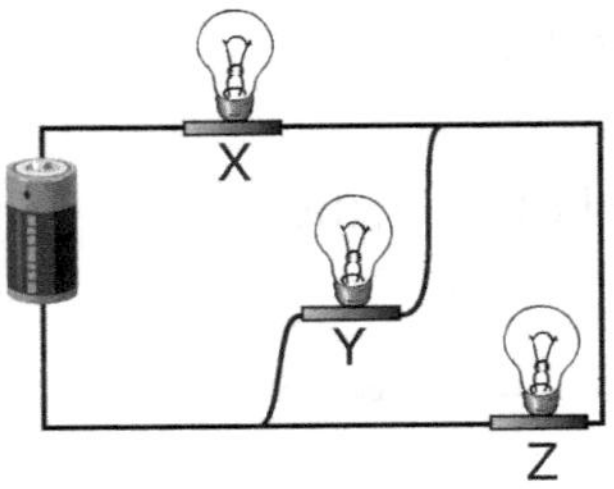

B.
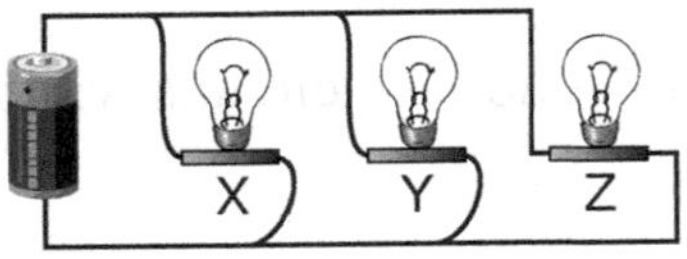

C.
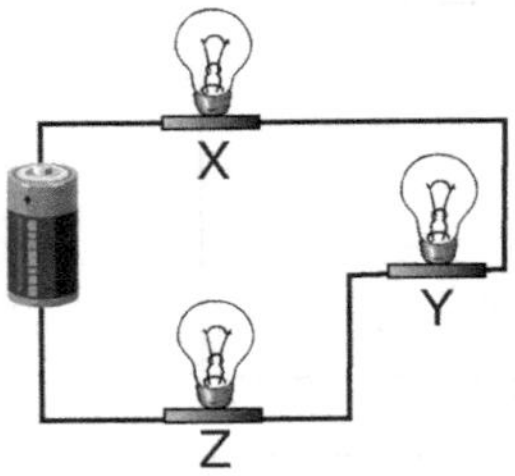

D.
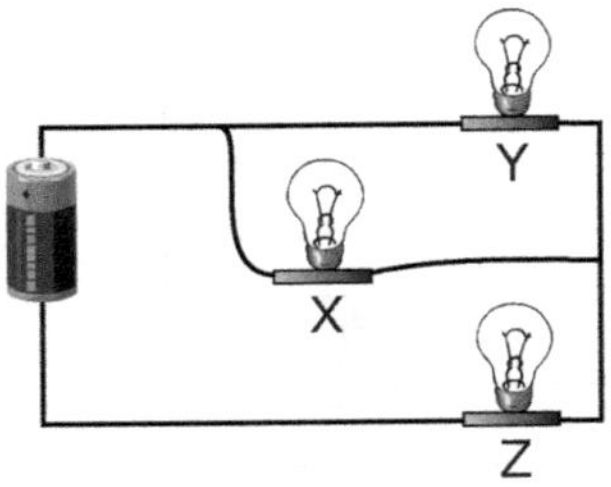

6ME3.8 describe ways in which the use of electricity by society, including the amount of electrical energy used, has changed over time

Changing Patterns in Electricity Use

In the past, people used very little electricity. Today, the average person in Canada uses a lot of electricity every day. Technology has changed so that people need to use more electricity. In the past, the same job or activity might not have used any electricity. For example, everybody used to hang their clothes up to dry on a clothesline. This uses no electricity. Now, many people put their wet clothes in a clothes dryer. A clothes dryer uses a lot of electricity. However, it is faster and easier to use a clothes dryer than hanging the clothes on a line.

In the past, people hung their washing on a clothesline.

Now, most people use a clothes dryer.

The following table lists some other ways in which electricity usage has changed in Canada over the years. The first column shows a job, activity, or task performed in the past that used little or no electricity. The second column shows how the same job or activity has changed because of electricity.

Changes in Electricity Use — Past and Present

In the past, people...	In the present, people...
used candles and lanterns for light	use light bulbs
played board games	play video games on television
washed dishes by hand	wash dishes using a dishwasher
washed clothes by hand	wash clothes using a washing machine
wrote letters to friends and family	use a computer to send emails
visited friends and family to talk	use a telephone to call friends or family
cooked food in a wood-burning stove	cook food in ovens and micro-waves
listened to news and music on the radio	watch the news and programs on a television
wound clocks and watches to keep time	use batteries and electricity to keep time in clocks and watches
boiled water for cooking and clean-ing over a fire or on the wood stove	boil water using a stove top or an electric kettle.
used cold storage rooms to store food that needed to stay cool	use a refrigerator to keep food cold

Use the following information to answer the next question.

Many years ago, before flashlights were invented, people carried lanterns to provide the light that they needed. Now, most people use flashlights instead of lanterns.

21. What is the **most likely** reason that flashlights replaced lanterns as a source of light?

A. The metal lanterns rust easily, so they do not last as long.

B. Flashlights are made of more durable materials than lanterns.

C. Lanterns use oil or candles, which are more expensive than batteries.

D. It is safer to use flashlights with batteries than to burn oil or candles in a lantern.

6ME2.1 follow established safety procedures for working with electricity

Electrical Safety

Before you begin any experiments that use electricity, review the safety procedures your class has in place. Here are some things to think about:

- Always have an adult present when working with electricity.
- Make sure your hands are dry before you touch an electrical device.
- Use batteries in any experiments that use electricity. Do not use the electricity from a wall socket to do experiments. The electricity coming from a wall socket is strong enough to kill you! Batteries carry very little electricity and will not hurt you.
- Make sure any wires you use are insulated. An insulated wire has a plastic or rubber coating around it. Never use bare wires for experiments, even if you are only using a battery for power. Never use wires that have cracked or frayed insulation.
- Draw a plan that shows all the parts you are going to use in your experiment. Research how the different parts of an electric circuit go together. Only wire your project once an adult has looked over your plans and says it is safe to continue.

A battery is the safest source of electricity to use when conducting experiments with electricity.

You should also consider the following safety procedures:

- Keep electrical devices away from water. It can carry an electric charge.
- Keep electric cords away from heat. It could melt the plastic cover on the wire.
- When unplugging a device from the wall, always pull it out from the plug. Never pull it out by the cord.
- Never open an electric device, even if it is unplugged! Some devices have parts that store electrical charges, even when they are turned off and unplugged.
- If you notice that a wall socket feels warm, it could be a sign that the wiring if faulty. Tell an adult so he or she can get the socket fixed.
- Tell your teacher or parents about devices that have broken, cut, or frayed cords. Do not use these devices until the cords have been replaced or repaired.
- Only put electrical plugs into wall sockets. At home, if you have younger brothers and sisters, put plastic covers over unused sockets. Do not insert anything else into an electrical socket.
- If an electrical fire starts, do not use water to put it out. Use baking soda instead. If it is safe to do so, unplug the device that has started the fire. Otherwise, get out of the house.
- Call 911 or your local emergency department if you see a fire has started, or if someone has been badly injured by electricity.

Only put electrical plugs into electrical sockets. You could be seriously injured otherwise.

Here are some safety tips to remember when you are outside:

- Never climb electrical poles or touch overhead wires with other objects like poles or sticks. Do not climb trees near electrical wires. Only fly kites and other toys in an open field. Keep these toys away from overhead lines.
- Do not play near substations. These are places where electricity is changed from a high voltage to the lower voltage used in your home. A substation is a very dangerous place.
- Do not open up electrical boxes in your neighborhood. These boxes will probably have signs that say "Danger" or "Danger—High Voltage". If you see a box that is open, have an adult call the power company and report it.
- Do not go outside during a lightning storm. If you are outside when one starts, try to find shelter as quickly as you can. Do not go swimming during a lightning storm.
- Stay away from fallen electrical lines. Call 911 or your local emergency department.

Avoid playing near power lines and poles. Never climb power poles or towers.

22. The **main** reason that batteries, rather than household current, are used for experimentation is that

A. batteries cost less than household power

B. household current is weaker than battery current

C. batteries hold more energy than household current

D. household current is more dangerous than battery current

Use the following information to answer the next question.

Felix was making a potato battery for a science experiment.

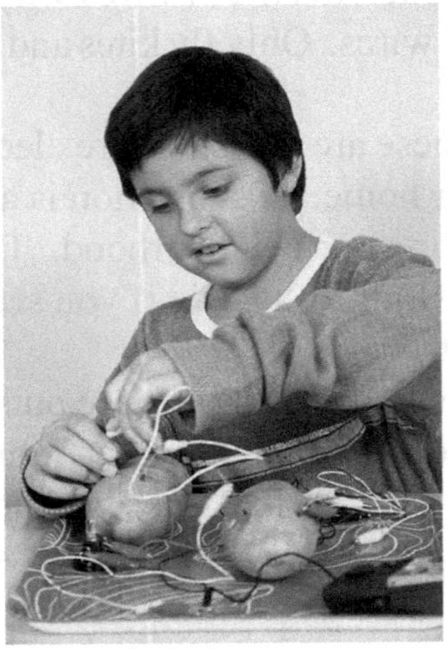

23. What is the **most important** safety precaution Felix must take in this experiment?

A. Wear safety glasses

B. Use wires that are insulated

C. Peel the potatoes before using them

D. Make sure the clips are fastened securely

6ME2.4 design, build, and test a device that produces electricity

BUILDING DEVICES THAT PRODUCE ELECTRICITY

You can make electricity at home using a lemon, wire, a paper-clip, and a penny. An illustration of a lemon battery is shown below.

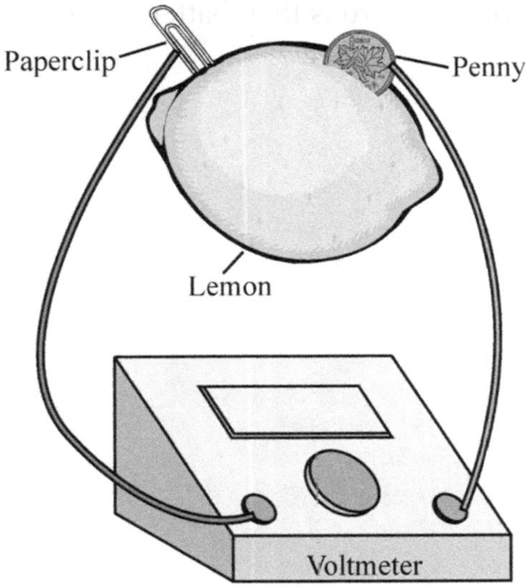

A lemon battery hooked up to a voltmeter.

Batteries work when the chemicals in them release electrons or negative charges. The electrons travel from the negative end of the battery, through the conductor and bulb and back to the positive end in a circuit.

In a lemon, the acid in the lemon juice reacts with the paperclip and the penny to release positive and negative charges. The lemon juice and paper-clip make a negative charge. The lemon juice reacts with the penny to make a positive charge. The electrons on the paper-clip travel up through the wire and back down to the copper penny. This flow of electrons is called electric **current**. Your lemon battery does not create a lot of electricity. Four or five lemons in one circuit can usually light up a Light Emitting Diode, or LED. You would need hundreds of lemons to make a regular light bulb glow!

Other fruits and vegetables that have acids in their juice can also be used to make a battery. The acid in the juice reacts with the metals to start the flow of electricity.

Use the following information to answer the next question.

Sania built a homemade wind turbine for the science fair. She turned a fan on medium and placed it in front of the turbine. Sania recorded 3 volts of electricity on the voltmeter.

Wind Turbine

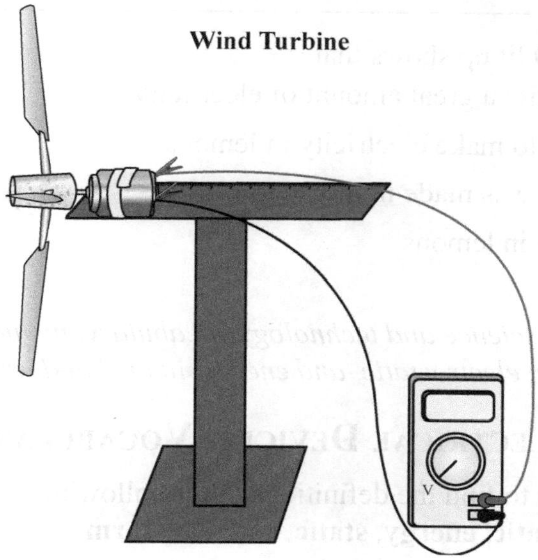

24. What would Sania need to do in order to get a reading of 5 volts of electricity?

A. Move the fan closer and change the angle of the blades

B. Increase the speed of the fan by turning it up higher

C. Turn the fan down and attach a bigger motor

D. Put the fan on the other side of the turbine

Use the following information to answer the next question.

Marco set up the following science fair experiment. When the end of the wire was attached to the paper-clip and the copper wire was placed in the lemon, the LED lit up.

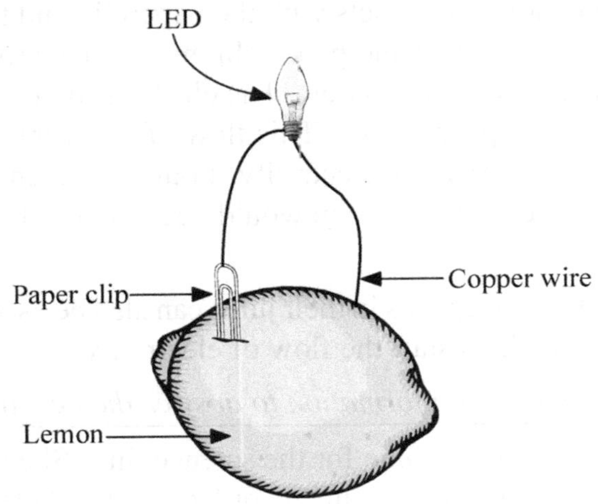

25. The fact that the LED lit up shows that

A. LEDs do not require a great amount of electricity

B. LEDs are needed to make electricity in lemons

C. current electricity was made in the lemon

D. there is electricity in lemons

6ME2.6 use appropriate science and technology vocabulary, including current, battery, circuit, transform, static, electrostatic, and energy, in oral and written communication

ELECTRICITY AND ELECTRICAL DEVICES: VOCABULARY

Please refer to the glossary to find the definitions of the following vocabulary words: **battery**, **current**, **circuit**, **electrostatic**, **energy**, **static**, and **transform**.

Use the following information to answer the next question.

Electricity changes into light and heat energy when a lamp is turned on.

26. When energy changes from one form to another, it

A. becomes current electricity

B. forms static electricity

C. is transformed

D. is stored

Use the following information to answer the next question.

After combing her dry hair, Nancy puts her comb on her dressing table near some scraps of paper. She observes that the scraps of paper are attracted toward the comb.

27. What force attracts the scraps of paper toward the comb?

A. Current

B. Magnetic

C. Frictional

D. Electrostatic

ANSWERS AND SOLUTIONS
MATTER AND ENERGY: ELECTRICITY AND ELECTRICAL DEVICES

1. B	7. B	13. B	19. B	25. C
2. A	8. C	14. C	20. B	26. C
3. C	9. A	15. A	21. D	27. D
4. A	10. C	16. B	22. D	
5. D	11. C	17. B	23. B	
6. B	12. A	18. A	24. B	

1. B

The construction of the four dams on the Nipigon River has lead to a decrease in the number of brook trout in the river since 1950.

2. A

In Ontario, nuclear and hydroelectric power would produce the large amount of electricity needed to make aluminum. Wind and solar power are available in Ontario, but they would not produce enough power needed to make aluminum.

3. C

Disabling the sleep mode feature on computers will not help energy because the computer will keep running for a long time. Turning the sleep mode feature on can save energy.

4. A

The increase of electricity in the summer months is most likely caused by the use of an air conditioner. This choice is the most reasonable because the biggest difference in energy use between the two houses occurs during the summer, when an air conditioner would be used.

If any of the other choices were true, the difference in energy use between the two houses would have been consistent throughout the whole year.

5. D

In static electricity, the electrons build up and move in sudden bursts. Current electricity is the continuous flow of electrons through a conductor.

6. B

Each balloon takes on a negative charge when rubbed. When both balloons are negatively charged, they will repel each other. Any two objects with the same charge will repel one another.

7. B

When pieces of clothing are tumbled together in a dryer, static electricity is produced.

8. C

Rubber is a poor conductor of electricity. This means that electric currents do not pass through rubber. This prevents a person working with electric circuits from getting shocked.

9. A

The ceramic objects Margaret sees are insulators. Overhead electric lines have high voltages of electricity moving through them. Ceramics are made of baked clay, which is a good electrical insulator. The ceramic insulators are used so the electric wires do not touch the poles and electricity is not lost to the ground.

10. C

Good Conductor	Poor Conductor
Copper	Plastic

Copper and iron are metals, which are good conductors of electricity. They allow electricity to pass through them easily. Plastic, rubber, and wood are poor conductors of electricity. Electricity does not travel through these types of materials.

11. C

A wind turbine converts wind energy into electrical energy. The force of the wind causes the large blades to spin. The turbine attached to a generator produces electrical energy.

12. A

Water released from a dam is sent through pipes. The water spins the turbine as it passes through. The turbine spins the generator, which generates electricity.

13. B

To make an effective burglar alarm, Timothy should move the light and battery inside his room. Otherwise it would be seen by anyone walking on the mat. It would be best to have the light off the floor and on the wall where it can be seen easily from anywhere in the room. So, the best place for Timothy to place the light and battery would be on to the wall away from the door inside his bedroom.

14. C

In the group of given pictures, there are two machines that change electrical energy into heat energy: the dryer (**IV**) and the stove (**V**). The dryer uses heat energy to dry clothes. The stove uses heat energy to cook food.

15. A

Brad is missing a switch in his window alarm. Without a switch, his alarm cannot be turned on or off. As this alarm is currently wired, the buzzer will ring all the time.

16. B

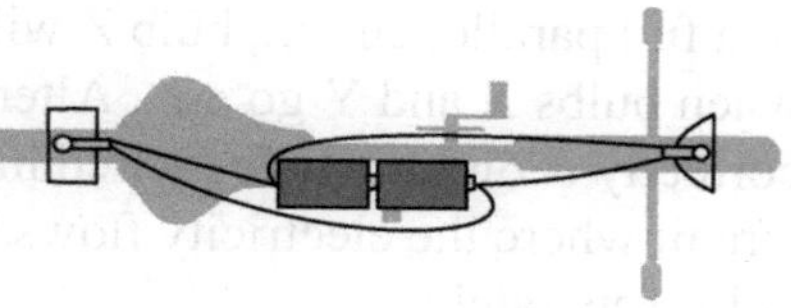

In this circuit, if one bulb burns out, the remaining bulb will stay on. This is because the bicycle lights are wired in parallel.

A parallel circuit has two or more paths for the electricity to follow. The electricity travels to each bulb separately. In this closed circuit, when one light burns out, the remaining bulb will stay on because it has a separate path for the electricity to follow. The diagram shows the correct circuit in which one bulb stays on if the other bulb burns out.

17. B

A series circuit is one in which all components are connected in series with each other. If bulb 4 burns out, then the circuit will be a series circuit, as shown in the following figure. No current will flow through the branch where bulb 4 is located.

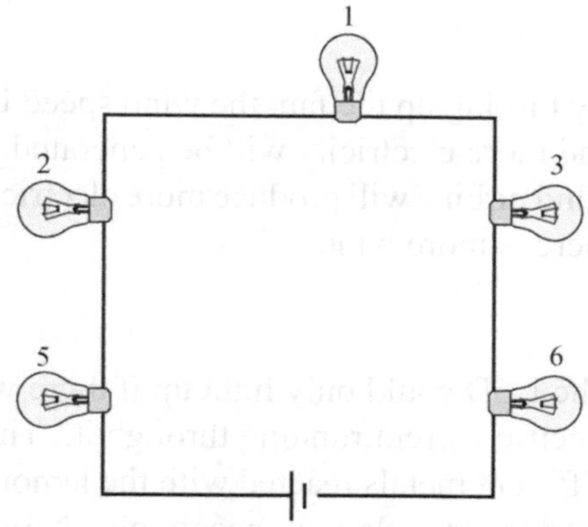

18. A

The series circuit is the circuit that will have both lights go out when the switch is opened. A gap is formed when the switch is opened. This means the electricity cannot flow to the bulbs wired in a row.

19. B

When one bulb burns out, the other bulb will not work until the first bulb is replaced. The bulbs shown are wired in a series circuit.

20. B

In a full parallel circuit, bulb Z will remain lit when bulbs X and Y go out. Alternative **B** correctly shows the bulbs wired in a parallel circuit where the electricity flows to all three bulbs separately.

21. D

The batteries in flashlights provide a safer source of light than burning oil or candles in a lantern.

22. D

It is much safer to experiment with batteries than an electric current. A household current is more dangerous than battery current.

23. B

It is important to use only insulated wires when conducting experiments with electricity. Insulated wires have a plastic or rubber coating around them. Never use bare wires for experiments, even if you are only using a battery for power. Never use wires that have cracked or frayed insulation.

24. B

By turning up the fan, the wind speed increases and more electricity will be generated. The wind turbine will produce more electricity when there is more wind.

25. C

The LED could only light up if there was an electric current running through it. The two different metals reacted with the lemon juice to produce free-flowing negatively charged particles or electrons. The electrons flowed through the conducting wires to the LED to light it up.

26. C

Transform means to change from one form to another. Electricity changes from electrical energy into other forms of energy.

27. D

Electrostatic force is the attractive or repulsive force between two charged particles.
The friction between dry hair and the comb produces static electric charges on the comb. When the charged comb is brought near the scraps of paper, the scraps of paper are attracted toward the comb as a result of electrostatic force.

UNIT TEST — MATTER AND ENERGY: ELECTRICITY AND ELECTRICAL DEVICES

Use the following information to answer the next question.

While there are many benefits to using nuclear power as a source of electricity, there are also some drawbacks.

1. Which of the following **negative** impacts does nuclear power have on the environment?
   A. Nuclear power plants create a lot of noise pollution.
   B. The steam from a nuclear power plant is so hot that it harms the surrounding habitat.
   C. The waste products from a nuclear power plant are toxic and may harm people or the environment.
   D. The people that work in nuclear power plants are exposed to high levels of radiation that can leak from the plant.

Use the following information to answer the next question.

Youseph visited the McLeod Dam in the Belleville area. The dam is used to generate electricity.

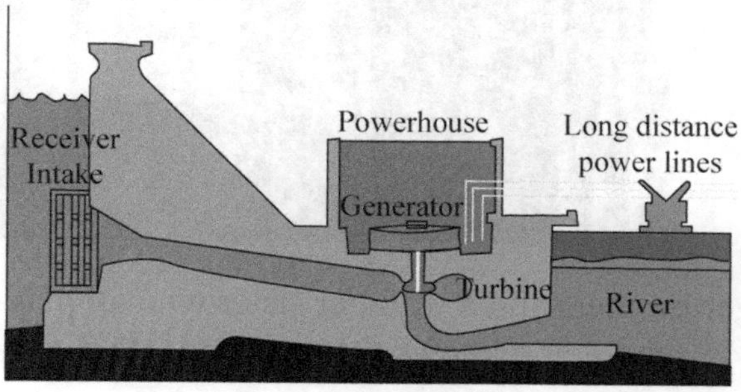

2. Which natural resource does the dam use to generate electricity?
   A. Oil
   B. Coal
   C. Wind
   D. Water

Use the following information to answer the next question.

Electricity in the home must be supplied as needed because no technology yet exists that can store all the electricity required. There are peak times of the day, afternoon and early evening, when a great deal of electricity is used. If too much electricity is needed at one time, supply cannot meet the demand and power outages happen.

3. Which of the following examples is an action that would help reduce the need for electricity at peak times?

A. Using the oven between 2 P.M. and 8 P.M.

B. Setting the dishwasher to wash the dishes after 11 P.M.

C. Draining the hot water tank and refilling it with clean water.

D. Presetting the furnace to run constantly at room temperature.

Use the following information to answer the next question.

This is the fuse box area in Tom's basement.

Tom has two younger brothers and a younger sister who all play in the basement. Tom is studying electricity in school and knows that it is not safe for children to play around electrical equipment.

4. To make the basement a safer place for his brothers and sister to play, Tom should ask his parents to

A. draw a line on the floor around the fuse box area and tell his brothers and sister that they are not allowed to cross the line

B. build a cupboard around the electrical box and lock it so that only his parents can access it

C. board up the electrical box so that no one has access to it

D. move the fuse box to a different location in the house

5. Which of the following circuits would **most likely** have one bulb glowing brighter than the other?

A.

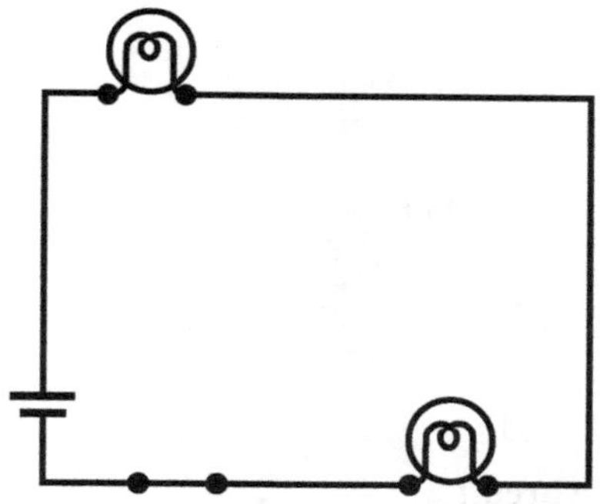

B.

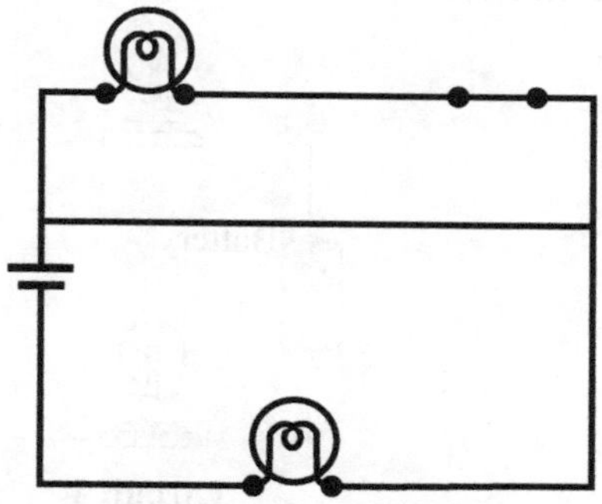

C.

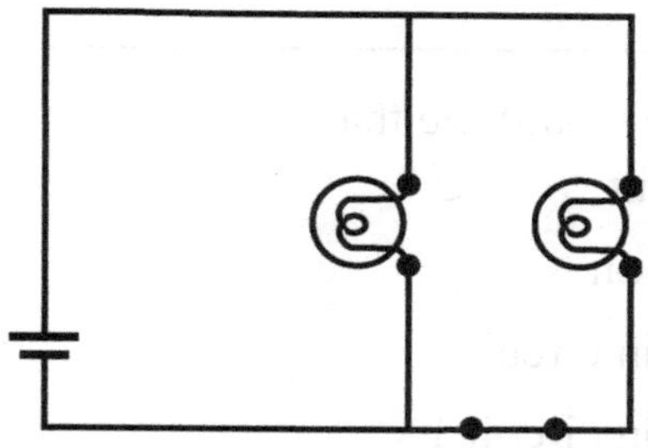

D.

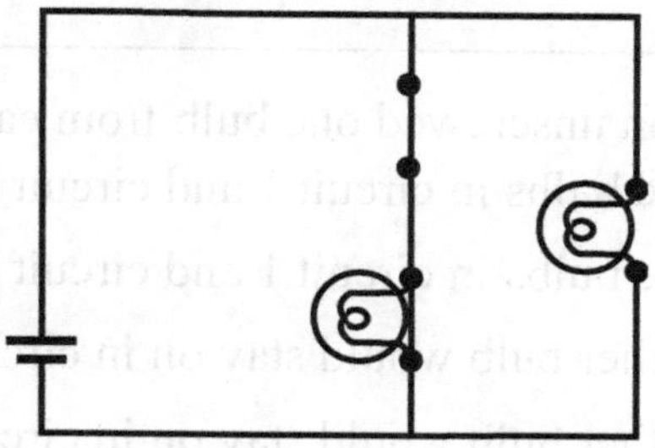

Use the following information to answer the next question.

Ricky set up this circuit.

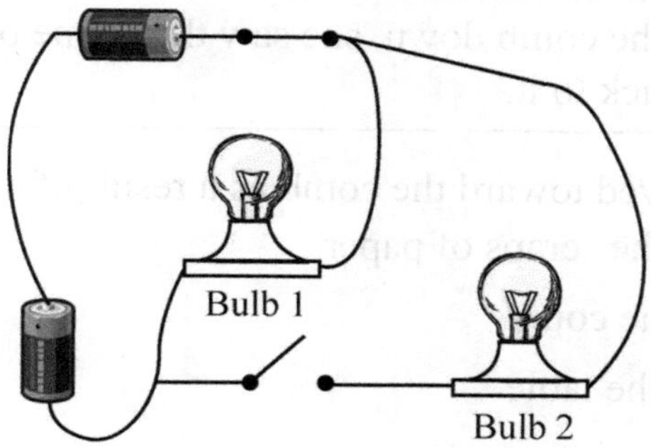

6. Which of the following statements **correctly** describes how the bulbs will be lit?
   A. Bulb 1 will be brightly lit, and bulb 2 will be dimly lit.
   B. Bulb 1 will be dimly lit, and bulb 2 will be brightly lit.
   C. Bulb 1 will be lit, and bulb 2 will be off.
   D. Bulb 1 will be off, and bulb 2 will be lit.

Use the following information to answer the next question.

Sheldon and Monique tested these circuits.

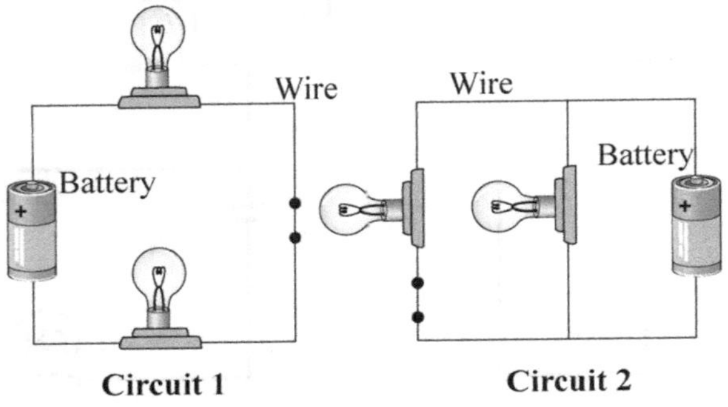

7. If Sheldon unscrewed one bulb from each circuit, he would see that

A. all the bulbs in circuit 1 and circuit 2 would go out

B. all the bulbs in circuit 1 and circuit 2 would stay on

C. the other bulb would stay on in circuit 1 but not in circuit 2

D. the other bulb would stay on in circuit 2 but not in circuit 1

Use the following information to answer the next question.

Maria combed her dry hair and then set the comb down on a table next to a few tiny scraps of paper. After setting the comb down, she saw that some of the scraps of paper moved toward the comb and stuck to it.

8. The scraps of paper moved toward the comb as a result of

A. chemical energy in the scraps of paper

B. static electricity in the comb

C. a magnetic field on the table

D. heat energy in the comb

Use the following information to answer the next question.

An Energy Producing Device

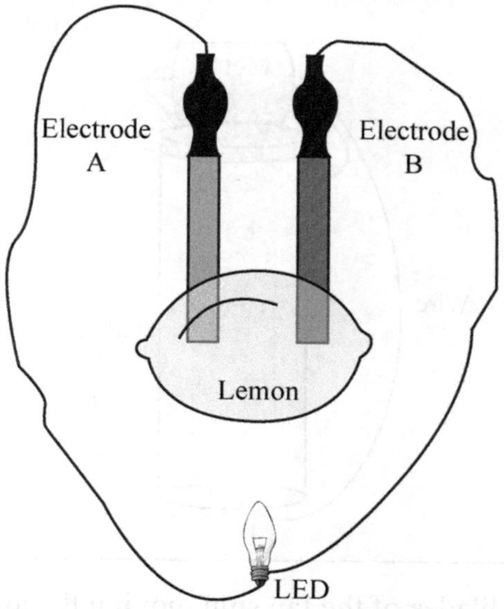

9. In order for this device to work, which of the following conditions must be met?

A. Electrode B must be longer than electrode A.

B. Electrode A must be longer than electrode B.

C. The electrodes must be made of the same metal.

D. The electrodes must be made of different metals.

Use the following information to answer the next question.

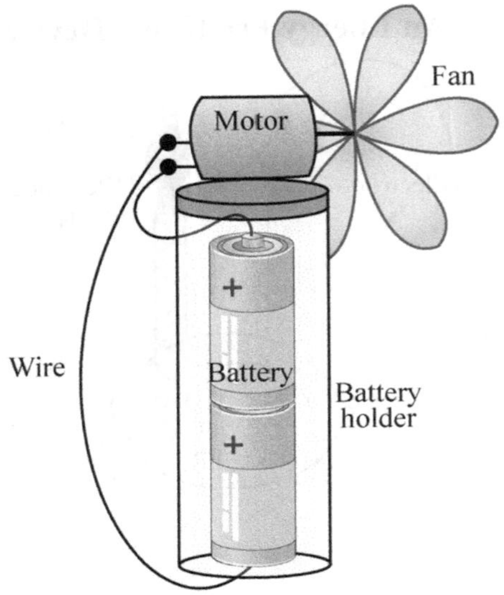

10. Amy built this fan. The blades of the fan spin moving the air around them. This type of fan transforms what kind of energy into mechanical energy?

A. Rotational energy
B. Electrical energy
C. Wind energy
D. Heat energy

11. Which of the following statements **best** describes a closed circuit?

A. The incomplete path that current electricity takes to provide electricity to a load.
B. The incomplete path that static electricity takes to provide electricity to a load.
C. The complete path that current electricity takes to provide electricity to a load.
D. The complete path that static electricity takes to provide electricity to a load.

Use the following information to answer the next question.

When Jim rubbed his feet along his carpet and touched a metal doorknob, he felt a small shock.

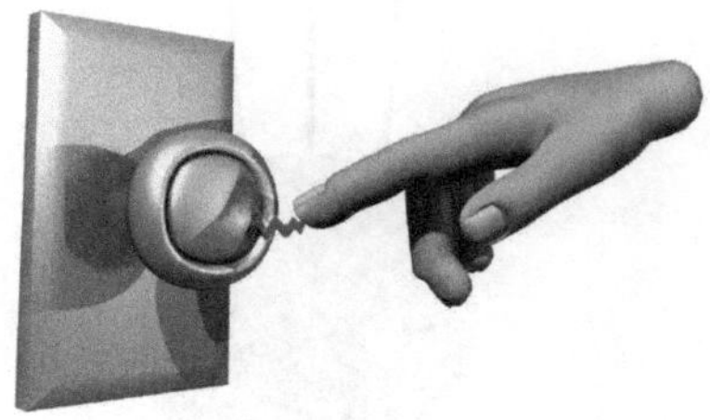

12. Why does Jim feel a shock when he touches the doorknob?

A. The current generated from rubbing his feet on the carpet produced a shock.

B. The electrons that had built up moved in a sudden burst and produced a shock.

C. The electrons flowed continuously from the carpet to his feet and gave him a shock.

D. The shock came from the current of electrons that were stored when he rubbed his feet.

Use the following information to answer the next question.

Amy knows that a Van de Graaff machine is an electrostatic generator. She attached three strands of yarn to the machine and turned on the generator. Amy noticed that the strands stood up on end and repelled each other.

13. Why did the yarn stand up on end above the generator?

A. The strands of yarn became positively charged.

B. The strands of yarn became negatively charged.

C. The positively charged yarn attracts to the positively charged machine.

D. The positive charges in the machine move to the positively charged yarn.

14. Which of the following materials **cannot** be used as an electrical insulator?

A. Wood

B. Plastic

C. Rubber tire

D. Pencil lead

Use the following information to answer the next question.

While Martin is constructing an electrical circuit, he notices that the metal electrical wires are covered with plastic.

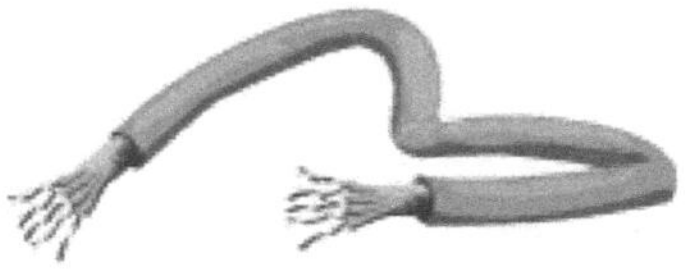

15. Metal electrical wires are covered with plastic because plastic is a good

A. electric conductor

B. electric insulator

C. heat generator

D. heat absorber

Use the following information to answer the next question.

The following diagrams show methods of generating electricity.

X	Y	Z

16. Which of the following tables correctly identifies the energy sources depicted in these diagrams?

A.

X	Y	Z
Solar energy	Hydroelectric energy	Nuclear energy

B.

X	Y	Z
Wind energy	Solar energy	Nuclear energy

C.

X	Y	Z
Nuclear energy	Hydroelectric energy	Solar energy

D.

X	Y	Z
Wind energy	Hydroelectric energy	Solar energy

Use the following information to answer the next question.

17. The illustration shows a circuit that consists of a bulb, a switch, and a battery. When the switch is closed, energy is converted from

A. heat and light to electricity
B. electricity to heat and light
C. light to electricity
D. heat to light

18. In an electrical circuit, a switch is used to

A. change the brightness of the bulb
B. prevent the wires from touching
C. close the gap in the circuit
D. save the battery's energy

Use the following information to answer the next question.

Daniel draws a diagram of the circuit in his room.

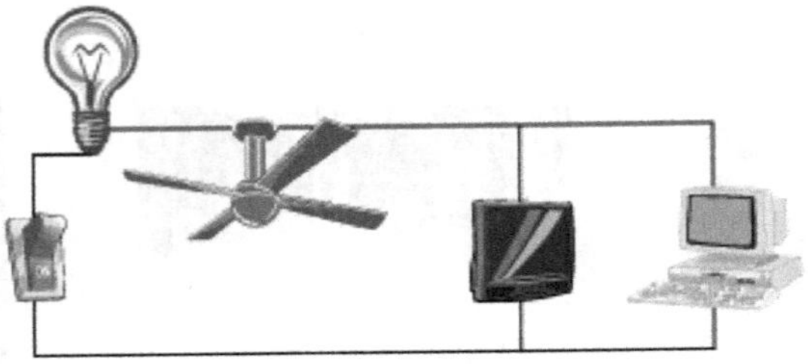

19. The television and the computer are connected according to what type of circuit?

A. Parallel
B. Simple
C. Series
D. Short

Use the following information to answer the next question.

Many years ago, every household used a wood stove to cook their meals. With the invention of current electricity, most wood stoves were replaced with electric ovens. While modern ovens use a great deal of electricity, they are still favoured over a wood stove for cooking purposes.

20. Why are more electric ovens now used for cooking than wood stoves?

A. Wood stoves can become very hot and often burn food.

B. Electric ovens cost less to operate than wood stoves.

C. Electric ovens heat up faster than wood stoves.

D. Wood stoves need a venting system.

ANSWERS AND SOLUTIONS — UNIT TEST

1. C	**5. A**	**9. D**	**13. B**	**17. B**
2. D	**6. C**	**10. B**	**14. D**	**18. C**
3. B	**7. D**	**11. C**	**15. B**	**19. A**
4. B	**8. B**	**12. B**	**16. C**	**20. C**

1. C

One negative impact on the environment from nuclear power plants is the waste products that are produced. This waste is difficult to dispose of because it is extremely toxic. Some people worry that an accident could happen where the toxic waste would harm the public and the environment.

2. D

Electricity is generated when moving water passes through the dam. The hydroelectric power plant supplies electricity to nearby areas.

3. B

You can reduce your need for electricity by reducing your use of electricity at peak times. One way to do this is to use the dishwasher later at night, when there is less demand for electricity.

4. B

To make the basement safer, Tom's parents should build a cupboard around the electrical box and lock it. That way only his parents can access it.

5. A

When two bulbs are wired in a series circuit, one bulb will glow brighter than the other. Both bulbs will be dimmer than the bulbs in the parallel circuits.

Diagram A shows a series circuit where one bulb would glow brighter that the other.

6. C

Bulb 1 and bulb 2 are wired in a parallel circuit. However, the switch next to bulb 2 is open, so bulb 2 will be off. Bulb 1 will be lit.

7. D

Circuit 1 is a series circuit, so if one bulb is taken out, the other will go out. Circuit 2 is a parallel circuit, so if one bulb is taken out, the other will stay lit.

8. B

The scraps of paper moved toward the comb as a result of static electricity in the comb. When Maria ran the comb through her hair, the comb rubbed against the hair and took electrons away from the hair. This left the hair with a positive charge and the comb with a negative charge.

9. D

In a lemon battery, the electrodes must be made of different metals. The metals react with the acid in the lemon to produce negative and positive charges. The negative charges move along the wire to light the LED.

10. B

This fan transforms electrical energy from the batteries into mechanical energy. The mechanical energy causes the blades of the fan to spin.

11. C

A closed circuit is the complete path that current electricity takes to provide electricity to a load.

12. B

When Jim rubbed his feet on the carpet he generated static electricity.

This form of electricity builds up and moves in sudden bursts.

13. B

Each strand of yarn became negatively charged by the generator. Since they have the same charge, the strands repel each other.

14. D

Pencil lead is a conductor of electricity that is actually made of graphite.
Wood, rubber, and plastic are poor conductors of electricity. They can be used as electrical insulators.

15. B

Electrical wires are coated with plastic because plastic is a good electric insulating material. The plastic prevents electricity from escaping from the wire. This protects a person working with electric circuits from getting a shock.

16. C

The nuclear reactors in diagram **X** show the steam that is released from an older nuclear power plant. Diagram **Y** shows a hydroelectric dam, and diagram **Z** shows solar panels that are used to generate solar electricity.

17. B

When the switch is closed, the battery will provide electrical energy to the bulb. This electrical energy will be changed or transformed into heat and light energy.

18. C

In an electrical circuit, a switch is used to close the gap in the circuit. When the switch is open, the current cannot flow. When the switch is closed, the current can flow through the circuit.

19. A

In a parallel electric circuit, electrons have a least two paths to follow. The television and the computer are wired in separate paths.

20. C

While electric ovens use a great deal of electricity, they are still used more today than wood stoves. The convenience of fast and even heat for cooking justifies the use of electric ovens.

Earth and Space Systems: Space

EARTH AND SPACE SYSTEMS: SPACE

Table of Correlations

Specific Expectation		Practice Questions	Unit Test Questions	Practice Test
6ESS1:STSE	Assess the impact of space exploration on society and the environment;			
6ESS1.1	*assess the contributions of Canadians to the exploration and scientific understanding of space*	1, 2	1, 2	1
6ESS1.2	*evaluate the social and environmental costs and benefits of space exploration, taking different points of view into account*	3, 4	3, 4	2
6ESS2:Skills	Investigate characteristics of the systems of which the earth is a part and the relationship between the earth, the sun, and the moon;			
6ESS2.1	*follow established safety procedures for handling tools and materials and observing the sun*	20	5	3
6ESS2.2	*use technological problem-solving skills to design, build, and test devices for investigating the motions of different bodies in the solar system*	21, 22, 23	6, 7	4
6ESS2.3	*use scientific inquiry/research skills to investigate scientific and technological advances that allow humans to adapt to life in space*	13	8	5
6ESS2.4	*use appropriate science and technology vocabulary, including axis, tilt, rotation, revolution, planets, moons, comets, and asteroids, in oral and written communication*	24, 25	9, 10	6
6ESS3:Concepts	Demonstrate an understanding of components of the systems of which the earth is a part, and explain the phenomena that result from the movement of different bodies in space.			
6ESS3.1	*identify components of the solar system, including the sun, the earth, and other planets, natural satellites, comets, asteroids, and meteoroids, and describe their physical characteristics in qualitative terms*	5, 6, 7, 8	11, 12, 13	7
6ESS3.2	*identify the bodies in space that emit light and those that reflect light*	9, 10	14	8
6ESS3.3	*explain how humans meet their basic biological needs in space*	11, 12	15	9
6ESS3.4	*identify the technological tools and devices needed for space exploration*	14, 15	16, 17	10
6ESS3.5	*describe the effects of the relative positions and motions of the earth, moon, and sun*	16, 17, 18, 19	18, 19, 20	11

6ESS1.1 assess the contributions of Canadians to the exploration and scientific understanding of space

Canadian Contributions to Space Exploration

Canadian scientists, astronomers, and astronauts have made many contributions to the study of space.

Canadarm

The Shuttle Remote Manipulator System, called the Canadarm, is a well-known Canadian invention. It is used on all the space shuttles. It was designed and built by the National Research Council and several Canadian companies. The Canadarm acts like a human arm. It has shoulder, elbow, and wrist joints, which are held together with an upper arm and a lower arm boom. It is 15.2 metres long, and weighs about 410 kilograms on Earth. It is used to grab and move heavy objects, support objects in need of repair, and support astronauts during space walks. It has special sensors and cameras to find damage to equipment and the space shuttle.

Dextre

Canada's most recent addition to space exploration is a new tool that will work in conjunction with the Canadarm aboard the International Space Station. This tool is called Dextre. Dextre's moving parts resemble the fingers of a hand that is attached to an arm. It will perform tasks that astronauts usually carry out, as well as other jobs that require very precise movements.

The Canadarm with Dextre

Microvariability and Oscillations of Stars Telescope (MOST)

The Microvariability and Oscillations of Stars Telescope was Canada's first space telescope. It is sometimes called the "Humble" space telescope. It is the smallest space telescope yet made. The telescope sits in a satellite about the size of a suitcase. MOST is designed to study stars to find out their age, behaviour, and composition. It also examines stars that have planets orbiting them. MOST can focus on a star for up to seven weeks in a row. This provides astronomers with more details about a star. Putting this telescope in space also helps avoid the distortion of Earth's atmosphere that is seen through telescopes on Earth.

Marc Garneau

Marc Garneau was the first Canadian astronaut in space. He started his career in the Canadian Navy before being accepted into the Canadian Astronaut Program. He made journeys into space in 1984, 1996, and 2000. He also worked as a capsule communicator, or CAPCOM, on several other space missions. A CAPCOM is a person on Earth who gives messages from the space shuttle crew to the Mission Control Centre. Marc Garneau was also president of the Canadian Space Agency from 2001 to 2005.

Roberta Bondar

Roberta Bondar became the first Canadian female astronaut to go into space in 1992. She is a neurologist and holds several degrees. Dr. Bondar worked for NASA for ten years as head of space medicine. She and her team studied how space flight affects the human body, and how the body recovers from being in space. This knowledge has helped doctors learn more about diseases on Earth. She now works as a speaker and consultant for businesses, scientists, and medical communities. She is also a writer and nature photographer, and has published several books.

Richard Bond

Richard Bond is an astronomer, university professor, and the director of the Canadian Institute for Theoretical Astrophysics (CITA). Bond's research explores how the universe was created, what size it is, and how old it is. To do this, he studies light and sound energy, that may have been made at the time the universe formed. Dr. Bond's work has helped scientists discover what the universe looks like. His work has helped scientists learn that the universe is flat and that it is expanding. It also supports the idea that some form of energy is causing the universe to expand. This energy is called dark energy. It is stronger than the force of gravity. Many scientists believe that it makes up most of the universe's mass and energy.

David Levy

David Levy is an astronomer and science writer. He has discovered more than 22 comets, as well as other space objects. He co-discovered the comet Shoemaker-Levy 9, which collided with Jupiter in 1994. This comet was captured by Jupiter's gravity, causing it to break apart. The pieces hit the surface of the planet, causing great fireballs to erupt. Dark marks were left behind.

The dark marks show where parts of comet Shoemaker-Levy 9 impacted on the surface of Jupiter.

Helen Hogg

Helen Hogg is an astronomer and university professor. Much of her work involved studying globular clusters. A globular cluster is a mass of stars bound together by gravity. There are 150 known globular clusters in the Milky Way. She taught astronomy at the University of Toronto and encouraged people, especially women, to study the stars and be interested in science. She died in 1993, but her contributions to astronomy will be remembered for years to come.

1. What did the Canadian astronomer Dr. Richard Bond help to discover?

A. What the universe looks like

B. The light given off by globular clusters

C. How space flight affects the human body

D. The distance to comets in our solar system

Use the following information to answer the next question.

Microvariability and Oscillations of Stars telescope (MOST) is Canada's first space telescope. It sits in a satellite about the size of a suitcase and is the smallest space telescope. MOST is used to study the age of stars and to search for any planets orbiting them.

2. What is the MOST telescope sometimes called because of its size?

A. Humble space telescope
B. Hubble space telescope
C. Suitcase telescope
D. Skylab telescope

6ESS1.2 evaluate the social and environmental costs and benefits of space exploration, taking different points of view into account

Benefits of Exploring Space

Some of the greatest benefits of exploring space have come from **artificial satellites**. Communication satellites allow radio and television shows to be broadcast around the world. They also allow people to talk to each other, no matter where they are in the world. Weather satellites help meteorologists make better forecasts about the weather and provide warnings to people about upcoming storms. Global positioning satellites (GPS) help with navigation. Other satellites have helped make accurate maps of Earth and its oceans.

MILSTAR, a communication satellite

Other inventions made for exploring space have helped life on Earth. Examples include the ear thermometer, artificial heart, cordless tools, lithium batteries, and robotic arms.

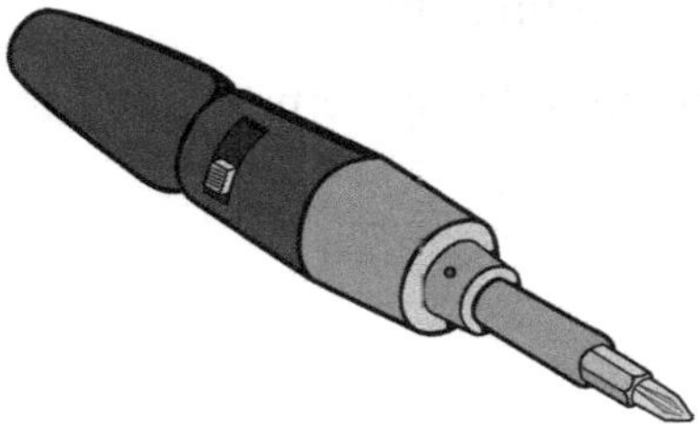

A cordless drill uses technology developed for space exploration.

Many experiments performed in space have helped humans better understand how things work on Earth. For example, insulin crystals grown in micro-gravity have helped to treat diabetes. Other experiments looked at how the human body reacts to space flight and micro-gravity. Astronauts also examine how space flight affects other living things such as plants.

An experiment being performed in space.

There are many resources in space that could be useful on Earth. Asteroids contain many minerals, including iron, gold, and platinum. These minerals would be worth billions of dollars on Earth. Scientists are also looking for methods of capturing the solar energy in space to use as a source of energy on Earth.

Costs of Exploring Space

Space exploration is dangerous. People have died during missions and training. People who work on the ground have also died in accidents. Many people believe that there are cheaper and safer ways of exploring space than are used now. For example, it is cheaper and safer to send up space probes or robots. An astronaut, however, might argue that there are certain jobs that a robot cannot do.

Some people are concerned about the number of space missions that fail. Many instruments have been damaged during space flight or have not performed as they should. An astronaut or astronomer, however, might argue that even these failed missions have some benefit. Scientists can learn from these failures to make sure they do not happen again. Many of these missions do succeed and provide scientists and astronomers with valuable information about space.

Exploring space is expensive. Canada spends about $300 million a year on exploring space, while the United States spends billions of dollars each year. Only a few countries can afford to explore space. Does this mean that these countries do not have the right to space resources and technologies? Many also wonder whether is it correct to spend money on exploring space instead of using the money to solve problems on Earth. For example, a doctor may believe the money used for space exploration could be better used to find cures for diseases like cancer.

Space exploration produces a lot of waste called space junk. Used rocket boosters, old satellites, and other materials litter the space around the planet. This space junk is a concern because it can collide with working satellites and spacecraft. People are also worried that this junk might fall to Earth and cause damage. Fortunately, most space junk is so small it would burn up in the atmosphere well before it reaches the earth. Larger materials, like satellites, are designed to fall to Earth in places where they will not cause damage. Still, many scientists and environmentalists worry that this space junk poses a threat to the planet, the space around Earth, and the solar system. Since many different countries have added to this space junk over the years, who should be responsible for cleaning it up? Where would all this space junk go once it is cleaned up?

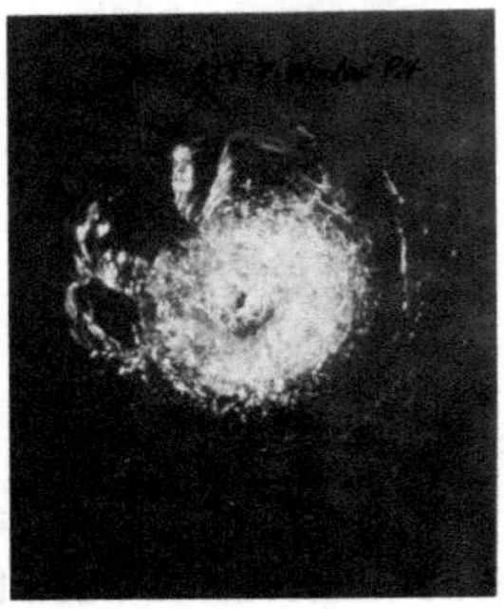

A piece of space debris caused this impact on a space shuttle window.

Many scientists and environmentalists also wonder whether it is a good idea to alter space. For example, what environmental damage might be caused by mining asteroids for their minerals? Who would be responsible for making sure that the space environment is not altered or damaged beyond repair? Do humans have the right to go to places like the moon and Mars and alter them for their own purposes, or should they be left as they were found? How will countries decide policies related to space? These are all important questions that will need to be answered before exploration in this area continues.

Use the following information to answer the next question.

Space exploration raises many different social and environmental issues. There are many points of view on space travel, such as those of the governments, families, and agencies involved.

3. What would you predict is the **most** important issue of space exploration to an astronaut's family?

   A. The increasing demand for information obtained by the astronauts in space

   B. The time the astronaut is away from family and friends

   C. The dangers to the astronauts when travelling in space

   D. The financial cost of being an astronaut

Use the following information to answer the next question.

Technology developed for space has also had an impact on Earth. Many different technologies used in space can be adapted to serve different purposes on Earth.

4. How has the technology used for space shuttle fuel pumps helped society?

A. It has made oil extraction safer.

B. It has helped develop better artificial hearts.

C. It helped to develop better navigational aids.

D. It has brought us higher quality satellite signals.

6ESS3.1 identify components of the solar system, including the sun, the earth, and other planets, natural satellites, comets, asteroids, and meteoroids, and describe their physical characteristics in qualitative terms

Members of the Solar System

The sun and all of the bodies that orbit it make up the solar system. This includes the planets and their moons, as well as comets, asteroids, meteoroids, and any other bits of rock and dust. The main bodies in the solar system are the eight planets, an asteroid belt, and three dwarf planets. All these bodies orbit around the sun.

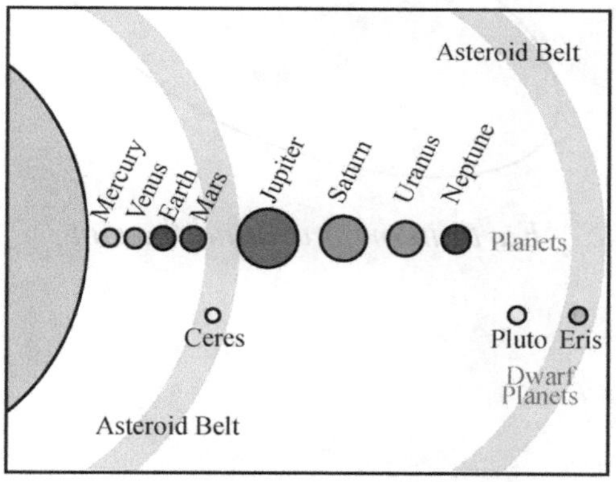

The solar system

The Sun

The sun is just one star of millions in Earth's galaxy. Even though it is small for a star, it is still 109 times larger than Earth. The sun has a diameter of 1 392 000 km. The temperature on the sun ranges from 4 000 to 9 000°C.

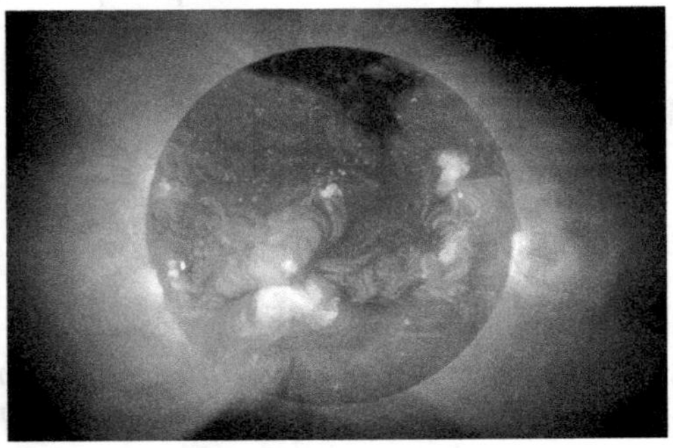

The sun

Because of its size, the sun has strong gravity. It keeps Earth and the other objects in the solar system in orbit around it.

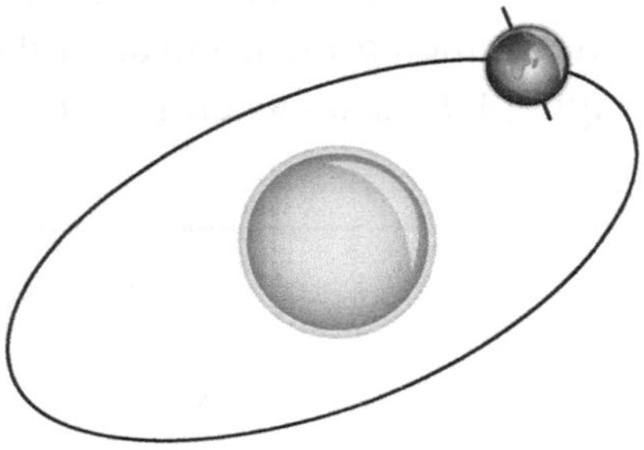

Earth in orbit around the sun

THE INNER PLANETS

Planets are balls made of rocks, gases, or both rocks and gases combined that orbit a star. The four planets closest to the sun are known as the inner planets. They are small, rocky planets. These planets are Mercury, Venus, Earth, and Mars.

- *Mercury* is the smallest of the eight planets. It is closest to the sun. Mercury is a small, rocky planet covered with craters. Mercury has almost no atmosphere. It also has no moons.
- *Venus* is the second planet from the sun. It is a small, rocky planet with no moons. It has a thick atmosphere that is mostly made up of carbon dioxide. There are also many miles of thick sulfuric acid clouds that completely cover the planet. The clouds and atmosphere trap heat on the surface of the planet. Venus is the hottest planet in the solar system, reaching temperatures well over 465°C. There is no chance that life can exist on Venus.
- *Earth* is the third planet from the sun. It receives a steady flow of heat and light from the sun, which allows for a gentle heating of the atmosphere. Earth is a small, rocky planet with a surface of rock and water. It is the only planet that is known to support life. One moon orbits Earth.

Earth and the moon in space

- *Mars* is the fourth planet from the sun. Mars has permanent ice caps at both of its poles. This ice is made up of frozen water and carbon dioxide. Very strong winds and dust storms occur regularly in Mars' atmosphere. Its surface is covered in iron-rich dust, which gives Mars its reddish appearance. Mars has two tiny moons that orbit very close to its surface.

THE ASTEROID BELT

An asteroid belt lies between the inner planets and the outer planets. It is a collection of rocks, ice, and metal. Just like the planets, the asteroid belt orbits the sun. Scientists believe that this material is the debris left over from the formation of the solar system.

The Outer Planets

The next four planets are called the outer planets. They are also called the gas giants because they are made up of mostly gas and are much larger than the inner planets. These planets are Jupiter, Saturn, Uranus, and Neptune.

- *Jupiter* is the fifth planet from the sun and the largest of all eight planets. It is made up of about 90% hydrogen and 10% helium. Jupiter is about 1 000 times the size of Earth. Jupiter is known for its Great Red Spot, which is believed to be a huge storm. Jupiter is so big that it can attract smaller bodies in space into its orbit because of this gravity. Jupiter has 63 known moons.
- *Saturn* is the sixth planet from the sun and the second largest planet. It is made up of materials that are lighter than water. It is about 75% hydrogen and 25% helium. Saturn's rings are mostly frozen water, but they may also include rocks that are covered in ice. Saturn has 59 moons.

Saturn

- *Uranus* is the seventh planet from the sun and the third largest of the eight planets. Uranus is made of rock and ice. Its atmosphere has hydrogen and a little helium in it. Uranus spins differently than most of the other planets. It seems to be tilted sideways instead of right side up. Uranus has 27 moons.
- *Neptune* is the eighth planet from the sun. At times, its orbit crosses over the orbit of the dwarf planet Pluto. It likely has an inner core made up of different types of ice and rocks. Neptune's blue colour comes from the gas methane that makes up its atmosphere. Neptune's winds are the fastest in the solar system, reaching 2 000 kilometres per hour. Neptune has 13 moons.

The Dwarf Planets

There are also some bodies in the solar system that are too small to be called planets, but are too large to be called asteroids. These are called **dwarf planets**. There are three dwarf planets in the solar system: Ceres, Pluto, and Eris. Ceres is found in the asteroid belt within the solar system. Pluto has three moons, and is usually found farther from the sun than Neptune. However, its orbit sometimes crosses over Neptune's orbit, bringing it closer to the sun than Neptune. Eris is in orbit even farther out in space than Pluto, and it has one moon. It is the largest of the three dwarf planets.

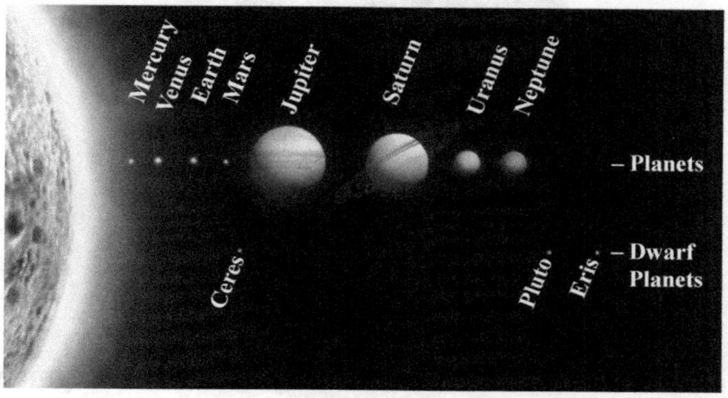

The eight planets and three dwarf planets of the solar system

The Moons

Moons are naturally occurring satellites that orbit these planets. Only the two planets closest to the sun, Mercury and Venus, do not have moons. However, each planet has a different number of moons. For example, Earth has only one moon, while Jupiter has 63. Scientists have found that these moons can be very different from each other. For example, Earth's moon is a rocky, dusty place with no atmosphere. Io, one of Jupiter's moons, is very different. It is the most volcanically active body in the solar system. Volcanic plumes rise 300 km above the surface of Io.

Earth's moon

Io, one of Jupiter's moons

Asteroids and Meteoroids

There are fragments of rock in the solar system that are too small to be planets. However, these fragments also revolve around the sun in their own orbits. These fragments can be classified as asteroids or meteoroids, depending on their size. The larger rocky fragments in the solar system are called **asteroids**. They are the rocky debris left over from the formation of the solar system. Most asteroids are found in the main asteroid belt in the solar system, which is located between Mars and Jupiter.

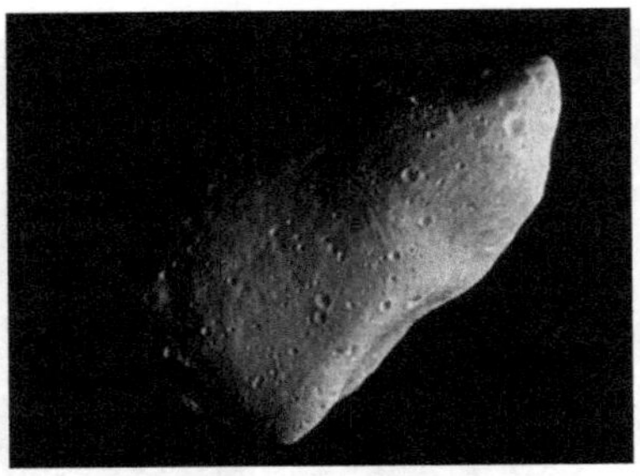

Asteroid

The smaller fragments of rock are called **meteoroids**. These smaller fragments can be pulled toward Earth by gravity. As meteoroids enter Earth's atmosphere, friction with the particles in the atmosphere causes the rocks to heat up. As a result, they can then be seen in a meteor shower. Some people call them shooting stars. These meteoroids may burn up in the atmosphere, or they might fall to Earth's surface as meteorites. When a meteorite hits the surface, it leaves behind an impact crater. The Manicouagan crater is found in Quebec. At 100 km across, it is the fifth largest impact crater in the world.

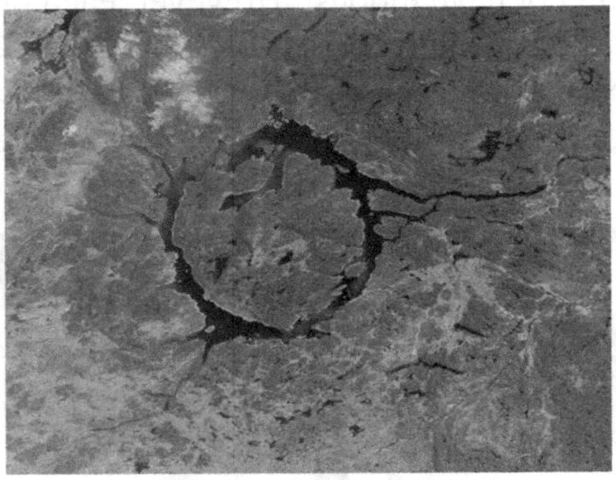

The Manicouagan crater

Comets

Comets consist mostly of ice, gas, and dust. They orbit the sun in large, oval orbits. As a comet approaches the sun, it begins to warm up. Some of the ice will begin to melt, releasing dust and gas into space. This is what forms the tail on a comet. The tail seen from Earth at night is the sunlight reflected off the the dust trail behind the comet. The gas tail can sometimes only be seen with a telescope. These tails can stretch out for millions of kilometres.

Comet Hale-Bopp. The bright tail on the right is the dust tail. The dim tail on the left is a gas tail.

As a comet approaches the sun, the tail grows longer. As it moves away from the sun, the tail grows shorter. The tail always points away from the sun.

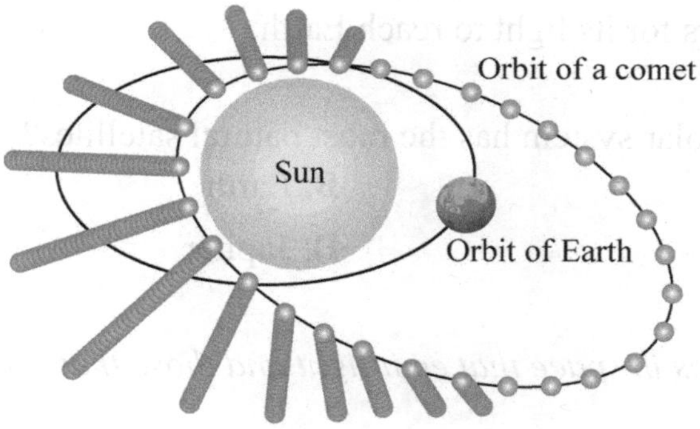

A comet orbiting the sun

Since comets have a regular orbit around the sun, their reappearance is predictable. For example, Halley's comet is visible from Earth every 76 years. It will next appear in 2033.

Use the following information to answer the next question.

Astronomers have classified the planets of the solar system into the inner planets and the outer planets. The inner planets are Mercury, Venus, Earth, and Mars, while the outer planets are Jupiter, Saturn, Neptune, and Uranus.

5. Which of the following statements describes a difference between the inner planets and the outer planets?

A. The inner planets tend to have more moons than the outer planets.

B. The inner planets have denser, rockier cores than the outer planets.

C. The inner planets receive less energy from the sun than the outer planets.

D. The inner planets take longer to revolve around the sun than the outer planets.

6. Other than Earth, scientists have only found water in the form of ice on the planet

A. Mars
B. Venus
C. Jupiter
D. Mercury

7. Which of the following statements about the sun is true?

A. It is the second closest star to Earth.

B. It has an average temperature for a star.

C. When compared with other stars, it is very large.

D. It takes eight hours for its light to reach Earth.

8. Which planet in the solar system has the most natural satellites?

A. Mars
B. Earth
C. Saturn
D. Jupiter

6ESS3.2 identify the bodies in space that emit light and those that reflect light

Objects that Emit and Reflect Light in Space

Many objects in the solar system are visible in the night sky. Some of these objects give off their own light. These objects **emit** light. Other objects can only be seen when they **reflect** the light from objects like the sun.

Objects in space that emit light	Objects in space that reflect light
Sun	Comets
Stars	Asteroids
Galaxies	Meteoroids in space
Nebulae	Moons or natural satellites
Meteors in Earth's atmosphere	Artificial satellites

Meteors in Earth's atmosphere emit light.

Meteoriods and asteroids in space reflect light.

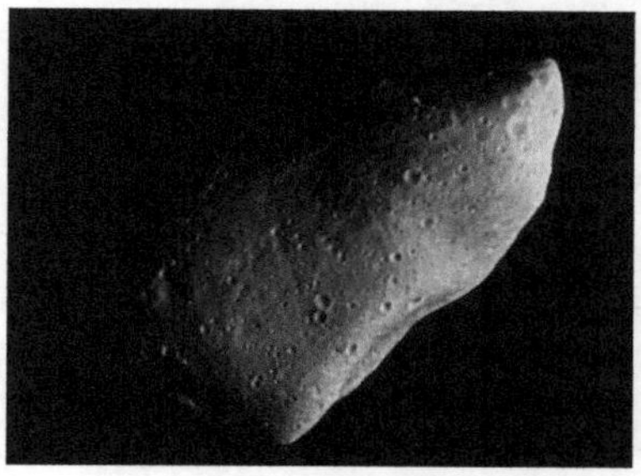

9. Which of the following statements explains why the moon does **not** light up the sky as much as the sun?

A. It is smaller than the sun.

B. It only reflects light from Earth.

C. It only reflects some of the light from the sun.

D. It is much farther away from Earth than from the sun.

Use the following information to answer the next question.

Jason's teacher asked him to make a chart to show which objects in space reflect light and which emit light.

Objects that emit light	**Objects that reflect light**
W	Planetoids
Stars	*Y*
Galaxies	*Z*
Nebula	Moons or natural satellites
X	Artificial satellites

Jason still has to place the following four labels into his chart:

- Sun
- Planets
- Meteors in the atmosphere
- Asteroids and meteoroids in space

10. Which of the following lists shows Jason's correct entries?

A. *W*—Sun; *X*—Planets; *Y*—Meteors in the atmosphere; *Z*—Asteroids and meteoroids in space

B. *W*—Planets; *X*—Asteroids and meteoroids in space; *Y*—Meteors in the atmosphere; *Z* —Sun

C. *W*—Sun; *X*—Meteors in the atmosphere; *Y*—Planets; *Z*—Asteroids and meteoroids in space

D. *W*—Meteors in the atmosphere; *X*—Planets; *Y*—Sun; *Z*—Asteroids and meteoroids in space

6ESS3.3 explain how humans meet their basic biological needs in space

6ESS2.3 use scientific inquiry/research skills to investigate scientific and technological advances that allow humans to adapt to life in space

THE CHALLENGES OF LIVING IN SPACE

Space is a hostile environment without air or water. When people go into space, they need to take all the things they need to survive with them. They must be prepared to adjust to living in space. There are also many hazards in space that they must prepare for.

When people go into space, their bodies go through many changes as they adjust to living in microgravity. Microgravity is a condition where the normal forces of gravity are reduced or no longer present. In space, a person is almost weightless. This can confuse the body's senses. Some astronauts sometimes feel like the world has turned completely upside down. Many astronauts also develop space sickness. This is like motion sickness on Earth. They feel nauseated and dizzy and have headaches. Sometimes they vomit, which can be very dangerous if they are wearing a space suit. Once the astronaut adjusts to microgravity, which can take two to four days, the symptoms go away. Many scientists and doctors have researched strategies and inventions to make the lives of astronauts easier while they are in space. For example, astronauts can wear a patch on their skin that releases medication into their body to fight nausea while on space walks.

Astronauts train to prepare for the feeling of microgravity in space.

Gravity also helps pull the liquids in your body, like water and blood, downward. In space, there is nothing to pull bodily fluids down. The fluids move from the legs to the upper body and head. This extra fluid can block a person's sinuses, just like when one has a cold. An astronaut's face and neck can also look puffy. A person's blood also spreads easily through the body in space.

A person's bones and muscles are used to working under gravity. In space, they do not have to work as hard. Both bones and muscles can lose some of their strength. Astronauts exercise in space to keep their muscles in good condition. When an astronaut returns to Earth, it can take several weeks before the body has returned to normal. The longer a person has been in space, the longer it takes for the body to return to normal.

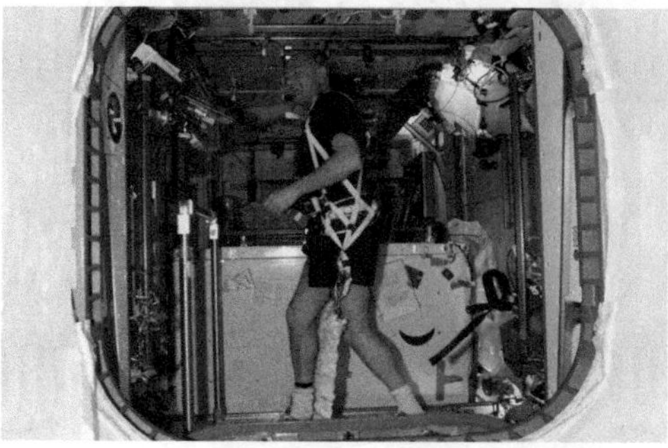

Exercising in space

A person in space also faces other challenges. There is very little room on a space craft. Living spaces are shared among the astronauts. Over time, it can be difficult to live and work with the same people day after day. It can also be difficult to get used to eating and sleeping in space. Even going to the bathroom is different.

One important piece of equipment used by astronauts is the space suit. The space suit allows a person to enter space safely. It is made up of many layers, is air tight, and protects the astronaut from the sun's radiation.The oxygen needed during a space walk is contained in the backpack attached to the space suits. The cabins in the space station have windows that are hermetically sealed. That means that the air in the cabin cannot escape into space. The cabin temperature and air quality are controlled to keep the astronauts comfortable.

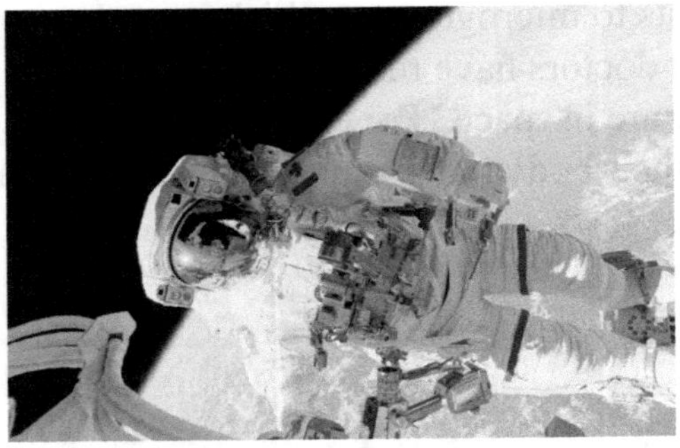

An astronaut in a space suit

Many things are recycled and reused on spacecraft to save room. Almost all space shuttles carry devices that can recycle water. Wastewater and moisture from the cabins is collected and cleaned, so it is safe to drink. A small supply of water for emergency use is carried in storage tanks. Sometimes oxygen is removed from wastewater and later used to breathe. The water is separated by a special generator. The oxygen is stored, and the hydrogen is vented out of the space craft. Carbon dioxide gas can also be separated so that the oxygen in it can be used.

A spacecraft like the space shuttle must bring enough oxygen, food, and water for all those on board. These things can take up a lot of room, so scientists have found methods to repackage them so they take up less space. For example, most spacecraft carry oxygen in the form of a liquid, not a gas. To turn oxygen into a liquid, it is cooled to –183°C. It is then stored in tanks. Oxygen takes up much less space when it is a liquid. Most of the food carried on board is dehydrated to remove most of the water from it. This makes the food much lighter. Astronauts use a device like a water gun to put the water back into these items before they eat them.

Most food eaten in space is dehydrated.

Use the following information to answer the next question.

Space stations need to be able to produce oxygen for the astronauts aboard to live. For almost ten years, the Russian space station Mir was able to produce oxygen for the different rotations of astronauts living aboard.

11. What technology did Mir use to generate useable oxygen?

A. Massive oxygen holding tanks

B. Ventilators to cycle air from space

C. Machines that removed the oxygen from wastes

D. A room filled with plants and trees to absorb carbon dioxide and produce oxygen

Use the following information to answer the next question.

Sometimes, astronauts have extended stays in space, such as missions aboard the International Space Station. Sometimes these astronauts stay in the low gravity environment of space for weeks or even months.

12. Which of the following effects on the bones and muscles is seen in astronauts who remain in space for extended periods?

A. They get stronger from lifting heavier weights.

B. They get weaker from not working as hard in space.

C. They lose all of their bloodflow from the low gravity environment.

D. They grow smaller from the lack of gravity and oxygen in the space environment.

13. Which of the following statements explains how the issue of limited water supply is dealt with on a spacecraft?

A. Water is reused several times before being discarded.

B. Ice is collected from outside the spacecraft.

C. Stored ice is melted into water.

D. Water is recycled continually.

6ESS3.4 identify the technological tools and devices needed for space exploration

Space Technology and Tools

There are different kinds of telescopes that are used to explore space.

Optical telescopes are used to view different objects in space. They hold mirrors and lenses that gather and focus light from the sky. The person looking through the telescope sees magnified images of objects in space. Some people have telescopes in their homes. Other optical telescopes are so large they are housed in their own buildings. These are used to view distant nebulae, stars, and galaxies. Some optical telescopes are in orbit in space. The Hubble Space telescope is an example of an orbiting satellite.

Optical telescopes can be small (left), large (middle), or put into space (right).

Radio telescopes collect different forms of energy to create images of distant objects.

A radio telescope

A *spectrum* is a group of bands of colour seen when white light passes through a prism. A rainbow is an example of a spectrum. Gases and other materials on Earth give off different spectra. Scientists can view and record these spectra. They are called spectral emissions. Objects in space also give off spectral emissions. Scientists compare the spectral emissions found on Earth to those from different stars. This helps a scientist find out what materials are in a star.

Spectral images of different gases

Scientists use different tools to study spectra.

- A *spectroscope* can be used to see spectra from different light sources. They use diffraction grating, a special material that has hundreds of tiny lines cut into it. This works like a prism to separate light into a spectrum.
- A *spectrograph* is the record or picture of spectral emissions from stars and other objects in space, as well as objects on Earth.
- A *spectrometer* is spectroscope that has a scale to compare and measure the wavelengths. It is seen below.

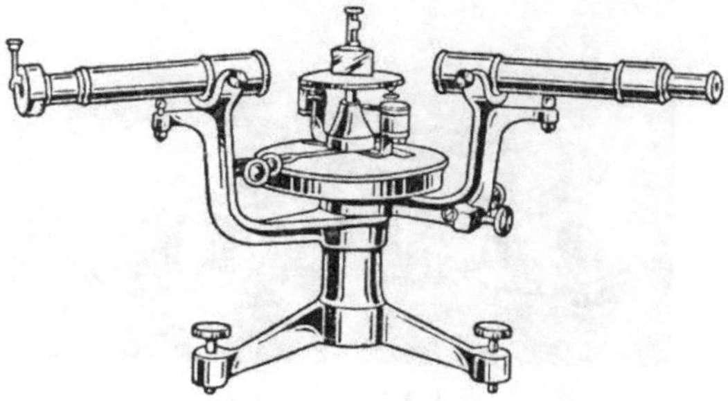

A spectrometer

Much of what people know about the solar system has been learned through space explorations. Rockets have allowed people travel into space and to the moon. Scientists have also sent unmanned spacecraft to other planets and objects in our solar system.

There are many different kinds of spacecraft that have been sent into space. A *space probe* is a robotic spacecraft that leaves Earth's orbit. Space probes may travel to the moon, other parts of the solar system, or even out of the solar system. Some the space probes return to Earth. Others send information back to Earth but will not return.

The Genesis space probe (left) was sent to orbit the sun and return to Earth with samples of solar wind. Other space probes send information back to Earth rather than return (right).

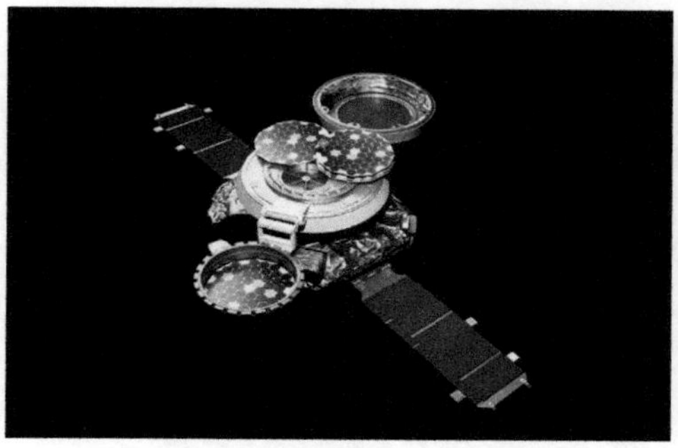

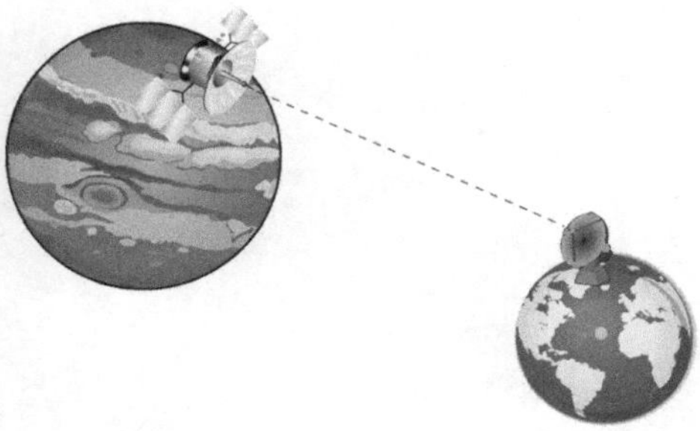

An *orbital spacecraft* orbits Earth. The International Space Station (ISS) is an example of a manned orbital spacecraft. The space shuttle is another. Sputnik is an example of an unmanned orbital spacecraft. Sputnik was the first artificial satellite put into space. Some spacecraft orbit the moon or other planets. Other spacecraft have landed on these planets. For example, the Mars Rovers have landed on the planet Mars. They collect data on rocks and soils on Mars. They helped to prove that water exists on Mars as ice.

A Mars rover

Space is a very dangerous place. In order for people to survive in it, special life support systems needed to be made. One of the most important life support systems is the space suit. A space suit has several important features. It is sturdy enough to withstand the harsh environment of space. It can withstand micrometeoroids, which are small bits of space dust and junk. It also protects the astronaut from radiation from the sun. However, the suit is also flexible enough so that an astronaut can move freely. It is specially designed with many joints that make it possible for an astronaut to pick up tools, bend, and move. The space suit has its own supply of oxygen and communication system. Since a suit can also get very hot, it also has a cooling system. It even has a portable bathroom.

The space suit is called an Extravehicular Mobility Unit (EMU). It is used by astronauts on the space shuttle and the International Space Station (ISS).

Use the following information to answer the next question.

Voyager 1, shown here, is the manmade object that has travelled the farthest from Earth.

14. Voyager 1 is a device classified as a space

A. satellite
B. shuttle
C. station
D. probe

Use the following information to answer the next question.

Radio telescope

15. How does a radio telescope create an image of distant objects?

A. By taking distant pictures

B. By combining sound waves

C. By collecting different forms of energy

D. By sending radar and sonar waves out to objects in space

6ESS3.5 describe the effects of the relative positions and motions of the earth, moon, and sun

THE MOTIONS OF EARTH AND THE MOON

Earth is always in motion. It rotates, or spins, on its axis once every 24 hours. Earth also revolves, or orbits, around the sun every 365.25 days. The moon is also in motion. It rotates on its axis and revolves around the Earth. It takes approximately 28 days for the moon to revolve around the Earth and rotate on its axis. Its rotation and revolution are synchronized. This is why you always see the same side of the moon.

The motion of Earth and the moon are responsible for certain events on Earth: eclipses, tides, and the phases of the moon.

Solar and Lunar Eclipses

If you could look at Earth, the moon and the sun from above, you would see that the three objects rarely line up in a straight line. They get close when the moon is in a full or new moon phase. But even then, they are often not completely aligned. Occasionally the sun, the moon, and Earth do line up perfectly. When this happens, an **eclipse** can occur. An eclipse happens when one body in space moves into the shadow of another body. This can create a solar eclipse or a lunar eclipse.

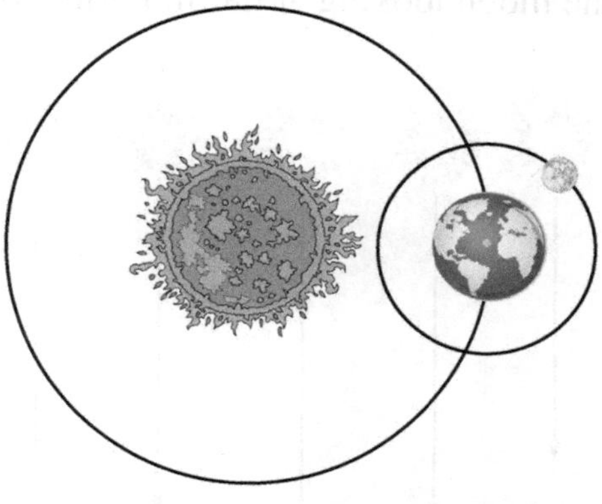

Earth and moon orbits

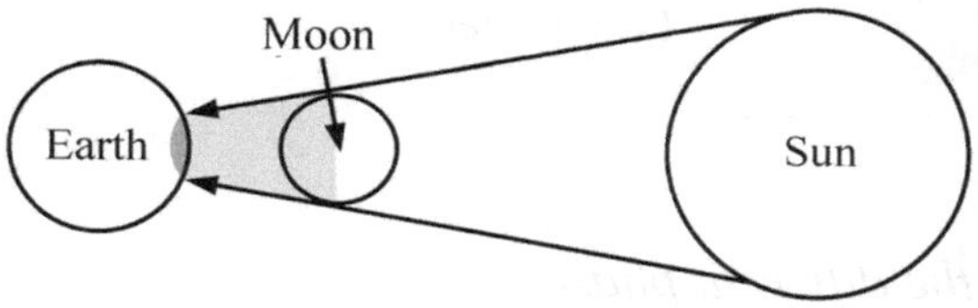

A solar eclipse

A *solar eclipse* happens when the moon comes in between Earth and the sun. The moon casts a shadow on Earth. Where the shadow falls, no sunlight reaches Earth's surface.

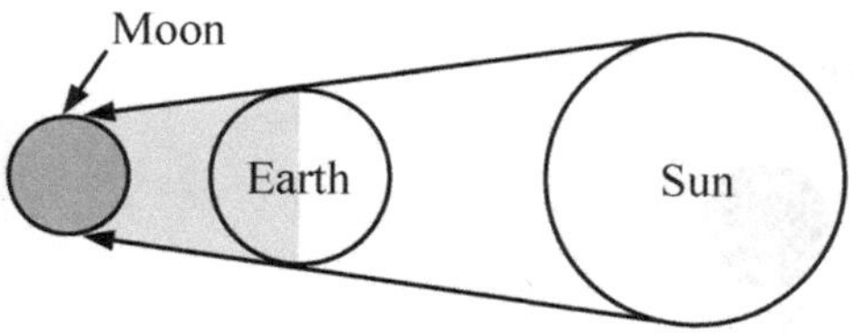

A lunar eclipse

A *lunar eclipse* happens when Earth comes in between the moon and the sun. In this case, Earth casts a shadow on the moon. Where the shadow falls, no sunlight reaches the moon's surface.

Phases of the Moon

The light you see from the moon is reflected sunlight. Just like Earth, half of the moon is lit by the sun and half is in darkness at any given time. As the moon orbits or revolves around Earth, you are able to see different portions of the reflected sunlight from the sunlit side of the moon. These are called the **phases of the moon**.

The cycle of the phases of the moon begins with a new moon. During this phase, you cannot see any of the sunlit side of the moon. As the moon moves in its orbit, you can gradually see more of its sunlit side. At this point, the moon is *waxing*. Eventually you can see all of the lit side of the moon. This phase is called the full moon. Throughout the next three phases, you can gradually see less and less of the sunlit side. During these phases, the moon is *waning*. Eventually you only see the unlit side of the moon. This phase is called the new moon. The cycle then begins all over again. This cycle takes approximately 28 days and repeats month after month as the moon orbits around Earth. If you were on the moon looking at Earth, Earth would appear to go through the same monthly phases.

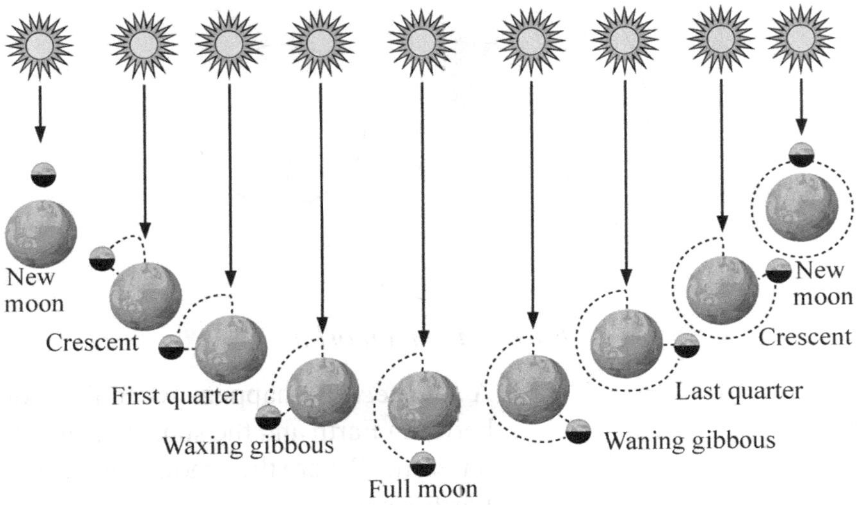

The position of the moon during the different phases.

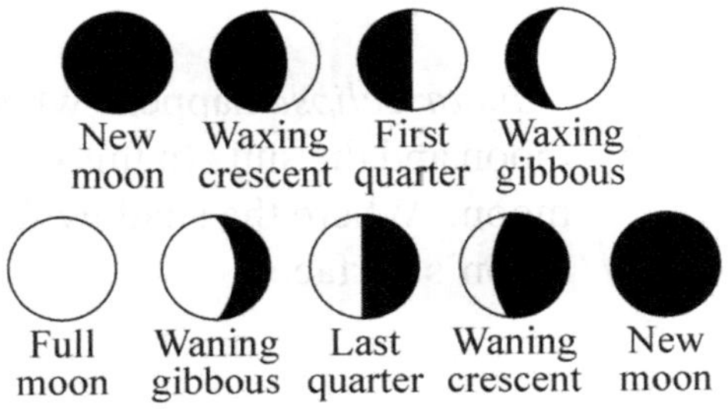

The different moon phases as viewed from Earth.

TIDES

The moons orbiting a planet affect that planet. This can be seen on Earth when the oceans go through high and low **tides**. Earth's gravity pulls on the moon. This is what keeps the moon in orbit around the planet. However, the moon's gravity also pulls on Earth. The pull of gravity from the moon affects water more than the land surface. The position of the moon above Earth's surface determines when the tide is high or low. There are two low tides and two high tides each day. This is because Earth rotates, and the position of the moon above Earth changes throughout the day.

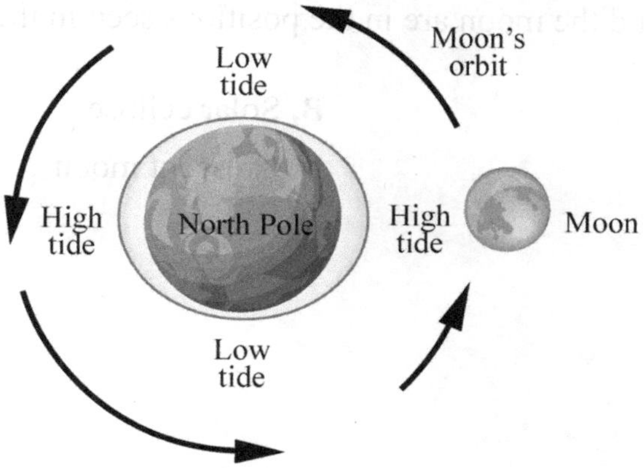

High and low tides

Very high tides occur when the moon, Earth, and the sun line up. This happens every 14 days.

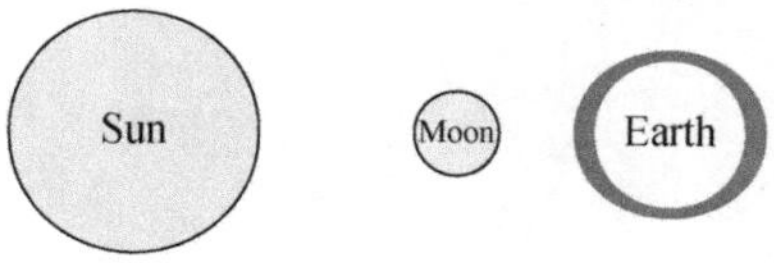

Weaker tides occur when the moon is at right angles with Earth and the sun.

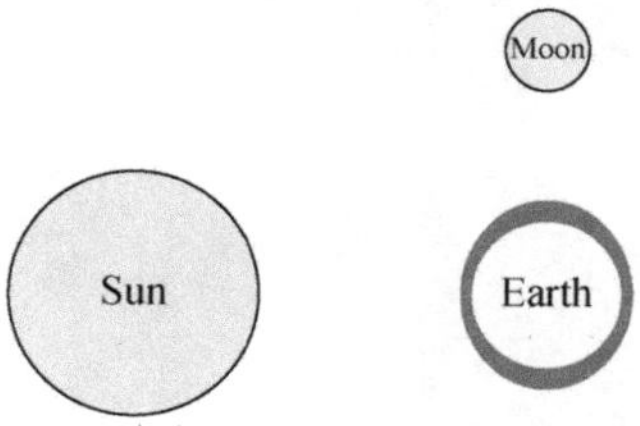

Use the following information to answer the next question.

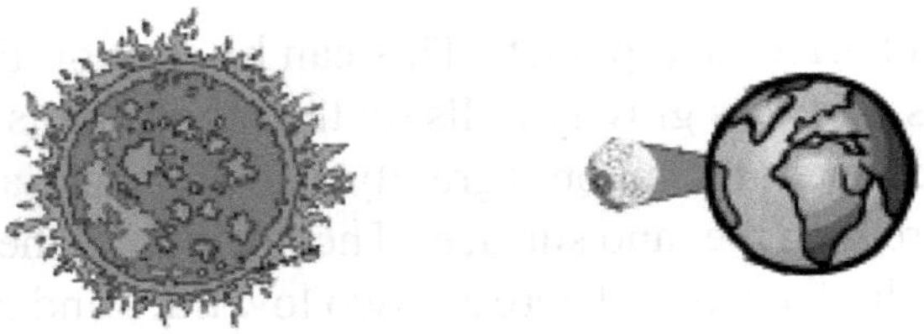

16. When the sun, Earth, and the moon are in the positions seen in the picture, what event occurs?

A. Full moon
B. Solar eclipse
C. Lunar eclipse
D. Crescent moon

Use the following information to answer the next question.

Andrew is modelling a lunar eclipse using pieces of fruit. He uses an apple, a lemon, and an orange to represent the sun, the moon, and Earth, as shown below.

17. Which of the following figures represents how the pieces of fruit should be arranged to represent a lunar eclipse?

A. 

B. 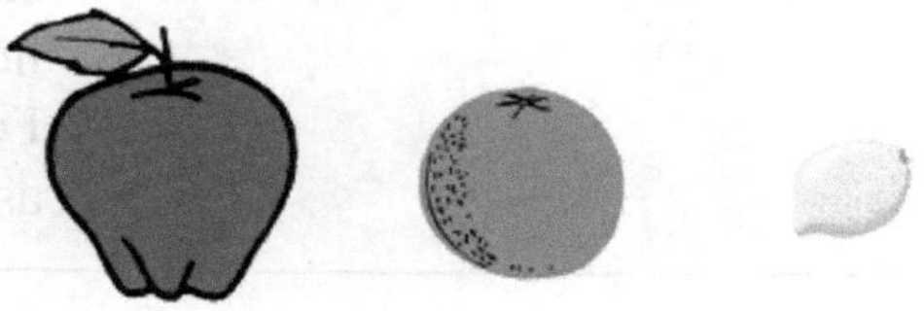

C. 

D. 

Use the following information to answer the next question.

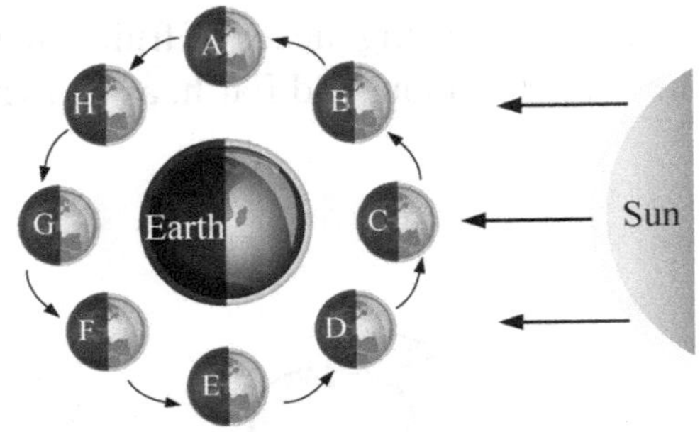

18. When the moon is in position **G**, what phase will the moon be in when viewed from Earth?

A. Third quarter **B.** First quarter

C. Half moon **D.** Full moon

Use the following information to answer the next question.

The positions of the moon, Earth, and the sun at a given time are shown in the picture. Tides are caused by the gravitational pull of the moon and sun on bodies of water on Earth's surface. The heights of tides vary with their locations on Earth. Four locations on Earth are marked in the picture as **I, II, III,** and **IV.**

19. What are the respective heights of the tides at points **I, II, III,** and **IV**?

A. Low, low, high, and high **B.** High, high, low, and low

C. Low, high, low, and high **D.** High, low, high, and low

6ESS2.1 follow established safety procedures for handling tools and materials and observing the sun

Safety Procedures for Studying Space and the Sun

Observing the sun can be dangerous. Your eyes can suffer temporary or permanent damage if you look directly at the sun. You need to use proper safety equipment to observe the sun. Sunglasses do not provide the proper protection from the sun. You should purchase the following special filter.

- For your telescope and binoculars before looking at the sun with them.
- Shade number 14 welding filter can be bought at a welding supply shop. Smoked glass is not the same as welder's glass, and it will not protect your eyes.
- Aluminized polyester filters made especially for looking at the sun can sometimes be bought at specialty photography shops. Otherwise, you may need to look on the Internet to find a source.

If you cannot find special filters, try these other methods. They are safe so long as you do not look directly at the sun while you are using them.

Projecting the Sun onto a Piece of Paper

Hold up a pair of binoculars so they are pointed toward the sun—do not look through them to find the sun! You can also cut out a piece of stiff paper and use a pin to make a small hole in the middle of the paper. In your other hand, hold a piece of white paper or stiff white card. Aim the binoculars or pinhole so that the sun shines through the lenses and projects onto the card. On the card, an image of the sun will appear. You can also use this method to watch the sun during a solar eclipse.

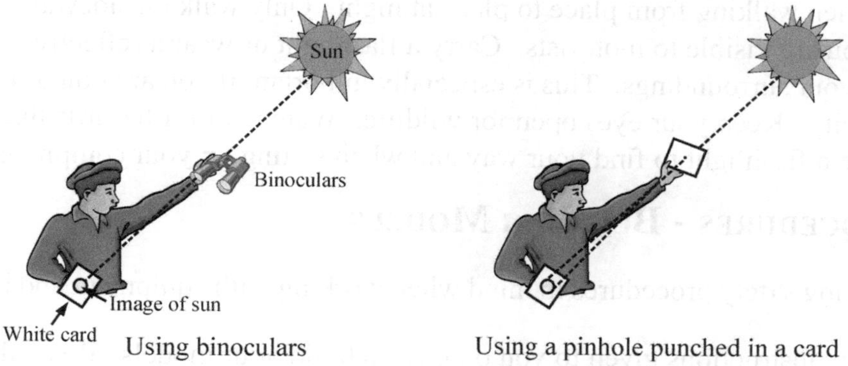

Two safe ways to observe the sun

Projecting the Sun onto a Screen

If you are at school, you can project the sun onto a white screen. Apply masking tape around a small mirror until only a small square of mirror is showing in the middle. The square should be about 5 mm by 5 mm. Hold the mirror by the window. Aim the image of the sun on the screen. Be careful not to shine the light in anyone's eyes. Turn off the lights in the room. The darker you can make the room, the brighter the image of the sun will be.

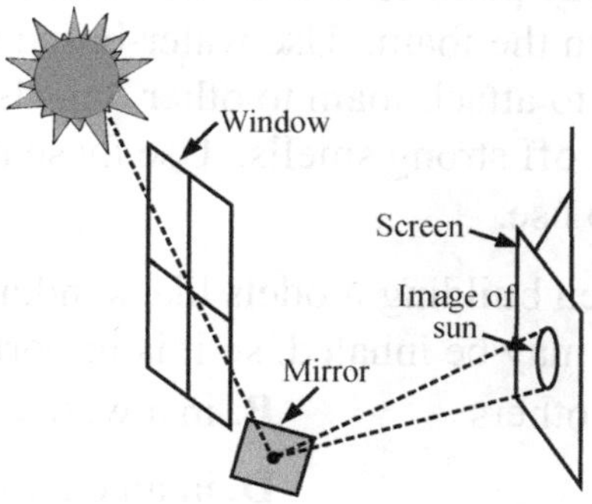

Projecting the sun onto a screen using a mirror

Observing the Stars and Other Space Objects at Night

Keep these safety tips in mind when you go out at night to observe the sky:

- Dress warmly for the weather. It can get cold at night, even in the summer.
- Always observe the sky with a friend or group. Never go out on your own. Always tell an adult where you are going and how long you expect to be gone.
- Be careful when walking from place to place at night. Only walk on sidewalks or footpaths. Make sure you are visible to motorists. Carry a flashlight or wear a reflective vest.
- Be aware of your surroundings. This is especially important if you are going into a natural area far from the city. Keep your eyes open for wildlife. Watch out for hazards like holes and roots in fields. Use a flashlight to find your way and when setting up your equipment.

Safety Procedures - Building Models

Keep the following safety procedures in mind when working with equipment and building models:

- Always follow instructions given to you on how to build your models. Read all instructions carefully. If you are unsure about something, ask your teacher or another adult.
- Wear proper safety protection as provided by your teacher. For example, you may need to wear safety goggles if you are cutting wood. Do not take off any safety equipment until your teacher tells you that it is safe to do so.
- Always cut away from yourself and others when using a knife or razor blade.
- Take care when cutting Styrofoam, as it can create fine to large dust particles. These particles can get into your eyes and cause itchiness or damage to the eye. Sometimes people breathe in these particles, which can be uncomfortable. Wear safety goggles when you cut Styrofoam. You also do not want to use spray paint on foam. This can cause the foam to break down. Some glues can also break down the foam. Use water-based paints when decorating anything made of foam. Use white glue to attach foam to other objects.
- Some glues and paints can give off strong smells. Use these materials in a room that has lots of airflow, or take them outside to use.

20. Styrofoam is often used when building models like sundials. Cutting Styrofoam can produce small particles that may be inhaled, so it is important to remember to cut it

A. away from yourself and others
B. in a well-ventilated area
C. as quickly as possible
D. in an enclosed area

6ESS2.2 use technological problem-solving skills to design, build, and test devices for investigating the motions of different bodies in the solar system

Modelling the Motions of Bodies in the Solar System

You can build a model to show how Earth moves around the sun. Here are some things to consider when building and using your model:

- If you are holding a globe, you will notice that the North Pole is not pointing straight up toward the ceiling. This is because the **tilt** of Earth's **axis** is about 23 °. If you are using a ball or marble to represent Earth, make a mark on it to show the North Pole. Tilt it so the mark is pointing toward the top area of a wall and not the ceiling.

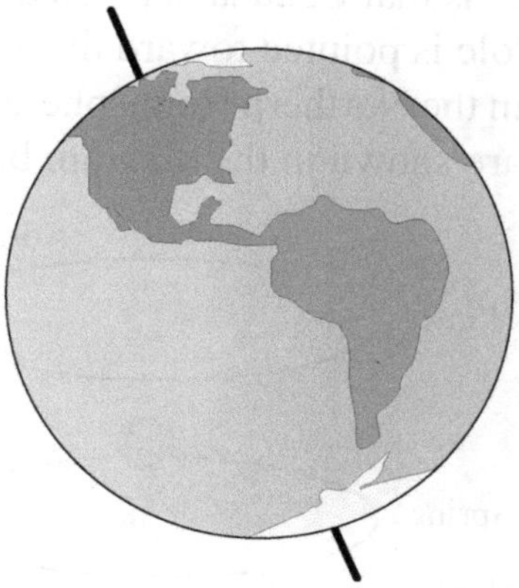

Earth's axis is tilted at a 23 degrees.

- Earth has two motions. It spins on its axis. This is called **rotation**. It also orbits the sun. This is called **revolution**. Earth revolves in a counter-clockwise direction around the sun.
- As you move your model Earth around the sun, make sure the North Pole always points toward the same wall. The North Pole is always pointed toward one point in space at all times of the year. This point is the North Star, which is also called Polaris.
- Earth's orbit around the sun is not a perfect circle. It is shaped more like an egg. Earth's orbit is called elliptical.

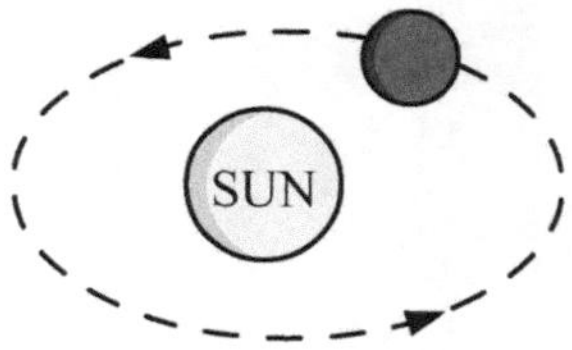

Earth's orbit is ellipti cal.

Here are some things to think about as you use your model:

- The light from the sun affects day and night on Earth as it rotates on its axis. Earth makes one complete turn every 24 hours, or once each day. As Earth rotates, some points on the planet are exposed to sunlight. These points are experiencing daytime. The points on Earth that are not exposed to sunlight are experiencing nighttime. Earth's rotation makes it appear as if the sun is moving across the sky. The sun seems to rise in the east and set in the west. However, it is Earth that is actually moving. If you spin the globe or model, are there parts of Earth that stay in darkness all the time? Are there parts that stay in the light all the time? How do these things change as you move Earth around the sun?
- The tilt, as Earth revolves around the sun, affects the seasons. For example, Canada is in the Northern Hemisphere. That means that Canada is located in the top half of Earth. When it is summer in Canada, the North Pole is pointed toward the sun. It is winter in the Southern Hemisphere. When it is winter in the Northern Hemisphere, the North Pole is pointed away from the sun. The different seasons are shown in the diagram below.

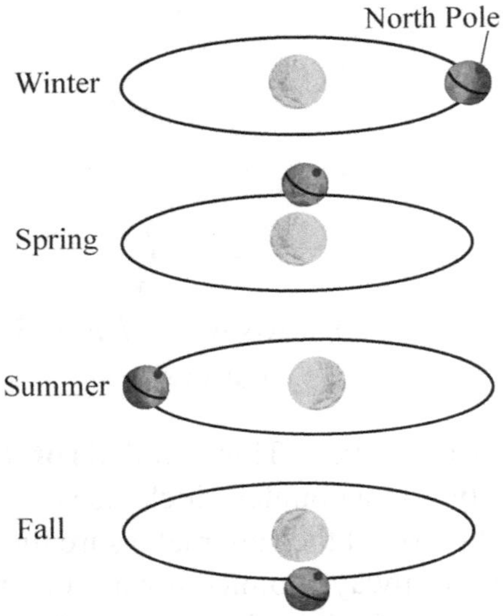

Positions of Earth during different seasons as Earth revolves around the sun.

Building a Sundial

People have used the sun's motion across the sky to help them tell time. They use an instrument called a **sundial**. The fin of the sundial, called a gnomon, casts a shadow on a disk. This shadow moves as the sun moves in the sky. On the disk are numbers that represent each hour. The number the shadow points to tells you what the time.

A large sundial

Setting up your sundial properly is important. Otherwise, it will not give the time accurately. The following hints will help you to set up your sundial:

- Place your sundial on a flat surface.
- Set up your sundial so that the gnomon points north. This will cast the gnomon's shadow on the disk correctly. Use a compass to help you find north.
- Compare the time shown on your sundial with the actual time. You may need to turn your sundial a little so that the shadow is pointing to the right time.
- It is best to set up your sundial at noon. At this time, the shadow from the gnomon should be directly underneath it.
- You may need to observe your sundial several times to get a true idea of how it works. Observe it early in the morning, around lunch time, and in the afternoon. Observe it at these times on two or three different days.

Here are some things to consider when using your sundial:

- How accurate is your sundial? Do you notice any differences in how the shadow moves from day to day?
- Daylight savings time will affect the time shown on your sundial. Your sundial will show the time of the sun, but your watch will be one hour ahead.
- Look carefully at the position of the shadow on the disk. Knowing that the sun rises in the east and sets in the west, where is the sun in relation to your sundial? Where is it in the morning? At noon? In the afternoon?

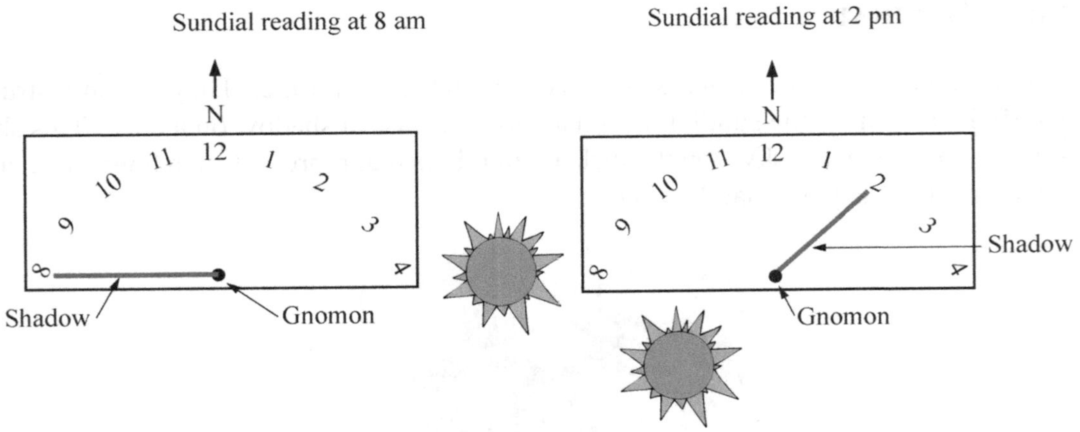

Two sundial readings, taken in the morning (left) and afternoon (right)

Use the following information to answer the next question.

While camping, Gianna used a ball and the campfire to set up the demonstration shown.

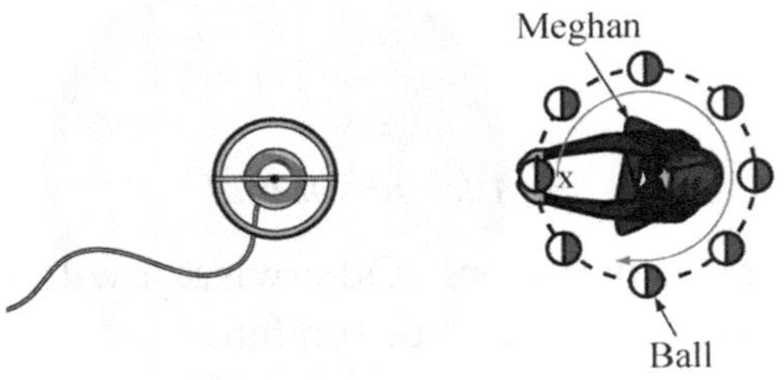

21. Which chart identifies **correctly** what Gianna, the ball, and the campfire represent?

A.

Ball	Earth
Gianna	Moon
Fire	Sun

B.

Ball	Moon
Gianna	Earth
Fire	Sun

C.

Ball	Moon
Gianna	Earth
Fire	Sun

D.

Ball	Moon
Gianna	Sun
Fire	Earth

Use the following information to answer the next question.

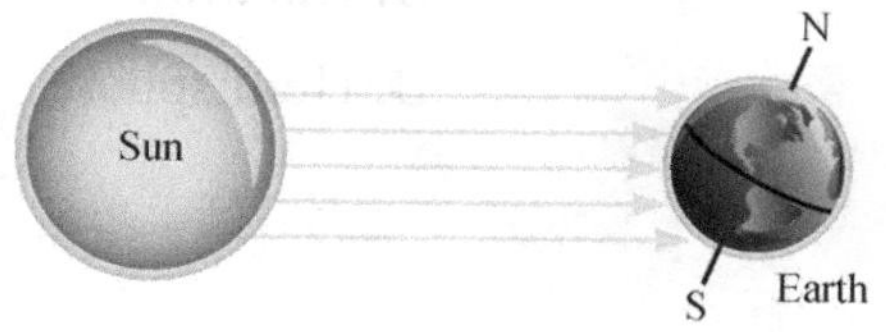

22. Which of the following conditions would a person in Northern Ontario experience when Earth has this orientation?

A. 24-hours of daylight
B. 24-hours of darkness
C. Long days and short nights
D. Short days and long nights

Use the following information to answer the next question.

23. When constructing and using the device shown above, it is important to remember to always point the arm

A. west
B. north
C. toward the sun
D. away from the sun

6ESS2.4 use appropriate science and technology vocabulary, including axis, tilt, rotation, revolution, planets, moons, comets, and asteroids, in oral and written communication

SPACE: VOCABULARY

Please refer to the glossary to find the definitions of the following vocabulary words: **asteroids**, **axis**, **comets**, **moons**, **planets**, **rotation**, **revolution**, and **tilt**.

24. What are enormous balls of rock, gases, or a mixture of rock and gas, that orbit a star called?

A. Stars
B. Planets
C. Comets
D. Asteroids

25. What is the term used to describe Earth completing one full spin on its axis?

A. Tilt
B. Rotation
C. Revolution
D. Hemisphere

ANSWERS AND SOLUTIONS
EARTH AND SPACE SYSTEMS: SPACE

1. A	6. A	11. C	16. B	21. C
2. A	7. B	12. B	17. B	22. C
3. C	8. D	13. D	18. D	23. B
4. B	9. C	14. D	19. D	24. B
5. B	10. C	15. C	20. B	25. B

1. A

Dr. Bond has helped scientists learn what the universe looks like. They learned that the universe was flat and that it was expanding. His research also supports the idea that some form of energy is causing the universe to expand.

2. A

MOST is also known as the "Humble" telescope.

3. C

The dangers of space travel would be the highest concern for the families of astronauts. Space travel is dangerous and people have died during missions and training.

4. B

Technology used in space shuttle fuel pumps has led to the development of better artificial hearts.

5. B

There are many differences between the inner planets and the outer planets. One of the most noticeable differences is that the cores of the inner planets are rocky and quite dense when compared to the cores of the outer planets. Even though the outer planets are very large, their cores are not very dense.

6. A

Mars is the only planet in the solar system besides Earth to possess polar caps. Mars' poles consist of solid water and dry ice.

7. B

The sun has an average temperature for a star. It is the closest star to Earth. It is a medium-sized star, meaning that there are stars in Earth's galaxy that are much bigger or much smaller than the sun. It takes approximately eight minutes for light from the sun to reach Earth.

8. D

Jupiter has the most satellites in the solar system; it has 63 moons.

9. C

The moon does not emit its own light; it reflects some of the light from the sun. This is why it appears lit in the night sky.

10. C

Asteroids, meteoroids in space, and planets reflect light. The sun and meteors in the atmosphere emit light.

11. C

Mir had machines to separate oxygen from wastewater. Oxygen could be produced for the crew and the hydrogen left over was pumped into space.

12. B

A person's bones and muscles are used to working under gravity. In space, they do not have to work as hard. Both bones and muscles can lose some of their strength in space. Astronauts exercise in space to keep their muscles in good condition.

13. D

Spacecraft are equipped with machines that enable the water used by astronauts to be recycled continually. This allows the astronauts to survive in space and also prevents the need to store large quantities of water onboard for missions.

14. D

Voyager 1 is a space probe. It was launched in 1977 and is expected to leave the solar system within years.

15. C

Radio telescopes collect different forms of energy from space to create images of distant objects.

16. B

The positions of the sun, Earth, and the moon will cause a solar eclipse. The moon is between the sun and Earth. Where the shadow falls, no sunlight will reach Earth.

17. B

A lunar eclipse occurs when Earth comes between the sun and the moon such that Earth's shadow falls on the moon. Andrew must place the orange (Earth) between the apple (the sun) and the lemon (the moon), as shown in the figure in **B**.

18. D

In position **G**, the moon would appear fully lit when viewed from Earth. This is called a full moon.

19. D

Tides are natural events that occur in patterns. Tides occur as a result of the gravitational pull of the moon and the sun on bodies of water on Earth's surface. The heights of the tides will be high toward the points facing the sun or the moon. In the given diagram, high tides will occur at points **I** and **III**, and low tides will occur at points **II** and **IV**.

20. B

When cutting Styrofoam it is important to do so in a well-ventilated area. This will protect against breathing in the particles produced by cutting the Styrofoam.

21. C

The ball represents the moon. Gianna represents Earth, and the campfire represents the sun. Gianna is showing the different phases of the moon. Scientists often use models to explain real situations.

22. C

The Northern Hemisphere is tilted toward the sun. This means that it would be summer in Northern Ontario, and a person there would experience longer days and shorter nights.

23. B

The sundial arm must point north to give the correct time.

24. B

Planets, such as Earth, are enormous balls of rock, gases, or a mixture of rock and gas, that orbit a star. At present, there are eight planets and three dwarf planets in the solar system.

25. B

Rotation is the spin of a body in space, such as a planet, on its axis. Earth completes a full rotation once every 24 hours.

UNIT TEST — EARTH AND SPACE SYSTEMS: SPACE

Use the following information to answer the next question.

1. The Canadian astronaut shown here is most famously known for being the first Canadian

A. woman in space

B. to perform a spacewalk

C. to operate the Canadarm

D. astronaut to visit the International Space Station

Use the following information to answer the next question.

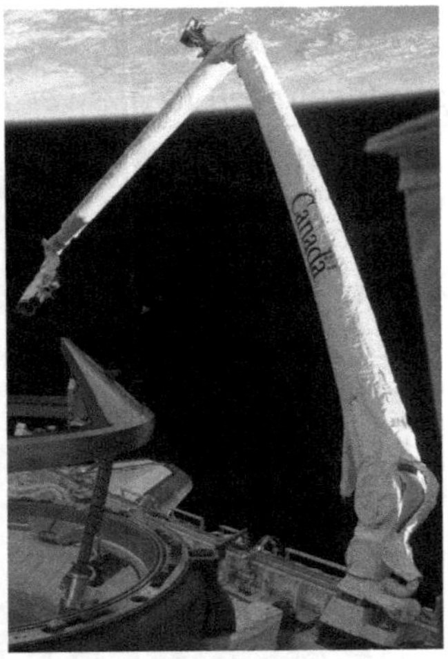

The Canadarm at work

2. Which of the following functions is the Canadarm **unable** to perform?

A. Grab hold of satellites orbiting in space

B. Help support astronauts performing space walks

C. Remove heavy objects from the shuttle and place them in space

D. Catch meteoroids passing close to Earth and take samples from them

Use the following information to answer the next question.

The costs and benefits of space bring up many different social issues. For example, space exploration is dangerous and expensive.

3. What is an argument a medical researcher would **most likely** have against space exploration?

A. The money used for space exploration could be used to find cures for diseases.

B. More research needs to be done on the effects of medical science in space.

C. Not enough medical technology is being tested on missions.

D. Medical experiments in space must first use animals.

Use the following information to answer the next question.

Geographical satellites in orbit send back detailed data to Earth, making navigation safer.

4. How does the data from geographical satellites make navigation safer?

A. It allows scientists to predict what weather patterns could affect transportation.

B. It takes the place of compasses and other direction-finding tools on Earth.

C. It improves the land and ocean maps so that they are more accurate.

D. It sends information to emergency vehicles about accidents.

5. Which of the following pictures shows a safe method to view the sun?

A.

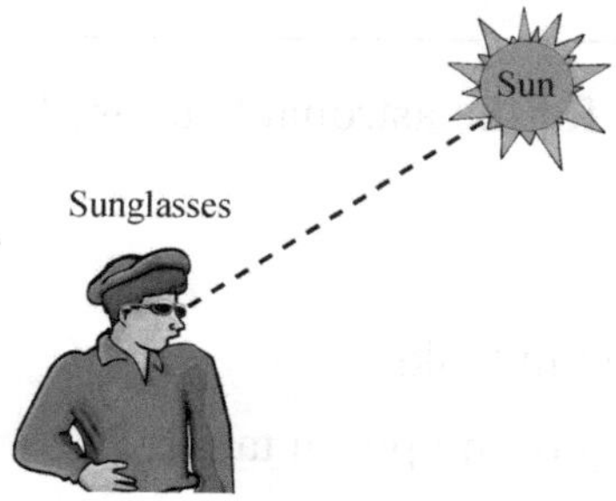

B.

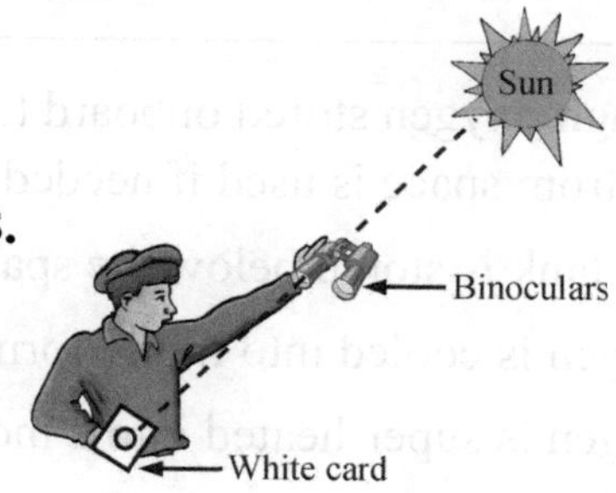

C.

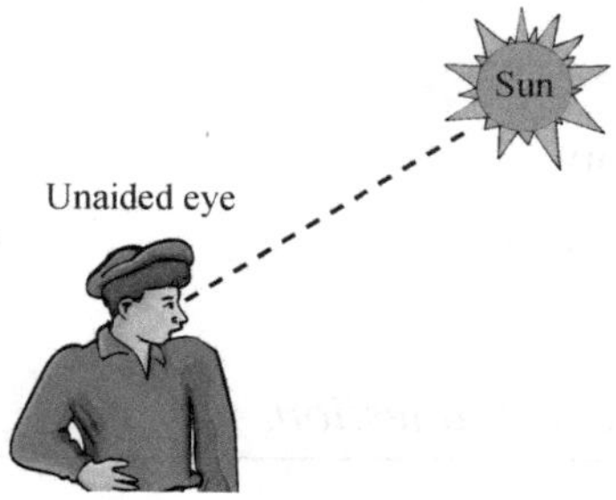

D.

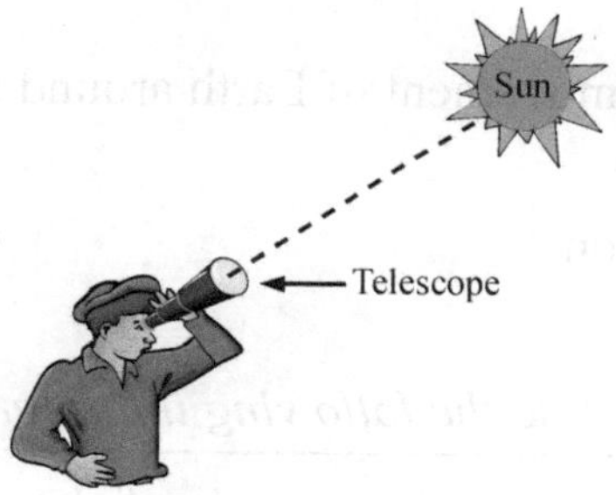

Use the following information to answer the next question.

In this figure, a globe and a candle are used to represent Earth and the sun.

6. According to the figure, what season is it in Earth's Northern Hemisphere?

A. Fall

B. Spring

C. Winter

D. Summer

7. The cycle of day and night on Earth is caused by

A. the tilt of Earth's axis

B. Earth's rotation about its axis

C. Earth's revolution around the sun

D. the relative movement between Earth, the moon, and the sun

Use the following information to answer the next question.

When the space shuttle is sent for missions in space, it must carry enough oxygen and food to sustain the astronauts aboard. There is not much space to store things onboard a space shuttle.

8. How is enough oxygen stored onboard the space shuttle for the astronauts to use?

A. Oxygen from space is used if needed.

B. An extra tank is stored below the space shuttle.

C. The oxygen is cooled into liquid form and then stored in tanks.

D. The oxygen is super-heated into a more compressed gas and put in tanks.

9. What is the movement of Earth around the sun called?

A. Rotation

B. Revolution

C. Oscillation

D. Circulation

Use the following information to answer the next question.

Earth's axis is tipped to a angle of about 23.5°.

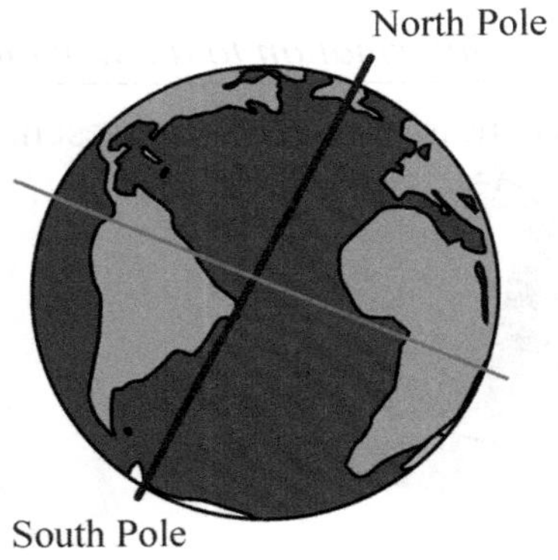

10. What is the term used to describe the degree to which a body in space, such as a planet, is tipped?

A. Tilt

B. Pole

C. Rotation

D. Revolution

Use the following information to answer the next question.

There are eight planets in Earth's solar system. There are also several known dwarf planets, three of which are Pluto, Ceres, and Eris.

11. Which statement best describes why Pluto, Ceres, and Eris are referred to as dwarf planets?

A. Their surfaces can only support small types of animal life.

B. They are thought to be smaller, broken pieces of a larger planet.

C. They have extremely short orbits around the sun and very short days.

D. They are too small to be called planets but too large to be called asteroids.

12. In Earth's solar system, a belt of asteroids lies between

A. Mars and Jupiter

B. Mercury and Venus

C. Saturn and Uranus

D. Neptune and Pluto

Use the following information to answer the next question.

Planet *X* is a member of the outer planets in the solar system. It is the second largest planet in the solar system and has a giant system of rings surrounding it.

13. Based on the given information, which planet is planet *X*?

A. Jupiter

B. Saturn

C. Uranus

D. Neptune

14. Which of the following charts has correctly classified three objects in space that reflect light and three that emit light?

A.

Emit light	Reflect light
sun	moon
asteroid	nebula
comet	galaxy

B.

Emit light	Reflect light
sun	moon
nebula	asteroid
galaxy	comet

C.

Emit light	Reflect light
sun	moon
galaxy	nebula
comet	asteroid

D.

Emit light	Reflect light
moon	sun
asteroid	nebula
comet	galaxy

Use the following information to answer the next question.

Doctors are able to use data brought back from past trips to space to try to improve life for humans in space in the future. For example, some astronauts had trouble with motion sickness when trying to compensate for the lack of gravity.

15. What have doctors done to help the astronauts with this condition?

A. Asked scientists to add a larger medical bay to the space shuttle

B. Given drugs to the astronauts that put them to sleep in the event of sickness

C. Not allowed astronauts who experience motion sickness in training to go to space

D. Prescribed patches for the astronauts to wear that release medication into the body

Use the following information to answer the next question.

Scientists use different tools for space exploration. One such tool is a spectrograph.

16. Which of the following statements **best** describes what a spectrograph does?

A. It measures the brightness of stars.

B. It measures the distance to remote objects from Earth.

C. It is the record of emissions from stars and other objects in space.

D. It records the forces acting on asteroids and comets that enter the solar system.

17. Which of the following telescopes would provide the **best** images for scientists on Earth?

A.

B.

C.

D.

Use the following information to answer the next question.

William wants to construct a model of a lunar eclipse. He has a bulb, a globe, and a tennis ball.

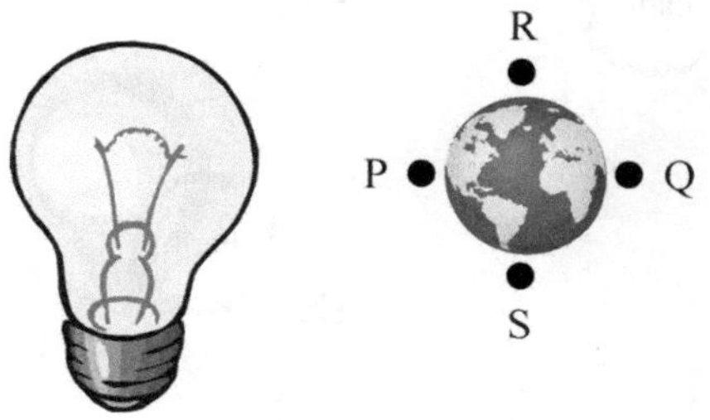

18. For William to correctly model a lunar eclipse, in the position of which letter should he place the tennis ball?

A. P **B.** Q

C. R **D.** S

Use the following information to answer the next question.

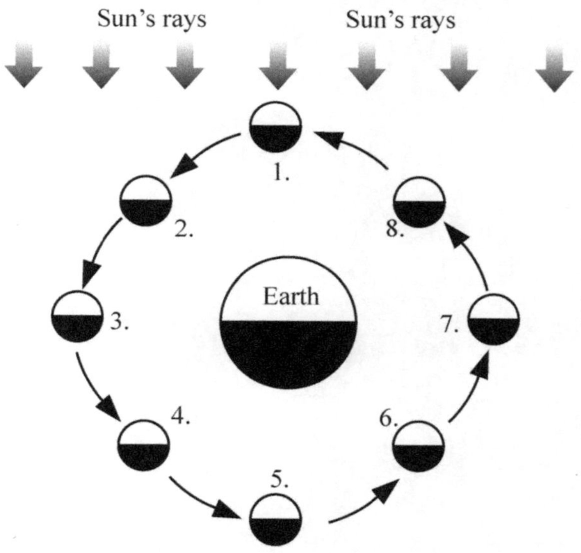

Phases of the moon over a period of one month

19. Beginning at the new moon phase, what happens to the portion of the moon that can be seen from Earth as the moon orbits Earth?

A. The sunlit portion disappears.

B. The sunlit portion remains the same.

C. The sunlit portion decreases and then increases.

D. The sunlit portion increases and then decreases.

20. Which of the following illustrations shows the relative positions of the sun, the moon, and Earth during the highest tides?

A. 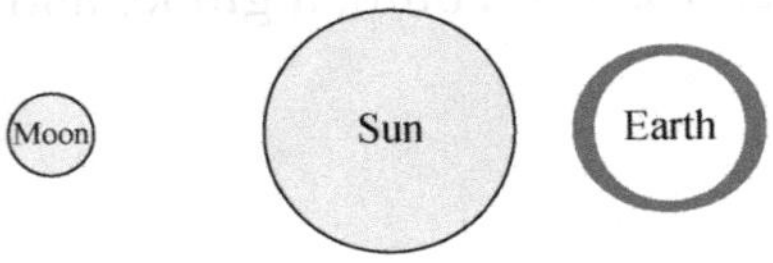

B. 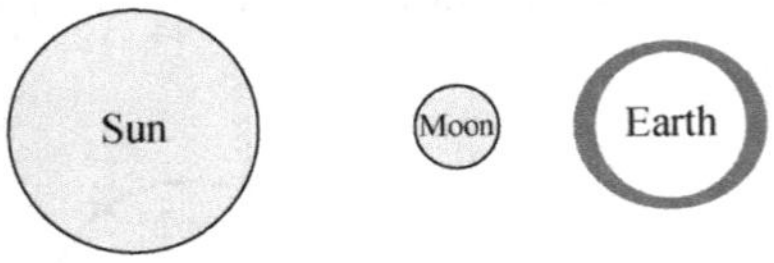

C. 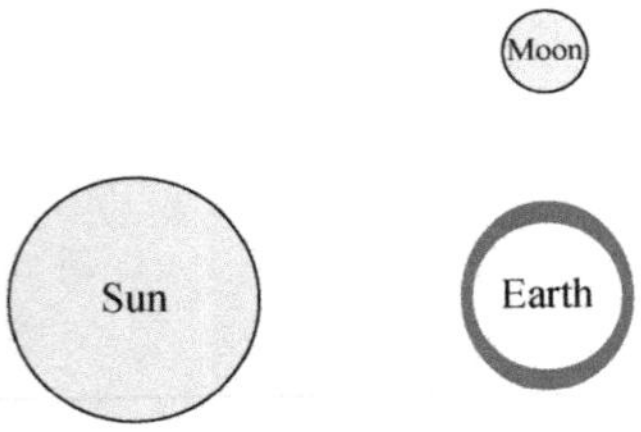

D. 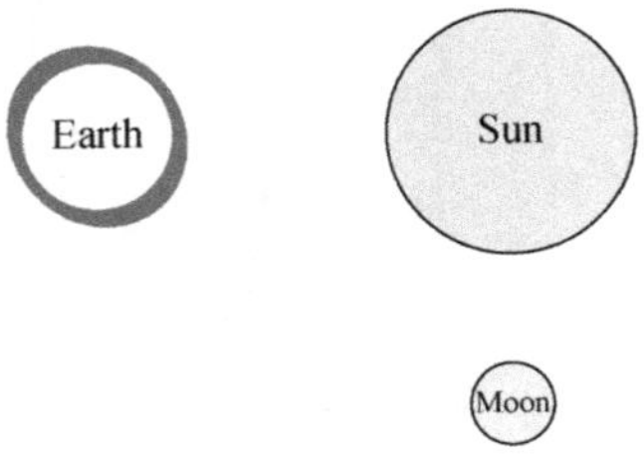

ANSWERS AND SOLUTIONS — UNIT TEST

1. A	**5. B**	**9. B**	**13. B**	**17. B**
2. D	**6. C**	**10. A**	**14. B**	**18. B**
3. A	**7. B**	**11. D**	**15. D**	**19. D**
4. C	**8. C**	**12. A**	**16. C**	**20. B**

1. A

This picture shows the first Canadian woman in space, Roberta Bondar. She is a neurologist and holds several degrees. She made her flight into space in 1992.

2. D

The Canadarm cannot catch meteoroids passing close to Earth.

3. A

Many diseases on Earth have yet to be cured, and the large amount of money used in space exploration could be used in medical research. A medical researcher would most likely be opposed to the use of money for space exploration rather than medicine.

4. C

Satellites have helped people make accurate maps of land and oceans. This helps make navigation safer, as it decreases the chances of getting lost.

5. B

To safely view the sun, hold up a pair of binoculars so they are pointed toward the sun—do not look through them to find the sun. Aim the binoculars so that the sun shines through the lenses and projects onto the card.

6. C

In the figure, Earth's northern hemisphere is tilted away from the sun. This means that the Northern Hemisphere will receive less direct sunlight than the southern hemisphere. Therefore, it is winter in the Northern Hemisphere.

7. B

The day and night cycle is caused by Earth's rotation about its axis. Earth rotates from west to east, making the Sun appear to rise in the east and set in the west. One rotation of Earth takes 24 hours, which is a full day.

8. C

Most spacecraft carry oxygen in the form of a liquid, not a gas, and store it in tanks. Liquid oxygen takes up about 800 times less volume than gaseous oxygen. This means a lot of oxygen can be taken on the spacecraft without having it take up too much space.

9. B

The movement of Earth around the sun is called a revolution. Earth takes 365.25 days to revolve once around the sun. This period of time is called a year.
Rotation is the movement Earth makes as it spins on its axis. It takes 24 hours for Earth to spin once on its axis. This period of time is called a day.

10. A

The degree to which a body in space, such as a planet, is tipped on its axis is called tilt.

11. D

Pluto, Ceres, and Eris are referred to as dwarf planets because they are too small to be called planets but too large to be called asteroids. Ceres is found in the asteroid belt between Mars and Jupiter. Pluto is usually found past Neptune, although at times its orbit brings it closer to the sun than Neptune. Eris is found past Pluto.

12. A

The asteroid belt separates the inner planets from the outer planets. The inner planets are Mercury, Venus, Earth, and Mars, while the outer planets are Jupiter, Saturn, Uranus, and Neptune. So, the asteroid belt lies between Mars and Jupiter.

13. B

Saturn is the second largest planet in the solar system. The four outer planets are Jupiter, Saturn, Uranus, and Neptune. Saturn also has a giant system of rings around it.

14. B

The sun, nebulae, and galaxies all emit light. Asteroids, comets, and the moon all reflect light.

15. D

To fight nausea while on space walks, astronauts can wear a patch on their skin that releases medication into their body. This medication is similar to motion sickness medication.

16. C

A spectrograph records spectral emissions from stars and other objects in space, as well as from Earth.

17. B

The Hubble space telescope provides far superior images than telescopes on Earth because it is in orbit above any weather or pollution that may affect telescopes on Earth.

18. B

A lunar eclipse occurs when Earth comes between the sun and the moon such that Earth's shadow falls on the moon. William should place the tennis ball at position **Q** such that the shadow of the globe falls on the tennis ball, as shown in the following figure.

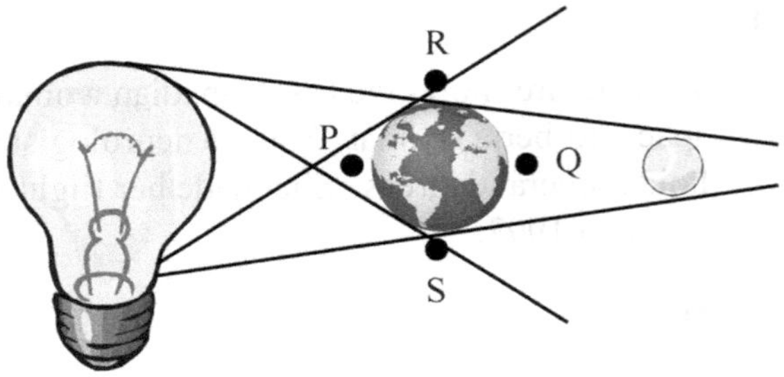

19. D

Beginning with the new moon phase, more and more of the sunlit side of the moon is visible each day. During this time, the moon is waxing. After the moon is full, less and less of the sunlit side will be visible until the moon is not visible at all or is in its new moon phase again. During this time, the moon is waning. So, the amount of light visible first increases and then decreases.

20. B

High tides occur when the moon, Earth, and the sun are lined up. Tides are caused by the gravitational pull of the sun and the moon on the water on Earths' surface. This gravitational pull will be at its maximum when the sun and the moon are on the same side of Earth, as shown in the illustration in alternative **B**.

Success on Tests

KEY STRATEGIES FOR SUCCESS ON TESTS

THINGS TO CONSIDER WHEN TAKING A TEST

It is normal to feel anxious before you write a test. You can manage this anxiety by using the following strategies:

- Think positive thoughts. Imagine yourself doing well on the test.
- Make a conscious effort to relax by taking several slow, deep, controlled breaths. Concentrate on the air going in and out of your body.
- Before you begin the test, ask questions if you are unsure of anything.
- Jot down key words or phrases from any instructions your teacher gives you.
- Look over the entire test to find out the number and kinds of questions on the test.
- Read each question closely, and reread if necessary.
- Pay close attention to key vocabulary words. Sometimes, these words are **bolded** or *italicized*, and they are usually important words in the question.
- If you are putting your answers on an answer sheet, mark your answers carefully. Always print clearly. If you wish to change an answer, erase the mark completely, and ensure that your final answer is darker than the one you have erased.
- Use highlighting to note directions, key words, and vocabulary that you find confusing or that are important to answering the question.
- Double-check to make sure you have answered everything before handing in your test.
- When taking tests, students often overlook the easy words. Failure to pay close attention to these words can result in an incorrect answer. One way to avoid this is to be aware of these words and to underline, circle, or highlight them while you are taking the test.
- Even though some words are easy to understand, they can change the meaning of the entire question, so it is important that you pay attention to them. Here are some examples.

all	always	most likely	probably	best	not
difference	usually	except	most	unlikely	likely

Example

1. Which of the following expressions is **incorrect**?

A. $3 + 2 \geq 5$

B. $4 - 3 < 2$

C. $5 \times 4 < 15$

D. $6 \times 3 \geq 18$

TEST PREPARATION AND TEST-TAKING SKILLS

HELPFUL STRATEGIES FOR ANSWERING MULTIPLE-CHOICE QUESTIONS

A multiple-choice question gives you some information and then asks you to select an answer from four choices. Each question has one correct answer. The other choices are distractors, which are incorrect.

The following strategies can help you when answering multiple-choice questions:

- Quickly skim through the entire test. Find out how many questions there are, and plan your time accordingly.

- Read and reread questions carefully. Underline key words, and try to think of an answer before looking at the choices.
- If there is a graphic, look at the graphic, read the question, and go back to the graphic. Then, you may want to underline the important information from the question.
- Carefully read the choices. Read the question first and then each choice that goes with it.
- When choosing an answer, try to eliminate those choices that are clearly wrong or do not make sense.
- Some questions may ask you to select the best answer. These questions will always include words like *best*, *most appropriate*, or *most likely*. All of the choices will be correct to some degree, but one of the choices will be better than the others in some way. Carefully read all four choices before choosing the answer you think is the best.
- If you do not know the answer, or if the question does not make sense to you, it is better to guess than to leave it blank.
- Do not spend too much time on any one question. Make a mark (*) beside a difficult question, and come back to it later. If you are leaving a question to come back to later, make sure you also leave the space on the answer sheet, if you are using one.

- Remember to go back to the difficult questions at the end of the test; sometimes, clues are given throughout the test that will provide you with answers.
- Note any negative words like *no* or *not*, and be sure your answer fits the question.
- Before changing an answer, be sure you have a very good reason to do so.
- Do not look for patterns on your answer sheet, if you are using one.

HELPFUL STRATEGIES FOR ANSWERING WRITTEN-RESPONSE QUESTIONS

A written response requires you to respond to a question or directive indicated by words such as explain, predict, list, describe, show your work, solve, or calculate. The following strategies can help you when answering written-response questions:

- Read and reread the question carefully.
- Recognize and pay close attention to directing words such as *explain*, *show your work*, and *describe.*
- Underline key words and phrases that indicate what is required in your answer, such as *explain*, *estimate*, *answer*, *calculate*, or *show your work.*
- Write down rough, point-form notes regarding the information you want to include in your answer.
- Think about what you want to say, and organize information and ideas in a coherent and concise manner within the time limit you have for the question.
- Be sure to answer every part of the question that is asked.
- Include as much information as you can when you are asked to explain your thinking.
- Include a picture or diagram if it will help to explain your thinking.
- Try to put your final answer to a problem in a complete sentence to be sure it is reasonable.
- Reread your response to ensure you have answered the question.
- Ask yourself if your answer makes sense.
- Ask yourself if your answer sounds right.
- Use appropriate subject vocabulary and terms in your response.

What You Need to Know about Science Tests

To do well on a science test, you need to understand and apply your knowledge of scientific concepts. Reading skills can also make a difference in how well you perform. Reading skills can help you follow instructions and find key words, as well as read graphs, diagrams, and tables.

Science tests usually have two types of questions: knowledge questions and skill questions. Knowledge questions test for your understanding of science ideas. Skill questions test how you would use your science knowledge.

How You Can Prepare for Science Tests

The following strategies are particular to preparing for and writing science tests:

- Note taking is a good way to review and study important information from your class notes and textbook.
- Sketch a picture of the process or idea being described in a question. Drawing is helpful for learning and remembering concepts.
- Check your answer to practice questions the require formulas by working backward to the beginning. You can find the beginning by going step by step in reverse order.
- Use the following steps when answering questions with graphics (pictures, diagrams, tables, or graphs):
  1. Read the title of the graphic and any key words.
  2. Read the test question carefully to figure out what information you need to find in the graphic.
  3. Go back to the graphic to find the information you need.
- Always pay close attention when pressing the keys on your calculator. Repeat the procedure a second time to be sure you pressed the correct keys.

Test Preparation Countdown

If you develop a plan for studying and test preparation, you will perform well on tests.

Here is a general plan to follow seven days before you write a test.

Countdown: 7 Days before the Test

1. Use "Finding Out about the Test" to help you make your own personal test preparation plan.
2. Review the following information:
   - Areas to be included on the test
   - Types of test items
   - General and specific test tips
3. Start preparing for the test at least seven days before the test. Develop your test preparation plan, and set time aside to prepare and study.

Countdown: 6, 5, 4, 3, 2 Days before the Test

1. Review old homework assignments, quizzes, and tests.
2. Rework problems on quizzes and tests to make sure you still know how to solve them.
3. Correct any errors made on quizzes and tests.
4. Review key concepts, processes, formulas, and vocabulary.
5. Create practice test questions for yourself, and answer them. Work out many sample problems.

Countdown: The Night before the Test

1. Use the night before the test for final preparation, which includes reviewing and gathering materials needed for the test before going to bed.
2. Most importantly, get a good night's rest, and know you have done everything possible to do well on the test.

Test Day

1. Eat a healthy and nutritious breakfast.
2. Ensure you have all the necessary materials.
3. Think positive thoughts, such as "I can do this," "I am ready," and "I know I can do well."
4. Arrive at your school early, so you are not rushing, which can cause you anxiety and stress.

Summary of How to Be Successful during a Test

You may find some of the following strategies useful for writing a test:

- Take two or three deep breaths to help you relax.
- Read the directions carefully, and underline, circle, or highlight any important words.
- Look over the entire test to understand what you will need to do.
- Budget your time.
- Begin with an easy question or a question you know you can answer correctly rather than follow the numerical question order of the test.
- If you cannot remember how to answer a question, try repeating the deep breathing and physical relaxation activities. Then, move on to visualization and positive self-talk to get yourself going.
- When answering questions with graphics (pictures, diagrams, tables, or graphs), look at the question carefully, and use the following steps:
    1. Read the title of the graphic and any key words.
    2. Read the test question carefully to figure out what information you need to find in the graphic.
    3. Go back to the graphic to find the information you need.
- Write down anything you remember about the subject on the reverse side of your test paper. This activity sometimes helps to remind you that you do know something and are capable of writing the test.
- Look over your test when you have finished, and double-check your answers to be sure you did not forget anything.

NOTES

Practice Test

PRACTICE TEST

1. Who was the first Canadian in space?
   A. David Levy
   B. Richard Bond
   C. Marc Garneau
   D. Roberta Bondar

2. Space junk is a term used for floating debris that orbits Earth. Why would space junk be dangerous to space travel?
   A. Astronauts have a hard time bringing it home to recycle.
   B. It pollutes the atmosphere, reducing visibility for astronauts.
   C. It can block the sun, leaving no source of heat for astronauts.
   D. It could hit and damage the spacecraft used to travel into orbit.

3. What is the **most** important thing to remember when viewing the sun?
   A. Use filters on binoculars.
   B. Never look directly at the sun.
   C. Wearing sunglasses is effective protection for viewing the sun.
   D. Project the sun onto a white piece of paper using binoculars or a telescope.

4. Which of the following statements **best** explains the reason for the changing of the seasons on Earth?
   A. Earth rotates on its axis.
   B. Earth revolves around the sun.
   C. Earth's axis is tilted, and Earth rotates on its axis.
   D. Earth's axis is tilted, and Earth revolves around the sun.

Use the following information to answer the next question.

> There is not much room for storage on a space shuttle. There are many supplies and machines on board, and the shuttle cannot be overloaded with excessive weight when being launched into space.

5. Which statement describes how the food used by astronauts is prepared for use in space?
   A. The food is dehydrated to make it lighter.
   B. The food is in liquid form and stored in tanks.
   C. The food is put into pill form to provide all vitamins and nutrients needed.
   D. The food is brought from Earth in a frozen state and stored in the shuttle bays.

Use the following information to answer the next question.

There is an imaginary line that goes through the North and South Poles and the centre of the planet. Earth rotates around this imaginary line.

6. What is the imaginary line called?

A. Tilt
B. Axis
C. Atmosphere
D. Hemisphere

7. Which of the following pictures shows a comet?

A.
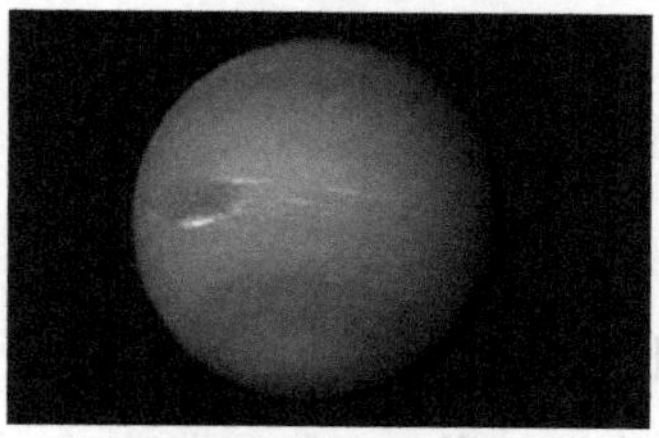

B.

C.
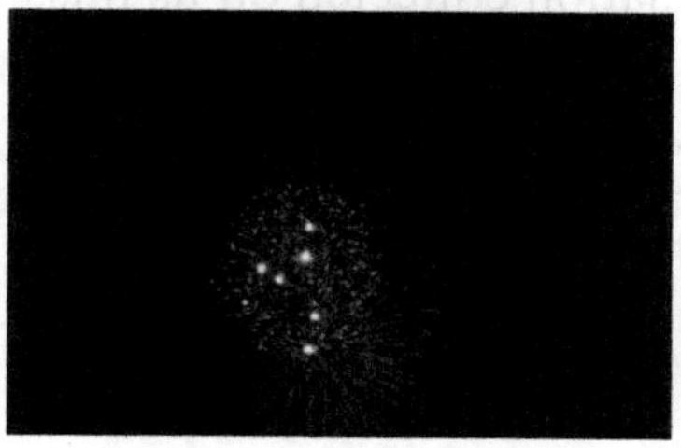

D.

8. Why can comets be seen in the night sky?

A. Comets emit their own light.
B. Comets reflect light from the sun.
C. Comets reflect light from the moon.
D. Comets burn up as they enter the atmosphere.

Use the following information to answer the next question.

9. Which necessity do space suits provide to allow astronauts to do space walks?

A. Water
B. Oxygen
C. Rocket packs
D. Artificial gravity

Use the following information to answer the next question.

Soujourner

10. What is unique about this type of technology?

A. It can help astronauts carry out repairs.

B. It can travel across the surface of other planets.

C. It can carry astronauts around the surface of other planets.

D. It can launch probes back to Earth, carrying information collected on its mission.

Use the following information to answer the next question.

Mr. Banks showed his science class this drawing of the sun, Earth, and the moon.

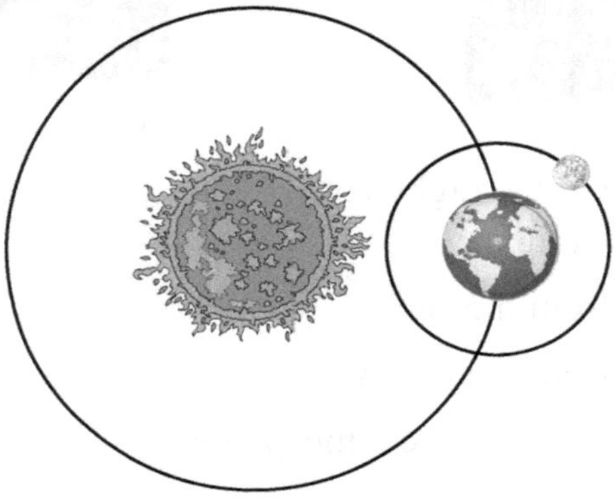

11. Which of the following statements explains what this drawing represents?

A. Earth revolves around the sun, and the moon revolves around Earth.

B. The moon revolves around Earth, and the sun revolves around Earth.

C. The moon revolves around the sun, and the sun revolves around Earth.

D. Earth revolves around the moon, and the moon revolves around the sun.

Use the following information to answer the next question.

Many years ago, ocean freighters and trains were the only means to transport goods to other countries.

12. How has the invention of the airplane changed how goods are transported?
A. Most goods are now transported by airplane.
B. It has made it more dangerous to transport goods.
C. People can buy and sell goods from anywhere in the world.
D. It takes longer to receive goods being flown from other countries.

Use the following information to answer the next question.

Paul builds a model airplane for the science fair. The glue that he uses has a strong odour and makes his eyes water when he uses it.

13. What should Paul do in order to finish his project safely?
A. Turn up the heat in the house
B. Pour the glue down the drain
C. Ask a friend to glue the plane for him
D. Open a window to let in some fresh air

Use the following information to answer the next question.

Eva uses a balance to measure the mass of a deflated balloon. She then inflates the balloon with air and measures its mass again. She records her observations in the table below.

Balloon	**Mass (g)**
Deflated	15
Inflated	25

14. What is the mass of the air inside the inflated balloon?

A. 10 g
B. 15 g
C. 25 g
D. 40 g

15. A special adaptation that helps birds to fly is that their bones are

A. flat
B. heavy
C. hollow
D. pointed

Use the following information to answer the next question.

Maxine is designing a paper glider. She wants it to fly straight and stay in the air for a long time.

16. Which factor is the **most** important one that Maxine should consider when designing her glider?

A. Using brightly coloured paper.
B. Choosing paper that has a shiny side and a dull side.
C. Bending the wings so that they have a slightly curved shape.
D. Making sure her name is on the glider so that she can find it after she throws it.

Use the following information to answer the next question.

The word **propel** means to move forward. A jet is propelled by its engines. A paper airplane is propelled by the thrower's arm.

17. What is another name for the aerodynamic force that propels an airplane?

A. Lift
B. Drag
C. Thrust
D. Gravity

18. The airflow around a bird's wing produces differences in air pressure. Where is the area of highest pressure locate?

A. Behind the wing
B. In front of the wing
C. Over top of the wing
D. Underneath the wing

19. What is the property of air that allows it to be used to fill tires?

A. It has mass.
B. It can be compressed.
C. It contracts as it cools.
D. It is made up of different gases.

Use the following information to answer the next question.

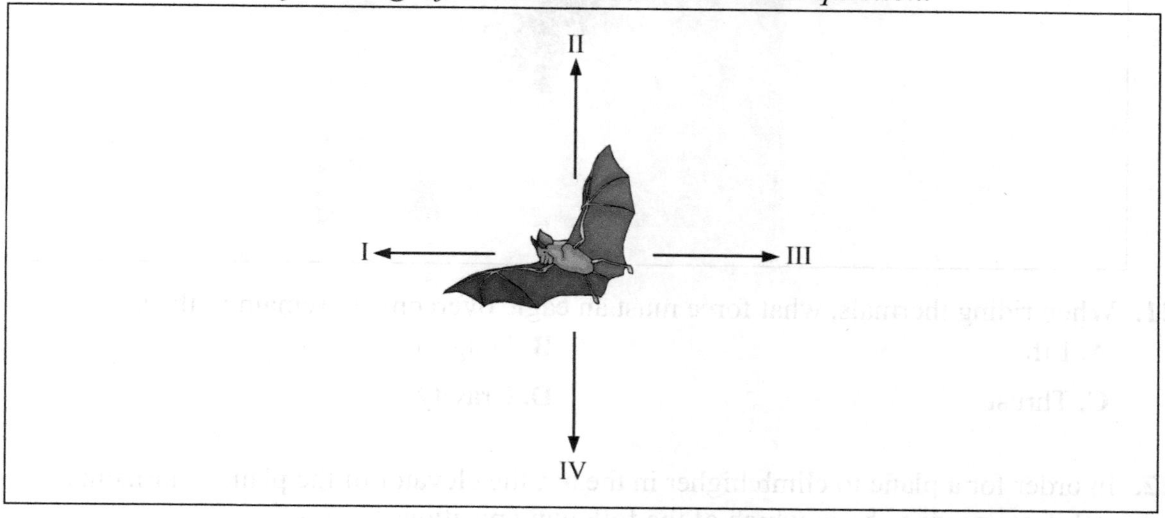

20. The forces of flight shown are

A.

I	lift
II	gravity
III	thrust
IV	drag

B.

I	gravity
II	thrust
III	drag
IV	lift

C.

I	thrust
II	lift
III	drag
IV	gravity

D.

I	drag
II	thrust
III	gravity
IV	lift

Use the following information to answer the next question.

An eagle will sometimes soar for hours in the air by riding thermals. A thermal is a small column of rising air.

21. When riding thermals, what force must an eagle overcome to remain in the air?

A. Lift

B. Drag

C. Thrust

D. Gravity

22. In order for a plane to climb higher in the air, the elevator of the plane's horizontal stabilizer needs to be in which of the following positions?

A.

B.

C.

D.

Use the following information to answer the next question.

Most airplanes have a cone-shaped nose.

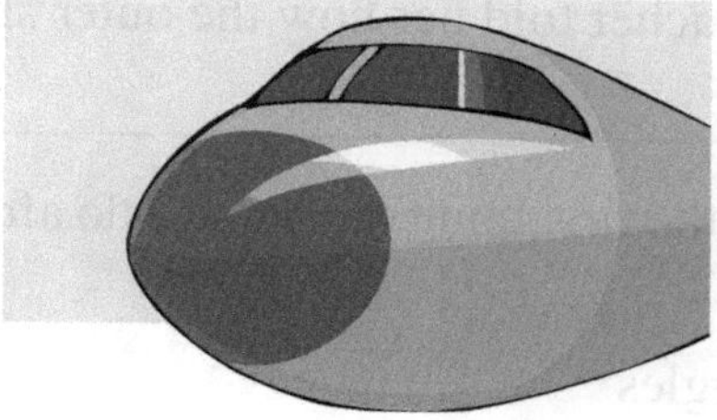

23. What is the reason airplanes have a cone-shaped nose?

A. To decrease the drag on the plane

B. To increase the thrust of the plane

C. To decrease the gravity on the plane

D. To allow the plane to fly at higher altitudes

Use the following information to answer the next question.

A shopping mall is to be built in a community. To make room for this shopping mall, the construction company has decided to cut down a local forest. A group of students in the local school decide to make others aware of this environmental issue.

24. Which action would be the **least** effective for making others aware of this issue?

A. Individually researching other areas to build the shopping mall

B. Writing a letter to the member of Parliament

C. Organizing a meeting to discuss options

D. Writing a letter to a local newspaper

Use the following information to answer the next question.

The great diversity of plant life on Earth has benefited people all over the world. Humans use plants for a wide variety of things.

25. Which statement does **not** state a use for plants?

A. Plants can be used to make shelter.

B. Plants can be used as medicine.

C. Plants are used to make plastic.

D. Plants are a source of food.

Use the following information to answer the next question.

Jen's class visited a zoo to learn about reptiles. Jen's teacher let her pick up a turtle to feel the outer shell. Her teacher told her how the outer shell of the turtle can protect it from predators.

26. In order to be safe, what is the first thing Jen should do after putting the turtle back down?

A. Wash her hands

B. Remove her safety goggles

C. Write detailed notes on her observations

D. Draw a picture on how to properly pick up a turtle

Use the following information to answer the next question.

Mike saw this tree.
He used the chart shown below the tree to classify it.

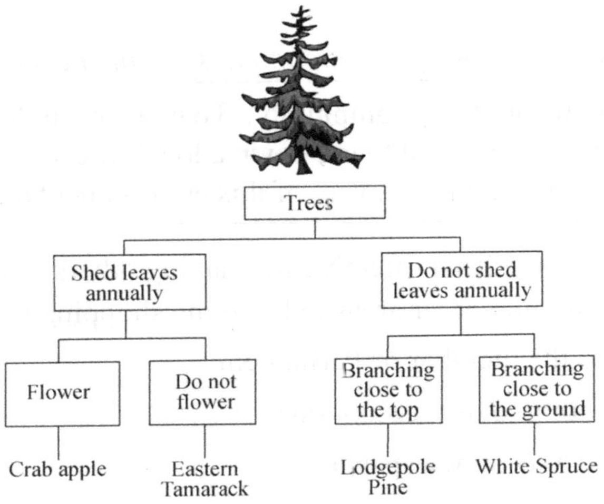

27. Based on the characteristics of the tree shown, what species of tree should it be classified as?

A. Eastern tamarack

B. Lodgepole pine

C. White spruce

D. Crab apple

Use the following information to answer the next question.

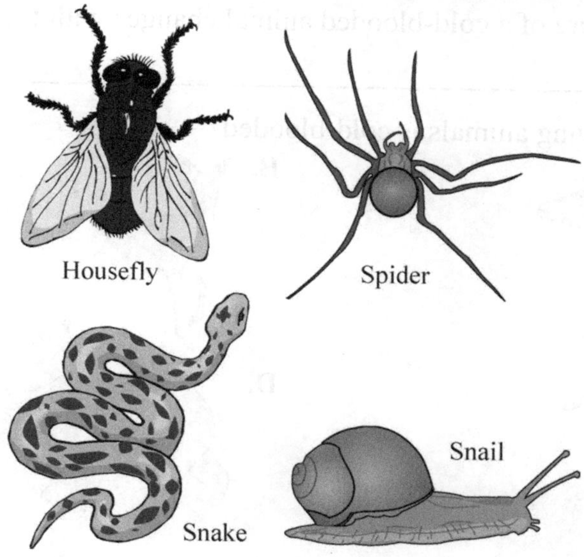

28. Which animal does **not** belong with the others in the group?

A. Housefly
B. Spider
C. Snake
D. Snail

29. What is an animal that has a backbone called?

A. Mammal
B. Arthropod
C. Vertebrate
D. Invertebrate

Use the following information to answer the next question.

Ronny found an animal on the ground under a tree in his yard. The animal has rough, scaly skin and moves quickly even though it has no legs or arms.

30. What type of animal did Ronny find?

A. Bird
B. Reptile
C. Mammal
D. Amphibian

Use the following information to answer the next question.

The body temperature of a cold-blooded animal changes with the temperature of its environment.

31. Which of the following animals is cold-blooded?

A. 

B. 

C. 

D. 

Use the following information to answer the next question.

32. What are all the populations that live together in a small area called?

A. Niche
B. Habitat
C. Ecosystem
D. Community

Use the following information to answer the next question.

Antibiotics are medicines that were invented to battle bacterial infections by killing or stopping bacterial growth. Over time, however, the effectiveness of these medicines has decreased. Some bacteria were able to survive and reproduce.

33. What do these bacteria show by adapting to and surviving changes in their environment?

A. Resilience
B. Respiration
C. Genetic material
D. Learned behaviour

Use the following information to answer the next question.

Honey bees get nectar from flowers. In return, as the honey bees fly from flower to flower, they carry pollen to pollinate other flowers.

34. The relationship between the flower and the bee is **best** described as

A. a parasitic relationship
B. a competitive relationship
C. an interrelationship within a species
D. an interrelationship between species

Use the following information to answer the next question.

Silkworms are used in the production of silk. Silk is a material used to make products like clothes but can also be used in making rugs, bedding, and even parachutes.

35. How are silkworms used in silk production?

A. They excrete silk as a waste product.
B. The eggs of the worm are processed.
C. Silk is obtained by unwrapping their cocoons.
D. The larvae of the worms naturally produce silk from their skin.

Use the following information to answer the next question.

Purple loosestrife, shown here growing in a field, is an invasive species that can quickly take over a habitat.

36. What is the **most likely** reason that purple loosestrife is a concern for farmers?

A. It can clog irrigation ditches and canals.

B. It adds foreign nutrients to the soil.

C. It cannot be fed to farm animals.

D. It cannot be harvested for sale.

37. Electrical power is generated by using different sources of energy. Which source of energy produce the **most** pollution?

A. Coal

B. Wind

C. Water

D. Sunlight

38. Which of the following actions will help reduce the amount of electricity used in the home?

A. Turning off the computer when it is not in use.

B. Turning on the dishwasher when it is half full.

C. Using the clothes dryer instead of a clothesline.

D. Leaving the television on when no one is watching.

Use the following information to answer the next question.

Joe mentioned to his classmates that is was not wise to fly a kite near power lines.

39. It is dangerous to fly a kite near power lines because the kite could

A. damage the power lines

B. create a pathway for electricity

C. be set on fire from touching the lines

D. become tangled and impossible to get down

Use the following information to answer the next question.

Alyssa designed this circuit.

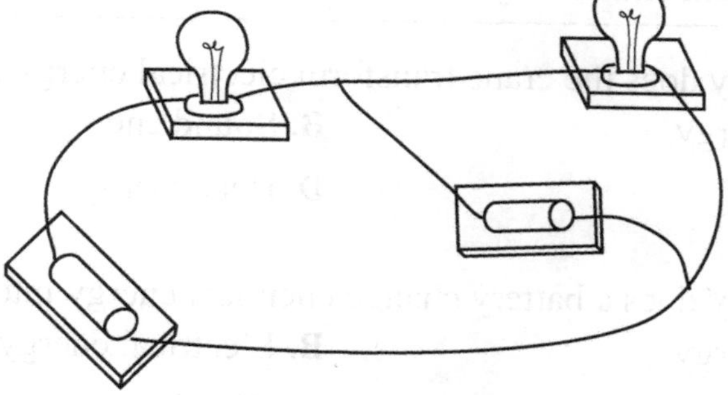

40. What type of circuit did Alyssa arrange the bulbs in?

A. Short circuit
B. Series circuit
C. Simple circiut
D. Parallel circuit

Use the following information to answer the next question.

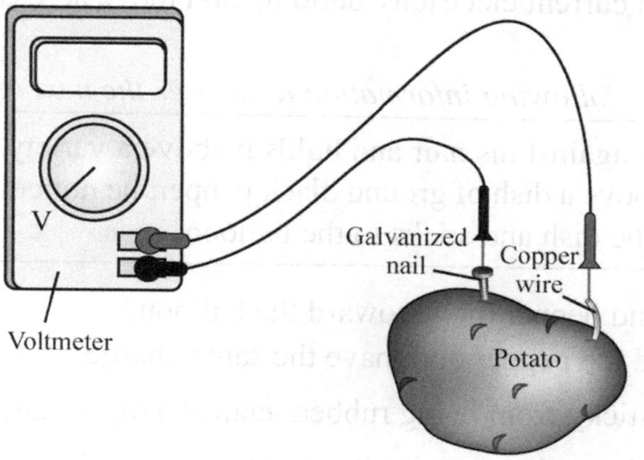

Jeremy builds a battery using a potato and two wires. He connects one end of each wire to the potato and the other end to a voltmeter as shown in the diagram. Jeremy notices that his potato battery produces 2 volts of electricity.

41. What would Jeremy have to do to increase the voltage of his battery?

A. Add more wires to the potato.

B. Create a parallel circuit and add another potato.

C. Switch the wires at the terminals of the voltmeter.

D. Connect more potatoes with wires in a series circuit.

Use the following information to answer the next question.

Selena wants to build a model crane to lift objects up and set them down. She uses a small electric motor, switch, and battery in the circuit.

42. What kind of energy does the crane transform electrical energy into?

A. Mechanical energy
B. Sound energy
C. Light energy
D. Heat energy

43. What kind of energy does a battery change chemical energy into?

A. Mechanical energy
B. Electrical energy
C. Potential energy
D. Kinetic energy

44. Which of the following statements about current electricity is **true**?

A. Current electricity moves in sudden bursts.
B. Current electricity flows continuously through a conductor.
C. The electrons in current electricity are all positively charged.
D. The electrons in current electricity build up and move across gaps easily.

Use the following information to answer the next question.

Troy rubs a balloon against his hair and holds it above a variety of materials. When he holds the balloon above a dish of ground black pepper, he notices that some of the ground pepper lifts out of the dish and sticks to the balloon.

45. Why does the ground pepper move toward the balloon?

A. The balloon and the pepper both have the same charge.
B. The balloon is sticky from being rubbed against Troy's hair.
C. The positively charged pepper is attracted to the negatively charged balloon.
D. The negatively charged balloon is attracted to the negatively charged pepper.

Use the following information to answer the next question.

Tomas tested the following materials in the science lab to find out if any would be insulators:

- foam cup
- glass rod
- steel nail
- nickel coin
- plastic straw
- brass button
- wooden stick
- copper penny

46. Which two materials act as insulators?

A. The foam cup and brass button

B. The glass rod and plastic straw

C. The plastic straw and steel nail

D. The steel nail and foam cup

47. In a solar cell, which of the following energy conversions takes place?

A. light energy to chemical energy

B. light energy to electrical energy

C. electrical energy to light energy

D. chemical energy to light energy

48. What part of an electrical circuit is responsible for conducting the electricity from one place to another?

A. Load

B. Wires

C. Switch

D. Battery

Use the following information to answer the next question.

Simone constructed a circuit as shown.

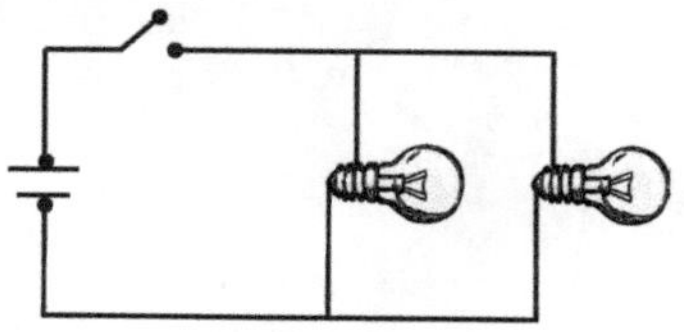

49. Simone connected the two bulbs according to what type of circuit?

A. Short

B. Series

C. Simple

D. Parallel

Use the following information to answer the next question.

Lucy was visiting her grandfather. He showed her a collection of old tools that had been passed down in his family. All of the tools were used before they had electricity.

50. Which tool was used to iron clothes without electricity?

A.

B.

C.

D.

ANSWERS AND SOLUTIONS — PRACTICE TEST

1. C	11. A	21. D	31. A	41. D
2. D	12. C	22. D	32. D	42. A
3. B	13. D	23. A	33. A	43. B
4. D	14. A	24. A	34. D	44. B
5. A	15. C	25. C	35. C	45. C
6. B	16. C	26. A	36. A	46. B
7. D	17. C	27. C	37. A	47. B
8. B	18. D	28. C	38. A	48. B
9. B	19. B	29. C	39. B	49. D
10. B	20. C	30. B	40. D	50. B

1. C

Marc Garneau was Canada's first astronaut in space. He started his career in the Canadian Navy before being accepted into the Canadian Astronaut Program. His first journey into space took place in 1984.

2. D

Space junk could hit spacecraft and damage it. This makes space travel dangerous for the astronauts. Space exploration makes a lot of space junk. Examples of space junk include used rocket boosters, old unused satellites, and other materials such as metals and solid fuel wastes.

3. B

Never look directly at the sun. Your eyes can suffer temporary or permanent damage if you look directly at the sun. Sunglasses are not effective protection against the sun. Filters are safe as long as you do not look directly at the sun when using them.

4. D

Earth's axis is tilted at an angle of 23.5°. The Northern Hemisphere is tilted toward and away from the sun at different times as Earth revolves around the sun. As a result, the tilt of Earth's axis and Earth's revolution around the sun are both responsible for the change in seasons on Earth.

Earth's rotation on its axis explains the difference between day and night, not the differences between the seasons.

5. A

Most of the food carried on board the space shuttle has had the water removed from it (been dehydrated) to make it lighter. Astronauts use a machine to add water to the food before eating it in space.

6. B

Axis refers to the imaginary line running through the centre of a planet. A planet rotates around its axis.

7. D

A comet is a celestial body that orbits the sun. It is a huge, dirty snowball in space. When it gets close to the sun, it melts and leaves a trail of gases and rocks. The trail of gases and rocks reflect sunlight and appear as a long tail. Figure D shows a comet.

8. B

While comets do lose some of their materials as they go around the sun, they do not burn up in a traditional sense because they remain in outer space and do not enter into any atmosphere. The sun is the only source of light in the solar system, and as the comet nears the sun, it becomes visible to humans because sunlight reflects off the comet. This reflected light is what reaches Earth.

9. B

Humans need oxygen to survive. Since there is no oxygen in space, space suits have been developed to carry oxygen with them. This allows astronauts to space walk for extended periods of time to accomplish tasks like repairing the space shuttle or satellites.

10. B

This type of rover can travel across the surface of other planets. The picture shown is of Sojourner, which was the first rover to successfully make it to another planet, which was Mars.

11. A

Earth revolves around the sun, and the moon revolves around Earth.

The drawing shows the movements of Earth and the moon. Earth revolves, or orbits, the sun. At the same time, the moon revolves around Earth.

12. C

People can now buy and sell goods from anywhere in the world. This has opened trade with other countries.

13. D

Some glues have a strong odour and fumes that can be harmful. It is important to make sure there is fresh air when you work with this type of glue. Opening a window is a good idea when using this glue.

14. A

The mass of the air in the inflated balloon is equal to the mass of the inflated balloon less the mass of the empty balloon.

25 g – 15 g = 10 g

The correct answer is 10 g.

15. C

Birds have adapted for flight by having lightweight, hollow bones.

16. C

Maxine should design her glider so that the wings are bent and have a slightly curved shape. This airfoil shape will help increase lift.

17. C

Thrust or propulsion is the force that moves the airplane forward.

18. D

The air moving over top of the wing moves faster than the air moving underneath the wing. The fast moving air has low pressure compared to the high pressure of the slower-moving air. The area of highest pressure is located underneath the wing.

19. B

Air is used to fill tires because it can be compressed. The air is pumped into the tire, and the tire inflates.

20. C

The forces in correct order from **I** to **IV** are thrust, lift, drag, and gravity. Lift is the upward force needed to overcome gravity. Thrust is the forward push force needed to overcome drag or air resistance.

21. D

The thermals provide the lift that the eagle needs to stay in the air, but the lift must overcome gravity or the eagle will fall to the ground.

22. D

A plane can climb higher in the air when the elevators on the horizontal stabilizers point upward as shown by illustration D. In this position, the air moving over the top surface moves slower and less lift is created. The tail then dips downward, and the nose of the plane points upward, allowing the plane to climb.

23. A

Most airplanes have a cone-shaped nose. This makes the airplane streamlined to reduce drag allowing it to move more easily through the air.

24. A

Individually researching alternate locations would be the least effective action. All the other choices would make others aware of the issue.

25. C
Plants are not used to make plastic. Plants are used to make shelter, medicine, and food.

26. A
Always wash your hands before and after handling organisms. This is for your health and the health of the organism.

27. C
This tree would be classified as a white spruce. It does not have leaves that shed annually and it branches close to the ground.

28. C
The housefly, spider, and snail are all invertebrates. These are animals that do not have a skeleton inside their bodies. The snake has a skeleton, so it is a vertebrate. Because of this, the snake does not belong with the others.

29. C
Vertebrates are animals that have a backbone or spinal column.

30. B
The animal Ronny found is probably a snake, which is a reptile. Reptiles have rough scaly skin and snakes do not have legs or arms for locomotion.

31. A
Fish are cold-blooded animals. Their body is the same temperature as the water in which they live.

32. D
The populations of living things that live together in a small area are called a community.

33. A
Resilience is an organism's ability to survive or adapt to changes in its environment. In this case, some bacteria became resistant to antibiotics used to kill them.

34. D
The bee and the flower have an interrelationship between species. The bee and flower depend on each other for survival, so both organisms benefit from the relationship.

35. C

The cocoons of silkworms are used to make silk. The threads from the cocoons are unravelled and woven into cloth.

36. A

Purple loosestrife can clog irrigation ditches and canals. It can also grow as weeds in fields. A lot of money is spent trying to get rid of this plant on farmlands.

37. A

Burning coal to generate electricity produces the most polluting byproducts. When wind, water, or sunlight are used to generate electricity, they do not produce as many polluting byproducts.

38. A

In order to reduce the amount of electricity used in the home, it is a good idea to turn off computers and televisions when they are not in use.

39. B

Flying a kite near power lines is very dangerous. If the kite touches the power lines it could create a dangerous pathway for electricity.

40. D

Alyssa assembled the bulbs in a parallel circuit. If one bulb burns out, electricity can still travel to the other bulb.

41. D

The voltage will increase by adding more potatoes in a series circuit.

42. A

Selena's crane transforms the electrical energy produced by the battery into the mechanical energy of movement.

43. B

A battery stores chemical energy that is changed into electrical energy.

44. B

Current electricity moves continuously along an unbroken path called a conductor.

45. C

When Troy rubs the balloon against his hair, it becomes negatively charged. The positively charged ground black pepper is attracted to this negatively charged balloon.

46. B

A glass rod and a plastic straw are both insulators—materials that do not allow electricity to flow through them.

47. B

Light energy can be converted to electrical energy using the photoelectric effect used inside a solar cell.

48. B

In an electrical circuit, the wires are responsible for conducting the electricity from one place to another.

49. D

A parallel electric circuit has two or more paths that the electricity can follow. Each bulb in this circuit will receive electricity.

50. B

A flat iron was used to iron clothes before electric irons were invented. The flat iron was heated, usually over a wood stove, and then used to press the clothes flat.

Appendices

GLOSSARY

adaptation something a living thing has or does that helps it survive in its environment

aerodynamics the study of how air moves on, over, under, and around an object.

artificial satellites human-made objects that orbit Earth to collect and transmit information.

asteroids small, rocky bodies that orbit the sun. Most exist in a belt between Mars and Jupiter.

axis the centre around which a planet rotates. It is often drawn as an imaginary line through the planet. On Earth, the axis would be drawn from the North Pole, through the centre of the planet, and out through the South Pole.

battery a device that stores electrical energy in chemical form.

biodiversity the variety of different organisms found in the different ecosystems on Earth.

characteristics the features of an organism or object that allow scientists to classify or identify it.

circuit the complete path current electricity takes in order to provide electricity to a load. A circuit includes different electrical devices, including wires (conductors), switches, loads, and a power source.

classify when scientists sort substances, objects, or organisms into different groups or categories.

comets frozen bodies in space that orbit the sun in elliptical orbits. Comets are usually made of ice, dust, rock, and gases. As a comet nears the sun, it forms a tail of dust and gases that can be millions of kilometres long.

compressed squeezed together. The particles of a substance may be squeezed together so they take up less space.

conductor a material that allows electricity to flow through it easily.

current the continuous movement or flow of electricity through a conductor.

current electricity electricity that moves continuously through a closed circuit.

drag the force that slows an object's movement through the air.

dwarf planets bodies in the solar system that are too small to be called planets but are too large to be called asteroids.

eclipse a phenomenon that happens when one body in space moves into the shadow of another body.

electrons the negatively charged particles present in atoms.

electrostatics the branch of physics that looks at the effects of static electricity on objects and how it passes between objects.

emit means to give out some form of energy. For example, the sun emits light.

energy the power to do work.

exoskeleton a shell or skeleton-like casing that covers the body of an invertebrate.

expand to spread out. Particles in a substance may spread out and take up more space when heated or released from a high pressure area to a lower pressure area.

extinct the status of a species of organisms that has died out completely everywhere in the world.

flight the process by which an object remains airborne for some time through the forces of lift and forward propulsion. A bird, for example, can remain airborne because its wings provide lift and propel it forward.

fungi multi-cellular organisms that cannot move on their own nor create their own food. They feed on dead organisms to survive.

generator a device that changes the energy of motion into electricity using magnets and coils of wire.

genes information in an organism's cell that is passed on from parent to offspring. Genes determine how an organism will look and how well it will survive in their environment.

glide the action of flying through the air without using an engine for propulsion. For example, a glider uses air thermals and the lift of its wings to remain aloft.

gravity the force that pulls an object down toward Earth's surface. Gravity is related to the weight of an object. The heavier the object, the greater the gravitational pull on the object.

insulator a material that does not allow electricity to flow easily.

interrelationship the connections formed between organisms in nature.

invasive species an organism that does not naturally occur in a specific area and that negatively affects the environment in some way.

invertebrates animals that do not have backbones.

lift the force that raises an object up into the air. This force opposes gravity.

load the device in an electric circuit that uses the electricity to do something. A bulb or motor are examples of loads.

meteoroids very small rocky bodies that orbit the sun. Sometimes they enter Earth's atmosphere and burn up. They are called meteors if they burn up. If they hit Earth's surface, they are called meteorites.

Monera single-celled organisms that do not have a nucleus and are neither plants nor animals.

monoculture the planting of only one type of crop on a farm.

moons large natural satellites that orbit around a planet.

natural community all the plants and animals that live in an area.

neutrons the neutral particles present in atoms.

non-native species an organism that has been introduced into a new environment.

non-renewable resources resources that cannot be replaced in a short period of time. They take millions of years to replace.

non-vascular plants plants that absorb water and nutrients through other parts of the plant rather than through tubes.

organism any single living thing. Examples of organisms are plants, animals, fungi, and protists.

parallel circuit an electrical circuit that has more than one path for the electricity to follow.

phases of the moon the different amounts of the lit side of the moon that can be seen from Earth. Half of the moon is always lit by the sun. The phases are the portions of reflected sunlight that can be seen from Earth as the moon revolves around Earth.

pitch the up or down attitude of the plane's nose caused by the elevators on the horizontal stabilizer.

planets are enormous balls of rocks, gases, or rocks and gases that orbit a star.

power source a device that provides electricity in a circuit.

pressure a continuous force applied to an object.

propel to move or push an object in a direction.

protists single-celled organisms that have a nucleus. They are neither plants nor animals but can act like plants or animals.

protons the positively charged particles present in atoms.

reflect to bounce energy off and away from an object. For example, the moon reflects light from the sun.

renewable resources resources that can be replaced within a short period of time such as a human lifetime.

resilience the ability of an organism or species to survive or adapt to changes in its environment.

revolution the movement of one object around another. For example, it takes the moon about 29 days to orbit, or complete one revolution, around the Earth.

roll the rotation of the fuselage (the dipping of the right or left wing) caused by the ailerons on the wings.

rotation a complete turn on an axis. For example, it takes Earth 24 hours to complete one full spin, or rotation, around its axis.

series circuit an electrical circuit that has only one path for the electricity to follow.

solar cell a device that transforms light energy into electricity.

stability when a species maintains a steady growth in its environment without sudden increases or decreases in its number.

static to stay still or not move. Static electricity is an electrical charge that builds up in one place and moves in short bursts.

static electricity a buildup of electrons on the surface of an object. The electrons can potentially move to a positively charged object.

sundial a device that shows the time of day by the shadow cast by a gnomon (pointer) onto a marked plate.

switch a device used to open and close a circuit.

thrust the force that pushes an object forward through the air.

tides are the periodic rising and falling of large bodies of water on Earth caused by the gravitational pull of the moon and sun.

tilt the degree to which a body in space, such as a planet, is tipped on its axis. Earth, for example, has a tilt of 23°.

transform to change from one form to another. Electricity transforms from electrical energy into other forms of energy.

turbine a device attached to a generator that moves the generator's coil or magnet to produce electricity.

vascular plants plants that have tubes to help carry water and nutrients to all of their parts.

vertebrates animals with a backbone and a skeleton inside their bodies.

wires metal threads that conduct electricity.

yaw the turning motion of the plane's nose to the left or right caused by the rudder on the vertical stabilizer.

NOTES

NOTES

NOTES

NOTES

SOLARO Study Guides
Ordering Information

The SOLARO Study Guides are specifically designed to assist students in preparing for unit tests, final exams, and provincial assessments.

SOLARO Study Guide—$29.95 each plus applicable sales tax

SOLARO
Study Guides

Ontario SOLARO Titles	
Mathematics 12, Advanced Functions, University Prep (MHF4U)	Civics 10, (CHV2O)
Mathematics 12, Calculus and Vectors, University Prep (MCV4U)	English 10, Academic (ENG2D)
Mathematics 12, Mathematics of Data Management, University Prep (MDM4U)	OSSLT, Ontario Secondary School Literacy Test
Physics 12, University Prep (SPH4U)	Mathematics 9, Academic, Principles of Mathematics (MPM1D)
Biology 12, University Prep (SBI4U)	Mathematics 9, Applied, Foundations of Mathematics (MFM1P)
Canadian and World Politics 12, University Prep (CPW4U)	Science 9, Academic (SNC1D)
Chemistry 12, University Prep (SCH4U)	Science 9, Applied (SNC2P)
English 12, University Prep (ENG4U)	Geography of Canada 9, Academic (CGC1D)
English 12, College Prep (ENG4C)	English 9, Academic (ENG1D)
World History 12, University Prep (CHY4U)	Science 8
Mathematics 11, Foundations for College Mathematics (MBF3C)	Mathematics 7
Mathematics 11, Functions and Applications, U/C Prep (MCF3M)	Science 7
Mathematics 11, Functions, University Prep (MCR3U)	Mathematics 6
Biology 11, University Prep (SBI3U)	Science 6
Chemistry 11, University Prep (SCH3U)	Language 6
English 11, University Prep (ENG3U)	Mathematics 5
World History 11, University/College Prep (CHW3M)	Science 5
Mathematics 10, Academic, Principles of Mathematics (MPM2D)	Mathematics 4
Mathematics 10, Applied, Foundations of Mathematics (MFM2P)	Science 4
Science 10, Applied (SNC1P)	Mathematics 3
Science 10, Academic (SNC2D)	Science 3
Canadian History 10, Academic (CHC2D)	Language 3
Canadian History 10, Applied (CHC2P)	

To order books, please visit
castlerockresearch.com or call
1.800.840.6224

Volume pricing is available. Contact us at orders@castlerockresearch.com

Student Notes and Problems
Workbook
Ordering Information

Student Notes and Problems (SNAP) Workbooks contain complete explanations of curriculum concepts, including examples and practice exercises

SNAP Workbook—$29.95 each plus applicable sales tax

Ontario SNAP Titles
Physics 12, University Preparation (SPH4U)
Physics 11, University Preparation (SPH3U)
Math 10, Academic, Principles of Mathematics (MPM2D)
Math 9, Academic, Principles of Mathematics (MPM1D)
Math 9, Applied, Foundations of Mathematics (MFM1P)

Total Cost

SOLARO Study Guides Ordered ________
SNAP Books Ordered ________
Cost Subtotal ________
Shipping and Handling
Please call for current rates ________
GST ________
Order Total ________

Payment and Shipping Information

Name ________
School ________
Telephone ________

SHIP TO:
School Code ________
School Name ________
Address ________
City: ________
Postal Code: ________

PAYMENT OPTIONS:
☐ By Credit Care VISA/MC
Name on Card: ________
Number: ________
Expirely Date: ________
☐ By Enclosed Cheque
☐ Invoice School
PO Number: ________

To order books, please visit
www.castlerockresearch.com

Volume pricing is available. Contact us at orders@castlerockresearch.com